Ulster
Gaelic Games Annual
1994

Jerome Quinn

Quinn, Jerome
Ulster Gaelic Games Annual 1994
Cataloguing is available from the British Library.

ISBN O 9524952 0 1

PHOTOGRAPH CREDITS

The author and publisher acknowledges with thanks the assistance received from the following both in research and in supplying photographs for this book. The pictures reproduced are sourced and identified as follows:

Oliver McVeigh (Tyrone Times, Dungannon) for photos on pages: 1, 4, 6, 8, 10, 14, 17 bottom, 19, 21, 23, 24, 29, 30, 31, 32, 33, 34, 36, 38, 39, 40, 42, 43, 53, 55, 57, 60, 66, 71, 72, 73, 74, 76, 80, 82, 100 bottom, 101, 104, 105, 108, 116, 117, 118, 133, 134, 136, 138, 139, 140, 141, 142 bottom, 143, 154, 158, 159, 160, 161, 163, colour pages 1, 2, 3, 4, 5 top, 6 top right, 7 bottom, and all Front Cover photos except top left.

John McAviney (Freelance, Monaghan 042-41164): 12, 26, 114, colour pages 5 bottom, 6 bottom, 8 top, Front Cover top left and Back Cover right.

The Irish News, Belfast, and photographers Brendan Murphy, Hugh Russell and Ann McManus: photos on pages: 17 top, 63, 83, 84, 87, 90, 111, 126, 132, 150 and 157.

Bass Ireland: 5, 145, 147, 148, 162 top, colour page 7 top and Back Cover left.

Brian Armitage (Lisnaskea Emmetts): 113 and colour page 8 bottom.

Jim Miskimmin (Down Recorder) : 46, 142 top and colour page 6 top left.

John (Curly) McElwaine (Ballymena Observer): 85, 93, 94 and 162 bottom.

Jimmy Davis (Newry Reporter): 110; **Peter Watson** (Fermanagh PRO): 64 and 97;

Liam McCartan (St Pauls): 98 and 100 (top); **Colm Connaughton** (Anglo-Celt, Cavan): 103;

Adrian McGuckin (St Pats, Maghera): 78.

Every effort has been made to identify and contact the copyright holders and where we have been unable to do so, we request that they contact the publisher.

Back Cover, left, Mickey Linden, with his neice, Courtney, the Sam Maguire Cup and the September Bass GAA Merit Award. *Right,* Ulster Captain Brian McGilligan with his son, Brian Og, and the Railway Cup.

Printed in Northern Ireland by Delta Print and Packaging Limited, Belfast.

CONTENTS

ACKNOWLEDGEMENTS

A supreme Ulster-wide effort has helped compile the information in this book. Individuals in each county have supplied results of county finals, players' christian names, etc.

My thanks go to: Gerry McClorey, Stephen Beacom and Jim McLean in Antrim, Pat Nugent in Armagh, Owen McConnon and Pat Fay in Cavan, Bernie and Seamus Mullan in Derry, Peter Campbell in Donegal, Michael Keenan in Down, Peter Watson and Michael Breslin in Fermanagh, John P.Graham in Monaghan, and Frank Rodgers in Tyrone. Considerable contributions were also made by Tony McGee of the Irish News, Adrian McGuckin, Brian McEniff and Maurice Hayes. One or two gaps remain in the list of club results so if you can help complete the list, then let me know.

Oliver McVeigh of the Tyrone Times is responsible for most of the excellent photographs (see example below). The other sources are listed on page 2.

Bass Ireland are the main sponsors. To Brian Houston, and all the staff on the Glen Road, thanks for having the faith in me to deliver. Other leading GAA sponsors have given their backing: Newry Building Supplies, Cavan Mart, Westenra Hotel, Carrickdale Hotel, Ulster Bank, Willie John Dolan, Mackies Foundry and Tracey Concrete.

Paddy O'Hara was my invaluable guide and friend last year, and again he warrants my greatest thanks. Last, but certainly not least, thanks to my wife Justine, for her patience, to the kids, Matthew, Kathryn and new addition Mark, and to new friends at Bredagh GFC.

Jerome Quinn, November 1994.

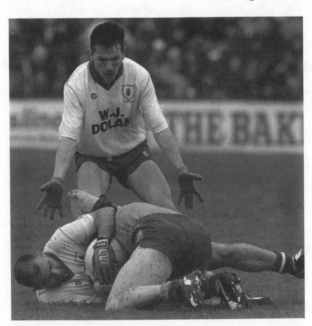

Tyrone's Adrian Cush appeals for the ball, but Paul Donnelly and a Donegal opponent seem unwilling to part.

BASS - A GREAT TRADITION

Bass Ireland are the Province's largest brewers and owners of Northern Ireland's only Brewery, the Ulster Brewery on the Glen Road in Belfast, where they produce Bass Ale, Tennent's Lager, Caffrey's Irish Ale, and Tuborg.

The company's links with the GAA in Ulster can be traced back more than a half a century, to Antrim's appearance in the 1943 All Ireland Hurling Final. Kevin Murphy played on the team and later became Chairman of Bass Ireland. The links continued for Antrim's next final, in 1989, when they were sponsored by Bass Ireland and managed by Jim Nelson, who is a key member of the Company's Technical Services Department.

Another famous GAA son of the Ulster Brewery is Tony Hadden, a former Director of Sales, who played in the great Down football team of the sixties, winning two All Ireland medals. Down and Ulster's more recent glories at Croke Park have also been acknowledged by Bass Ireland, largely through the Ulster GAA Writers Association, which the company helped set up in 1988. The Bass GAA Monthly Merit Awards have recognised many on-the-field achievements, while the Annual Banquet is the highlight of the GAA's social calendar. (See Chapter 19). Bass has also sponsored Armagh Championships, Players of the year, the Antrim Championships, and the St Johns Top Four Tournament.

August 1994 Bass GAA Merit Award Winner Conor Deegan accepts his trophy from PR Manager Brian Houston. In the background, GAA writer Eamonn O'Hara and Conor's father, Paddy Deegan.

Author Jerome Quinn is to be congratulated on compiling such a comprehensive review of the GAA in Ulster in 1994. The quality of this annual stands as testimony to the author's skills and the ever-increasing popularity of Gaelic Games in the province.

Brian Houston
Public Relations Manager,
Bass Ireland

Armagh defender Kieran McGeeney shrugs off two Fermanagh challenges.

Armagh in the Preliminary Round. *Back, left to right,* N.Smyth, D.Clarke, K.McGeeney, M.McQuillan, J.Burns, G.Reid, K.McGurk, C.O.Rourke, J.Grimley. Front, D.Horisk, B.Tierney, G.Houlahan, D.Marsden, J.McConville, J.Rafferty.

DAMP SQUIB AT ARMAGH

Ulster SFC Preliminary Round, May 15
Armagh 1-6   Fermanagh 0-6

"We're on fire for the Sam Maguire" proclaimed an Armagh banner, but the imagination and ambition of the supporters who devised the slogan was not matched by the performance of their team. In fact, neither side played to their potential as persistent rain ensured the Championship got off to a damp, dismal start at the Athletic Grounds.

Armagh had lost the National League Final to Meath only two weeks before, and some of the weaknesses exposed in Croke Park re-appeared here. Ironically, the main problems were in the same forward unit that had taken Armagh to the league final in such spectacular fashion. The forwards had accounted for every single score against Dublin (2-13) in the quarter-final and against Laois (3-11) in the semi-finals. In the final, they contributed just five points against Meath and now managed 1-6 against Fermanagh.

Ger Houlahan's loss of form ran parallel. The team captain scored 2-6 against Dublin and ended the league with a tally of 4-23 from ten games, yet he would total a mere 1-1 from two games in the Ulster Championship. It later emerged that health problems may have been to blame, as the demands of everyday work, on top of two football careers, took their toll on Houlahan. He had previously managed to play a major role in the progress of Sligo Rovers to the FAI Cup final, as well as leading Armagh to the National League Final. (Houlahan missed the soccer final as it fell on the same day as the Fermanagh game).

Certainly, it was a rather subdued Houlahan who missed simple free-kicks and was well-marshalled by full-back Paddy McGuinness, apart from two vital minutes at the start of the second half. First he took a difficult pass on the run and powered a shot towards goal just sixteen seconds after the throw-in. Cormac McAdam saved at point-blank range, but the goalkeeper was helpless ninety seconds later when McGuinness misjudged a high ball and gave Houlahan the few yards he needed to catch and side-foot the ball under McAdam for a goal.

Before the final whistle, Houlahan would miss another two free-kicks. Indeed, his team would add just two more points, yet it was enough to win a best-forgotten contest. Armagh badly needed a recognised place-kicker,

	Armagh	Fermanagh
7 mins Marsden	0-1	
9 mins C.O'Rourke	0-2	
11 mins McCreesh		0-1
12 mins Gallagher (F)		0-2
20 mins McConville	0-3	
22 mins Gallagher (F)		0-3
28 mins Gallagher		0-4
32 mins McCreesh		0-5
36 mins Marsden (45)	0-4	
HALF-TIME 36:30		
39 min Houlahan	1-4	
48 mins Gallagher		0-6
51 mins Marsden (F)	1-5	
60 mins Mackin	1-6	
FULL-TIME 73:00		

someone like John Toner who had fallen out of favour after scoring 1-15 in the group stages of the league.

Hugh McCabe's Fermanagh team featured many of the side involved in the dramatic collapse to Armagh a year before (Paul Greene the only debut) yet there was no repeat of the stylish football which had resulted in a tally of 1-16 on that occasion. Significant absentees from the forwards were Simon Bradley and Mark Gallagher, so when Collie Curran struggled, young Raymond Gallagher was left to lead the attack. He did score four times but only one of his colleagues, Colm McCreesh, joined him on the scoresheet. The worst statistic of all is the one that says Fermanagh scored just one point in the second half.

Their best period was the second quarter of the first half, when they edged in front by two points, 0-5 to 0-3. Gallagher scored twice and McCreesh once, yet Gallagher also missed a couple of frees, Collie Curran was wide twice and Paul Brewster once. And, when Diarmuid Marsden sent over a marvellous 45 in added time, all Fermanagh had to show for their efforts was a slender lead.

Fermanagh's last score came eleven minutes into the second half, courtesy of Gallagher, after which they were restricted to long-range efforts by a hard-working Armagh defence in which McQuillan, Rafferty and substitute McNeill all excelled. Des Mackin, another substitute, livened up the action for a time at the other end with some direct play, and the last score of the game.

Mackin's influence was brief however as the contest closed with the dismissal of Fermanagh's Michael O'Brien for a second bookable offence, and with two more wides from McGeeney and McGurk. The whole contest was littered with fouls and free-kicks, 59 of them awarded in total and 33 in the first half. Referee Pat McEneaney first blew his whistle after only eleven seconds, and later booked eight players. It wasn't so much a bad-tempered game, more a case of frustrated players struggling to cope with the conditions.

The Fermanagh team beaten by Armagh.

FERMANAGH

Cormac McAdam
(Lisnaskea)

Tommy Callaghan	Paddy McGuinness	Tony Collins
(Roslea)	(Devenish)	(Lisnaskea)
Raymond Curran	Michael O'Brien	Bart O'Brien
(Enniskillen)	(Devenish)	(Devenish)

Fergal McCann   Paul Brewster
(Irvinestown) (c)   (Enniskillen)

Colin Curran	Raymond Gallagher 0-4	Malachy O'Rourke
(Lisnaskea)	(Erne Gaels)	(Derrylin)
Paul Greene	Brian Carty	Colm McCreesh 0-2
(Derrygonnelly)	(Devenish)	(Lisnaskea)

SUBS: Martin Greene (Derrygonnelly) for Carty (55).

ARMAGH

Benny Tierney
(Mullabawn)

Dominic Clarke	Ger Reid	John Rafferty
(Harps)	(Eire Og)	(St Galls, Antrim)
Damien Horisk	Kieran McGeeney	Martin McQuillan
(Eire Og)	(Mullabawn)	(St Patricks)

Neil Smyth   Jarlath Burns
(Mullabawn)   (Silverbridge)

Cathal O'Rourke 0-1	John Grimley	Diarmuid Marsden 0-3
(Dromintee)	(Harps)	(Clan na Gael)
Kieran McGurk	Ger Houlahan 1-0	Jim McConville 0-1
(Sarsfields)	(Pearse Og) (c)	(Crossmaglen)

SUBS:Mark McNeill (Killeavey) for Clarke (36 mins),
Des Mackin (St Patricks) 0-1 for Burns (57).

Referee: Pat McEneaney (Monaghan).
Linesmen: Gerry McClorey (Antrim), Raymond Graffin (Antrim).
Bookings: Malachy O'Rourke, Tony Collins, Jarlath Burns, Dominic Clarke, Tommy Callaghan,
Michael O'Brien, Paddy McGuinness, Ger Reid.
Sending-off: Michael O'Brien (2 bookings) (69 mins).
Man of the Match - Neil Smyth.

CAVAN COLLAPSE

Ulster SFC First Round, May 22
Cavan 1-12 Monaghan 3-10

For Cavan 1994, read Tyrone 1986 in the All Ireland final, for just as Tyrone surrendered a sizeable lead in a dramatic second half collapse, so did Cavan in this year's championship.

The worst thing they both did was to score a goal right at the start of the second period. Back in '86 Paudge Quinn netted within 45 seconds of the restart to put Tyrone six points ahead of Kerry; in '94 Peter Reilly goaled for Cavan after just 16 seconds to give them a six-point advantage over Monaghan.

Cavan Co-op Mart

FARNHAMROAD, CAVAN   Telephone 049-31083, 31323

OFFICIAL SPONSORS OF THE CAVAN SENIOR AND MINOR FOOTBALL TEAMS

But, despite their big leads, both Tyrone and Cavan were pegged back well before the finish and both ended up losing by some distance - Tyrone by eight points, Cavan by five. Another identical statistic is the fact that they both managed to add only three points after their early goals. Tyrone lost the rest of the game to Kerry by 2-11 to 0-3 while the score from the Cavan goal to the final whistle was Cavan 0-3, Monaghan 2-7.

Some of the reasons offered for the collapses are also similar. "We scored our goal too early" offered Cavan manager PJ Carroll, "there were still thirty-five minutes to play but we stopped and they stepped up their game".

Reilly's goal, in the first minute of the second half, had come direct from the throw-in. Taking a pass from Damien O'Reilly, the former minor captain confidently sent a left-foot shot to the Monaghan net. The Breffni faithful among the crowd of 8,427 braced themselves for a first championship win in

		Cavan	Monaghan
11 secs	McEneaney		0-1
7 mins	O'Reilly	0-1	
9 mins	Carolan (F)	0-2	
10 mins	Cahill	0-3	
12 mins	Lambe (F)	0-4	
13 mins	Carolan (F)	0-5	
15 mins	McCarron (F)		0-2
19 mins	McGinnity		1-2
24 mins	Carolan (F)	0-6	
26 mins	Cahill	0-7	
27 mins	Carolan (F)	0-8	
33 mins	Carolan (F)	0-9	
37 mins	Slowey (F)		1-3
HALF-TIME 37:00			
38 mins	Reilly	1-9	
45 mins	F.Hartin o.g.		2-3
47 mins	Carolan (F)	1-10	
48 mins	Smyth		3-3
49 mins	T.Smith	1-11	
51 mins	Smyth		3-4
60 mins	Slowey		3-5
61 mins	Smyth (F)		3-6
63 mins	Smyth (F)		3-7
66 mins	Slowey (F)		3-8
69 mins	Cahill	1-12	
71 mins	Slowey		3-9
75 mins	Smyth (F)		3-10
FULL-TIME 75:00			

seven years, but by the end of the game, the same supporters stared on with disbelieving eyes at a humiliating defeat by their neighbours.

Cavan's midfield had been dominant up to Reilly's goal but as they relaxed, ever so slightly, Monaghan began to find an extra yard. Suddenly, the Cavan full-back line came under serious pressure as Monaghan pumped long and accurate balls towards their full-forwards.

From the first of these, after seven minutes, Gregory Flanagan's low shot was kicked into the corner of his own net by Fergal Hartin. Cavan raided upfield but only long enough for Ronan Carolan to point a free and for Monaghan goalkeeper Glenn Murphy to make an excellent diving block on John Brady.

Within a minute, Monaghan tried route one again. This time young Declan Smyth, on his championship debut, calmly took the high, dropping ball in his stride and shot to the net. Monaghan were right back in the game at 3-3 to 1-10.

Gerard McGuirk was so encouraged by the success of the long-ball, that he sent in another couple. The first bounced into the arms of Smyth who picked off a super point, the second won Monaghan a penalty. A bad fumble in the Cavan defence presented the ball to Ray McCarron who was sent crashing to the ground by goalkeeper Paul O'Dowd.

McCarron himself took the kick but failed to get any direction or power into his kick. He admitted afterwards that he had a hamstring problem and "shouldn't have taken the penalty but nobody else wanted to take it!" The drama took another twist seconds later as three players were sent off. Bernard Morris and Phil Smith

Peter McGinnity presents Declan Smyth with the BBC's Man of the Match Trophy

of Cavan, and Noel Marron from Monaghan, were dismissed after off-the-ball incidents. Reduced to thirteen men, Cavan soon lost the lead for the first time since the opening minute of the game. Two points each by Michael Slowey and Declan Smyth gave Monaghan a three-point advantage entering the closing stages. Fintan Cahill pulled one back but after Ronan Carolan missed two scoreable free-kicks, Monaghan's terrible twins, Slowey and Smyth, put Cavan out of their misery with further scores.

One of the after-match talking points reflected the kind of day it had been for Cavan. Television replays clearly showed Monaghan defender Gerard McGuirk lifting the ball clean off the ground in his own square in the 27th minute of the second half. The referee's view was blocked by a crowd of players.

Further controversy arose from Peter McGinnity's selection of Declan Smyth as Man of the Match on the BBC's Championship programme. The debut boy had displayed maturity beyond his years in scoring a goal and four stylish points, yet viewers saw a replay of Smyth aiming a kick at Cavan goalkeeper Paul O'Dowd in the fourth minute. Smyth was reacting to an incident where his colleague Stephen McGinnity appeared to be punched while on the ground, after having had a shot saved by O'Dowd. A number of viewers wrote to the BBC, arguing that Smyth should have been sent off and certainly not given the Man of the Match Award. McGinnity replied, "Those people who wrote in had the advantage of replays. At the game there were very few people who disagreed with the choice of Man of the Match. They didn't have access to different camera angles. The view we had was that Declan Smyth had a significant impact on the game".

Monaghan enjoyed their victory regardless. They had been written off after being consigned to Division Four of the National League while Cavan had nearly won promotion to Division Two (and beaten Monaghan in the process). Many of their own supporters prepared for the worst when Monaghan fielded with no fewer than seven Under-21 players, four of them making their Senior debuts (Glen Murphy, Pauric McShane, Declan Smyth and Vincent Martin). Yet, with a win behind them and the return to full fitness of McCarron, Gerry Mone and David Byrne, Michael

McCormick's team were full of optimism as they looked ahead to a semi-final with Derry or Down.

For Cavan these were desperate times. Everything had appeared to go well in the run-up to the game yet they had failed to win a championship game for the seventh year in-a-row. Manager PJ Carroll ultimately carried the can by resigning, though after watching his team crumble when faced with victory, he made a pertinent parting shot, "after seven years of losing in the first game you have to ask of this Cavan team...Are they winners?"

CAVAN
Paul O'Dowd
(Bailieboro)

Ciaran Brady	Fergal Hartin	Gerry Sheridan
(Gowna)	(Gowna)	(Mullahoran) (c)
Gerry Sheridan	Bernard Morris	Philip Smith
(Bailieboro)	(Gowna)	(Crosserlough)

Stephen King   Maurice Murphy
(Killeshandra)   (Ramor United)

Peter Reilly 1-0	Ronan Carolan 0-6	Fintan Cahill 0-3
(Knockbride)	(Cuchullains)	(Cuchullains)
Adrian Lambe 0-1	Damien O'Reilly 0-1	John Brady
(Bailieboro)	(Mullahoran)	(Laragh United)

SUBS: Tommy Smith (Denn) for Murphy (half-time),John Donnellan (Bailieboro) for G.Sheridan (Mullahoran) (59), Joe McCarthy (Kingscourt) for Reilly (61).

MONAGHAN
Glenn Murphy
(Emyvale)

Brendan Murray	Seamus Mullan	Edwin Murphy
(Clones)	(Scotstown)	(Castleblayney)
Gerard McGuirk	Declan Loughman	David King
(Scotstown) (c)	(Castleblayney)	(Aughnamullen)

Pauric McShane   Frank McEneaney 0-1
(Clontibret)   (Corduff)

Gregory Flanagan 1-0	Ray McCarron 0-1	Michael Slowey 0-4
(Cremartin)	(Scotstown)	(Clones)
Declan Smyth 1-4	Vincent Martin	Stephen McGinnity 1-0
(Carrickmacross)	(Killeevan)	(Drumhowan)

SUBS:Noel Marron (Donaghmoyne) for Mullan (half-time), Gerard Hoey (Iniskeen) for Flanagan, Gerard Mone (Clontibret) for Martin.

Referee: Damien Campbell (Fermanagh).
Linesmen: Mick McGrath (Donegal), Dessie Slater (Tyrone).
Bookings: Declan Smyth, Ciaran Brady, Damien O'Reilly.
Sendings-off: Philip Smith, Bernard Morris, Noel Marron.
Man of the Match - Declan Smyth.

GAME OF THE YEAR!

Ulster SFC First Round, May 29
Derry 1-12   Down 1-14

Game of the Year! A classic contest of quality football at a sun-drenched Celtic Park with enough dramatic twists to keep the capacity crowd (and a live television audience) on the edge of their seats right up to the final whistle. Better still, it was contested by the two best teams in the country in the First Round of the Ulster Championship.

Derry were All Ireland champions, Down would go on to become All Ireland champions, yet few really expected Derry to lose. Yes, Down still felt sore from losing by eleven points in Newry in the previous championship, but it was surely asking too much for the same men to go into the lion's den and reverse the decision.

Derry in fact were widely tipped to retain the Sam Maguire. They had a fairly young and talented squad which had romped through their league programme until losing to Dublin and crashing sensationally to Westmeath from Division Four. But, isn't that kind of setback supposed to give a side preparing for the Championship less distraction, and more time to focus properly on the main objective of the year? Furthermore, many tongues within Down had been wagging at a tremendous rate since Peter McGrath's team selection.

1. Barry Breen at centre-half-back? Wasn't he a midfielder and anyway, hadn't he missed the entire National League?

2. Conor Deegan and Gregory McCartan at midfield against the best pair in the country - Tohill and McGilligan? Wasn't Deegan a full-back and hadn't McCartan only just established himself as a right-half-back? Neither Deegan nor McCartan had played midfield in a major game for their county.

3. Eamonn Burns at number five? Wasn't he a midfielder?

4. John Kelly in the left corner of the defence? Wasn't he a half-back?

It's fair to assume that the knives were well sharpened among the sceptics in the kingdom of Mourne, many of whom were quietly predicting that this would be McGrath's last game as manager of Down. The enormity of his contribution towards winning the 1991 All Ireland appeared to have been almost forgotten as they anticipated an early championship exit to Derry for the third time in three years. Worse still, hadn't he lost the support of the players? Hadn't Greg Blaney asked County Board officers at a meeting in the summer not to re-appoint Peter McGrath?

"James the Brave" McCartan dives to block Karl Diamond.

Didn't a group of players gather at a hotel one winter's evening to discuss their unhappiness with McGrath? And, didn't two of Down's favourite sons - Blaney and James McCartan - leave the panel for three months?

When Blaney left, in October, he said "I believe the team management would prefer if I wasn't involved in the squad". He was unhappy at having to play full-forward in a game with Donegal but also felt he was being victimised for his request to the Board, though he was not speaking purely on his own behalf.

Being manager of Down was not easy for Peter McGrath. Living in Rostrevor, working in Newry and training in Hilltown, there was no escape from the controversy. However, he held firm until mid-February when Blaney and McCartan returned to training on a snow-covered Hilltown pitch.

McCartan re-appeared in a Down shirt against Dublin in Croke Park on February 20 as a substitute, Blaney returned against Kildare on March 13, but there was no magical change in Down's fortunes. Beaten by Donegal and then Meath in the league quarter-finals, McGrath was a long way off his Championship team.

Only three of the team that lost to Meath would line-out in the same position at Celtic Park - Collins, Blaney and Linden. Seven others were to be found in new positions - Michael Magill who had played six games in-a-row at full-back,. Conor Deegan who had taken over at centre-half after an injury to John Kelly, Brian Burns who played six straight games at midfield, Greg McCartan who had settled at number five, Eamonn Burns, Gerard Deegan and James McCartan.

DOWN TEAM V MEATH IN NATIONAL LEAGUE				
		N.Collins		
C.Murray		M.Magill		R.Starkey
G.McCartan		C.Deegan		E.Burns
	B.Burns		G.Colgan	
Ggy.Deegan		G.Blaney		Grd.Deegan
M.Linden		C.McCabe		J.McCartan

Of the remaining four players to come in, Aidan Farrell had started just four league games out of ten (none at full-forward), Ross Carr had missed the last four games with an injury that threatened his availability for the championship, John Kelly was injured against Donegal and Paul Higgins was on the bench against Meath.

Much the same thing happened in 1991 when a deliberate policy of experimentation through the winter left Down apparently disjointed. However, just as in '91, McGrath's Championship formula began to fall into place during April and May.

Against Fermanagh in the McKenna Cup we saw James McCartan given a roving commission from left-half-forward. One minute he fielded a 45 in his own square, the next he burst through for a point. Around the same time, I saw McCartan score 1-9 in a Division Two league match between Tullylish and Bredagh, rescuing his team from a six-point deficit. No doubt about it, James was back with a point to prove to those who dared suggest he was a one-season wonder. "He really pushed himself in training, always up at the front and very determined", recalls Peter McGrath.

Another piece of the jigsaw fell into place the weekend before Derry, when Barry Breen showed up extremely well at centre-half-back. He was confident of his individual battle with former college-mate Dermot McNicholl, who was flanked by Brian McCormick and Eamonn Burns on a new Derry half-forward line. Damien Barton and Damien Cassidy were relegated to the bench while Dermot Heaney was switched to full-forward. In defence, Johnny McGurk was judged not to have fully recovered from injury, so Karl Diamond had the job of marking James McCartan.

After one minute's play, Brian McCormick set the standard when he picked off the first score of the game from near the sideline; sixty seconds later Karl Diamond's curling shot came off the Down upright; in the third minute Greg McCartan pointed a free; in the sixth minute the same player scored from play to give Down the lead; a minute later Neil Collins made the "Save of the Championship" when he twisted acrobatically to deflect Anthony Tohill's drive over the Down crossbar.

FIRST HALF		Derry	Down
1 min	McCormick	0-1	
3 mins	G.McCartan (F)		0-1
6 mins	G.McCartan		0-2
7 mins	Tohill	0-2	
10 mins	Linden		0-3
12 mins	McCormick	0-3	
14 mins	Brolly	0-4	
16 mins	Brolly	0-5	
17 mins	Farrell		0-4
20 mins	Gormley (F)	0-6	
22 mins	Gormley (F)	0-7	
24 mins	Linden		0-5
25 mins	G.McCartan (F)		0-6
27 mins	Gormley (F)	0-8	
28 mins	Linden		0-7
29 mins	J.McCartan		0-8
30 mins	Linden		0-9
32 mins	Linden		0-10
HALF-TIME 37:30			

It didn't seem possible but Joe Brolly spent the next ten minutes trying to raise the standard even higher. Alert to a short free by Gormley, the Derry cornerman danced in front of John Kelly before sending the ball over the bar from an almost impossible angle out on the right. Two minutes later, he was quickest to react again when Tohill's shot came off a post; Gormley tapped over a simple free after Kelly had fouled Brolly and when another free came from his quick-thinking, the Down bench acted decisively. As Gormley lined up Derry's seventh point, Paul Higgins replaced John Kelly. Brolly still won the next ball but from then on Higgins had more success, partly because the supply of ball became less accurate.

But if Down had an answer to Brolly, then Derry had no answer to Mickey Linden. Five scintillating points he scored in the first half, four of them coming in the last eleven minutes, Down's best spell of the match. First, Linden teased the Derry defence before choosing his right foot to kick Down's fifth point, then he used his left foot after a pass from Blaney, and added the last two scores of the half, again courtesy of quick deliveries from Blaney. Derry manager Eamonn Coleman admitted within minutes of the end of the game that he had left his son Gary "too long on Mickey Linden".

James McCartan proved equally elusive in this period, being fouled for a simple free and then scoring the equalising point himself. Catching the ball straight from McCusker's kick-out, McCartan threw a brilliant dummy to Diamond, ambled forward and cooly tapped over his point.

Scoring apart, the main feature of Down's play was their work rate. Whenever a Derry player gained possession, he found himself under serious pressure to release the ball. Henry Downey was robbed while looking where to send his pass, Gary Coleman was hounded into kicking straight into touch. At midfield, McGilligan and Tohill were surrounded by red and black shirts. DJ Kane remembers the plan working, "one time big Brian caught a ball above his head and tried to turn. He couldn't. He tried to pass but couldn't do that either. Tommy Sugrue gave a free for overcarrying and Brian's expression said it all, as if to ask what else could he do".

SECOND HALF		Derry	Down
39 mins	Tohill	0-9	
44 mins	Burns	0-10	
47 mins	Heaney	0-11	
49 mins	G.McCartan (F)		0-11
50 mins	Linden		0-12
54 mins	F.McCusker	1-11	
58 mins	J.McCartan		0-13
61 mins	Tohill (F)	1-12	
67 mins	McCabe		1-13
72 mins	G.McCartan (F)		1-14
FULL-TIME 74:00			

Conor Deegan looks to set up an attack.

"Now we'll see what we're made of" said Eamonn Coleman as Derry began the second half two points in arrears. The All Ireland Champions responded with the first three scores of the half, from Tohill, Eamonn Burns and Heaney. Derry had taken the lead, but all the while Down were winning private battles over most of the field.

Even three-time All Star Tony Scullion was so pre-occupied in trying to curb young Aidan Farrell that the Derry defender did not kick the ball once in the entire match. Admittedly, Scullion wasn't fully fit, but it's still a surprising and revealing fact.

The tables were also turned on '93 hero Henry Downey as he tussled with a revitalised Greg Blaney. Down's oldest player did what he does best, scrapping for loose ball and distributing it quickly to speed merchants like Linden. On one occasion, Blaney travelled deep into his own defence to perform the second part of a brilliant Down "double-block" by Brian Burns on Heaney and then Blaney on Gormley.

But, for all their endeavour, Down didn't score until the twelfth minute. After watching Ross Carr's closer-in free strike a post, Greg McCartan made sure of his kick from 44 metres (James McCartan having drawn the free from Diamond). A minute later Linden regained the lead for Down with a classic point, turning and teasing new marker Kieran McKeever before kicking left-footed over the bar.

Derry responded with a goal. Eamonn Burns and Brolly worked the ball to left-half-back Fergal McCusker who had made his way to the right-corner-forward position. Stepping inside DJ Kane and Ross Carr, and with three more Down defenders converging, McCusker clipped the ball over the advancing Collins and into the Down net, aided slightly by a touch from Breen. 1-11 to 0-12. Down immediately signalled for Peter Withnell to warm up. Ross Carr's man had scored the goal and the Clonduff man was struggling after taking a knock early on.

Derry moved in for the kill but they simply couldn't penetrate the Down rearguard. After several "sideway" passes DJ Kane grabbed the ball and cleared to Greg McCartan who in turn found his namesake James, 45 metres from the Derry goal. What followed was the "Score of the Season".

With Tommy Sugrue keeping a close eye on things, as usual, McCartan wrestled his way inside Karl Diamond. In so doing he took as many as 13 steps, but was being held for part of his run. Once clear, the player soloed and took another seven steps as McKeever made his tackle. McCartan dropped the ball, regained it, bounced it once and, shrugging off the Derryman, he angled a beautiful kick over the bar. The steps taken were questionable but for balance, skill and pure determination it was a breathtaking score. Moreover, it raised Down hopes and dimmed many Derry hearts. If you were looking for a watershed in this match, then look no further.

Tohill wiped out McCartan's point with a 44-metre free soon after, but the initiative lay with Down. Eamonn Coleman made his third substitution inside fifteen minutes to the Derry attack after Tohill, carrying the fight from midfield, missed two further chances. The first came from an interception, but for once Tohill lost his balance and screwed a left-foot shot wide.

With seven minutes remaining and Derry still two points in front, Mickey Linden sent in a high ball towards Down substitutes Ciaran McCabe and Peter Withnell. McCabe got a touch to divert it into the path of Withnell who resisted a challenge and shot narrowly wide from 12 yards.

Down supporters barely had time to curse their luck. A poor kick-out fell to Blaney wide on the left. He moved inside and delivered a pass into Linden's chest, a swift transfer to McCabe gave the debut boy from Castlewellan a clear run on goal. He took one bounce and slotted the ball expertly over Damien McCusker and into the net. 1-13 to 1-12 to Down.

Derry still had time to level the game, but Declan Bateson's sideline free just missed the target. From the kick-out McGilligan made a clean catch, but four Down men blocked his path and Blaney knocked the ball out of his hands. Eamonn Burns gave it to McCartan, James sent it long to Withnell who drew a free from Heaney just 25 metres from the Derry goal. The fact that such industry came in the 72nd minute, on a sweltering day, was a credit to Down's fitness.

Greg McCartan pointed the free, and seconds later the final whistle sent Down people into raptures of delight. Hundreds raced onto the pitch while Ross Carr, who had clearly not been impressed with the management decision to replace him twenty minutes earlier, lifted little Peter McGrath right off the ground in a bear-hug of joy! When he eventually escaped, the manager who had been interpreted twelve months before in Newry as criticising his players after the defeat by Derry, put the record straight. "All credit to the players. They worked extremely hard for the last ten weeks and played like lions today. They never gave up, even when we went behind and eventually got what they deserved".

Derry's reign had come to an end. They had been worthy and sporting champions (not a single player booked) but had not played to their considerable potential on the day. Yet, they could have won, even in the dying moments. It was that sort of game.

DOWN

Neil Collins
(Carryduff)

Michael Magill .... Brian Burns .... John Kelly
(Warrenpoint) .... (Bryansford) .... (Carryduff)

Eamonn Burns .... Barry Breen .... DJ Kane (c)
(Bryansford) .... (Downpatrick) .... (Newry Shamrocks)

Gregory McCartan 0-5 .... Conor Deegan
(Ballymartin) .... (Downpatrick)

Ross Carr .... Greg Blaney .... James McCartan 0-2
(Clonduff) .... (Carryduff) .... (Tullylish)

Mickey Linden 0-6 .... Aidan Farrell 0-1 .... Gerard Deegan
(Mayobridge) .... (Rostrevor) .... (Downpatrick)

SUBS: Paul Higgins (Ballymartin) for Kelly (21), Peter Withnell (Drumaness) for Carr (53), Ciaran McCabe (Castlewellan) 1-0 for G.Deegan (63).

DERRY

Damien McCusker
(Glen)

Kieran McKeever .... Tony Scullion .... Gary Coleman
(Dungiven) .... (Ballinascreen) .... (Magherafelt)

Karl Diamond .... Henry Downey .... Fergal McCusker 1-0
(Bellaghy) .... (Lavey) (c) .... (Glen)

Anthony Tohill 0-3 .... Brian McGilligan
(Swatragh) .... (Dungiven)

Brian McCormick 0-2 .... Dermot McNicholl .... Eamonn Burns 0-1
(Lavey) .... (Glenullin) .... (Ballinascreen)

Joe Brolly 0-2 .... Dermot Heaney 0-1 .... Enda Gormley 0-3
(Dungiven) .... (Castledawson) .... (Glen)

SUBS: Damien Cassidy (Bellaghy) for McNicholl (49), Declan Bateson (Ballinderry) for Gormley (59), Seamus Downey (Lavey) for Burns (65).

Referee: Tommy Sugrue (Kerry). Linesmen: Pat McEneaney, Damien Campbell.
Bookings: Ross Carr, Paul Higgins, Eamonn Burns (Down).
Man of the Match - James McCartan.

QUOTES

PRE-MATCH : "You don't know how good you are until the championship. You can lose a match so suddenly, somebody can sneak a goal and it's gone, you just don't know" - Joe Brolly.

POST-MATCH : "We were like cornered rats going into Celtic Park. We had nowhere to go except fight for our footballing lives" - Greg Blaney.

"I feel sick inside but I'll enjoy a good holiday now" - Eamonn Coleman.

"Eamonn came across extremely well after the game. He said they (management team) intend to carry on, that he will stay as manager, to bring what still is a very good Derry side back again next year" - Derry PRO Bernie Mullan.

SAME OLD STORY FOR ANTRIM

Ulster SFC First Round, June 5
Antrim 1-9   Donegal 1-12

Missed chances, over-elaborate build-up and only themselves to blame. The same old story for Antrim footballers, though this was arguably their best championship performance since their last victory, against Cavan in 1982.

In the intervening years, Antrim suffered some very heavy defeats. Monaghan beat them 2-18 to 0-4, Tyrone by 3-13 to 1-4 and Fermanagh by 3-12 to 1-8, though their recent record does show signs of improvement under the management duo of PJ O'Hare and Gerry Higgins. Beaten by a single point away to Fermanagh, then by three points away to the then All Ireland champions Donegal and again by three points this year.

"We prepared well and did quite well today, but it's the same old story of too many wides", lamented O'Hare at Casement Park. "Lack of belief" offered midfielder Paul McErlean as a reason for Antrim coming so near yet so far. "We need to learn how to win and we seem to be getting closer, but it's difficult gaining championship experience when you only get one match a year".

		Antrim	Donegal
14 mins	Heatley (F)	0-1	
6 mins	Heatley	0-2	
8 mins	Heatley (F)	0-3	
10 mins	Bonnar (F)		0-1
11 mins	Kennedy (F)	0-4	
13 mins	Bonnar (F)		0-2
18 mins	T.Boyle		0-3
19 mins	Bonnar		0-4
21 mins	Heatley (F)	0-5	
23 mins	M.McHugh		0-5
23 mins	Molloy		0-6
26 mins	Heatley (F)	0-6	
30 mins	Kennedy (F)	0-7	
31 mins	T.Boyle		1-6
33 mins	Bonnar		1-7
HALF-TIME 37:00			
41 mins	Armstrong	0-8	
45 mins	Hegarty		1-8
48 mins	McGowan		1-9
56 mins	Bonnar (F)		1-10
60 mins	Donnelly	0-9	
63 mins	M.Boyle		1-11
64 mins	M.McHugh		1-12
65 mins	Heatley (Pen)	1-9	
FULL-TIME 74:00			

Television analyst Sean McCague pinpointed Antrim's problems. "Their defence was good apart from one, midfield was good too but only two forwards of the starting team scored. They had no confidence and passed the buck too often". Time and time again Antrim weaved complex patterns in their approach play only to miss the target, especially in the crucial period midway through the second half when Donegal appeared to be on the rack. In the first minute of the half Conal Heatley shot wide after a four-man move. Joe Kennedy did the same sixty seconds later.

Ironically, the only score that did come in this period was from a difficult angle out on the right. Donal Armstrong fired over a super point, though it was to be the only one from play in the entire half by the forwards, as the affliction soon spread to the Rossa man as well. Armstrong was a little too ambitious from a narrow angle on sixteen minutes, and wasted two easier chances when put through by Charlie McStravick, and in the twentieth minute when he went for a difficult goal when a simple point was on. After watching Heatley rushing his shot following a six-man move, half-back Aidan Donnelly decided enough was enough. Off he went on a direct, darting run before kicking expertly over the bar for Antrim's first point in nineteen minutes.

For all their huffing and puffing, Antrim trailed by 1-10 to 0-9. Donegal's half-backs Noel Hegarty and Barry McGowan had both found the target, while Bonnar tapped over an easy free after McCurdy had held onto the lively Tony Boyle. McEniff's men also responded to Donnelly's point with Martin McHugh and Manus Boyle extending their lead to six points with eight minutes left.

Seconds later Matt Gallagher hauled Mickey Boyle to the ground as he bore down on the Donegal goal. Penalty to Antrim; Heatley gave his side a fighting chance by smashing his kick to the net. Joyce McMullan took possession from Walsh's kick-out and sent a relieving ball upfield but his team-mates could only record three consecutive wides. Opportunity still knocked for Antrim, but Heatley and Kennedy both missed scoreable frees.

Harbinson tried something different; the St Galls' man slipped the ball to the unmarked Heatley, ten yards from the Donegal goal. However, John Joe Doherty did just enough to close down the forward's sight of goal and his shot blazed wide, Antrim's tenth wide of the half, twice as many as Donegal.

There was another major reason for Antrim's defeat - Tony Boyle. The former All Star scored Donegal's goal and had three different markers over the seventy minutes. "He was the one man we couldn't cope with

Listen and Learn. Tony Boyle (top) listens to advice, Matt Gallagher gives it.

in the first half", admitted PJ O'Hare, "his goal came at a crucial time coming up to half-time. We were 0-7 to 0-6 ahead but went in 1-7 to seven points down".

In the run-up to the game, O'Hare had questioned Boyle's championship fitness. After all, he hadn't played for more than a year and not in the championship since the 1992 final, but the Antrim boss was first to admit he had been proved wrong. Young Ronan Hamill was initially given the job of marking Boyle on only his second senior appearance. The Donegal man continually managed to win possession in front of Hamill, once scoring a great point from an acute angle and also drawing a free for Donegal's first score in the tenth minute.

Conal Heatley had given Antrim a dream start with three points in-a-row. His team played some good, direct football, with Murphy and McErlean on top at midfield, and they were further rewarded by a couple of long-distance frees from Joe Kennedy. However, Donegal's wing half-backs were cleaning up on break-ball around the middle of the park, and they went to have a major say in the contest. One of them, Barry McGowan, played a lovely ball in to Tony Boyle for their goal, though Antrim felt that the free-kick at the start of the move should have gone the other way. McErlean had been penalised for not releasing the ball after a high fetch. He felt he had been fouled by Brian Murray, but while he appealed Tony Boyle tucked away a classy goal.

TYRONE RELIEF

Ulster SFC Semi-final, June 12
Tyrone 3-10 Armagh 1-10

Five years of frustration ended for Tyrone at Omagh as they won their first Ulster Championship match since the 1989 final replay. That victory, over Donegal, gave Tyrone the Ulster title and also marked the end of the county's greatest decade. Now, their supporters eagerly forecast the beginning of a new era.

Their optimism was based on the emergence of many of Tyrone's All Ireland Under-21 winners, and one man in particular - Peter Canavan. He had captained both All Ireland successes and been labelled "the best forward in Ireland" by his manager Art McCrory after brilliant performances for club, county and province.

In February, Canavan almost led Errigal Ciaran to the All Ireland Club final, and a day later he scored the goal that effectively won the Railway Cup for Ulster in Ennis. In March, he scored 1-3 at Croke Park to book Tyrone's promotion to Division Two of the National League.

The one place Canavan had not performed in, surprisingly enough, was the Senior Championship. He had played in all of Tyrone's four consecutive defeats since 1989 withoutever hitting peak form. Now was the time!

Inside two minutes, Canavan had the ball in the Armagh net from a penalty, and he was centrally involved in the next four Tyrone attacks. Adrian Cush benefitted from the first, pointing from a free at the end of the move, then Plunkett Donaghy took a Canavan pass to score, then Canavan scored himself after a wonderfully balanced run and he was again fouled for a free. The kick was missed but Tyrone had raced into a lead of 1-2 to 0-0 within ten minutes.

Armagh manager Jim McCorry switched Damien Horisk onto Canavan, a fairly successful move but the damage had been done. Canavan had already given his team-mates a dream start and the confidence to take the game to the National League finalists. They conjured up the next score without Canavan's help, Donaghy making it 1-3 to 0-0.

Armagh hit back with two Diarmuid Marsden points before Tyrone scored a second goal. John Rafferty ran into trouble in front of his own goal, Adrian Kilpatrick slipped the ball to Stephen Lawn who picked his spot superbly in the corner of Benny Tierney's net.

Tyrone were seven points ahead, but Art McCrory and Eugene McKenna might have flashed their minds back twelve months to the Athletic Grounds, when Tyrone had a six-point lead at the same stage. By half-time in 1993 the advantage had been cut to two, but this time Joe Cassidy came off his line quickly to prevent a Des Mackin goal and Armagh were restricted to two more points from frees by Marsden. The fact that Marsden was the only Armagh player to score in the first half, speaks for a hard-working home defence in which Fay Devlin was outstanding.

		Tyrone	Armagh
2 mins	Canavan (Pen)	1-0	
5 mins	Cush (F)	1-1	
9 mins	Canavan	1-2	
12 mins	Donaghy	1-3	
14 mins	Marsden		0-1
15 mins	Marsden (F)		0-2
22 mins	S.Lawn	2-3	
25 mins	Marsden (F)		0-3
29 mins	Marsden (F)		0-4
HALF-TIME 36:00			
37 mins	Grimley		0-5
40 mins	Marsden		0-6
40 mins	Houlahan		0-7
43 mins	Smyth		0-8
47 mins	Canavan (45)	2-4	
48 mins	Donaghy	2-5	
54 mins	Canavan (F)	2-6	
55 mins	Gormley	2-7	
57 mins	Marsden (45)		0-9
59 mins	Cush (F)	2-8	
61 mins	Rafferty		0-10
63 mins	Canavan (F)	2-9	
64 mins	Donaghy	3-9	
70 mins	Marsden		1-10
71 mins	McGleenan	3-10	
FULL-TIME 74:00			

Fay Devlin races away from Martin McQuillan.

Trailing by 2-3 to 0-4 at the break, Armagh had to do something, and quickly. In the first minute John Grimley pointed. Marsden, Houlahan and Smyth all followed with long-range scores and suddenly there was only the bare minimum between the sides with 28 minutes still to play. Could Tyrone respond or would they crack under the pressure?

The next chance fell to Peter Canavan, a 14-yard free just to the left of the posts and a gift for someone of his ability, yet Armagh supporters behind the goal couldn't believe their eyes as his kick went wide. Fortunately for Canavan and Tyrone, he was handed a chance to make amends only ninety seconds later. The crowd held it's breath as Canavan steadied himself and kicked a 45 off a post and over the bar. Relief for Tyrone - their first score of the half.

Two minutes later, Ger Houlahan missed a simple 25-yard free in a central position. Tyrone seemed to have won the psychological contest; they outscored Armagh in the remainder of the match by 1-6 to 0-3.

Donaghy moved to full-forward with immediate dividends, scoring a point after taking a pass from substitute Brian Gormley, who added another himself. Lady Luck then decided to make up for the past four years by dishing out another helping to Tyrone.They had been thankful for the early penalty - most people agreed, even before the TV replays, that Ciaran Loughran was tackled (maybe not even fouled) a couple of yards outside the square - but this time the good fortune almost seemed too much to accept.

Tyrone's Plunkett Donaghy jumps for joy in front of glum faces in the Armagh support.

A long ball into the Armagh full-back line seemed set to arrive safely in Kieran McGeeney's lap when it took a wicked bounce straight to Donaghy, who was conveniently lurking behind the defender. He took one bounce, rounded the goalkeeper and shot into an empty net while Armagh protested at the number of steps taken. Closer inspection (more TV replays) supported their protest. Donaghy took seven steps between bouncing the ball and shooting to the net.

Seconds later John Grimley was sent off, and he was followed to the line by Martin McQuillan, who vented his frustration at not have being selected to start the game. Armagh had also been without Kieran McGurk from the start (chipped shoulder bone) and Jarlath Burns, who broke a finger in a challenge game with Kildare and aggravated it in a club game.

Tyrone also had serious pre-championship problems with their defence. Sean Teague suffered a broken leg, while goalkeeper Finbarr McConnell, John Lynch and Colm Donaghy were all suspended, and Chris Lawn, injured. 19-year-old Donaghmore goalkeeper Patrick McKenna and 31-year-old Gerry McGuigan, a brother of Frank, were called up. McGuigan was a recognised full-forward but he impressed when marking Plunkett Donaghy in two club championship games for Moortown, and was brought in to cover Tyrone's full-back problem. Chris Lawn recovered and did a fine job, though he ruined the fairytale story of the year for McGuigan!

TYRONE

Joe Cassidy
(Galbally)

Gareth McGirr	Chris Lawn	Fay Devlin
(Omagh)	(Moortown)	(Ardboe)
Paul Donnelly	Fergal Logan	Aidan Morris
(Beragh)	(Stewartstown)	(Newtownstewart)

Ciaran Corr   Plunkett Donaghy 1-2
(Coalisland) (c)   (Moy)

Adrian Cush 0-2	Adrian Kilpatrick	Stephen Lawn 1-0
(Donaghmore)	(Dungannon)	(Moortown)
Eamonn McCaffrey	Peter Canavan 1-4	Ciaran Loughran
(Errigal Ciaran)	(Errigal Ciaran)	(Carrickmore)

SUBS: Brian Gormley (Carrickmore) 0-1 for McCaffrey (23),
Mattie McGleenan (Eglish) 0-1 for Loughran (51).

ARMAGH

B.Tierney

M.McNeill	G.Reid	J.Rafferty 0-1
D.Horisk	K.McGeeney	Colm Hanratty

N.Smyth 0-1   Paul McGrane

C.O'Rourke	G.Houlahan 0-1 (c)	D.Marsden 1-6
D.Mackin	J.Grimley 0-1	J.McConville

SUBS: M.McQuillan for Mackin (half-time), K.McGurk for O'Rourke (53),
Barry O'Hagan for Reid (60).

Referee: Tommy McDermott (Cavan).
Linesmen: Gerry McClory, Kevin Brolly (Derry).
Bookings: Gareth McGirr, Ger Reid.
Sendings-off: John Grimley, Martin McQuillan.
Man of the Match - Fay Devlin.

Westenra Arms Hotel

In the Heart of Monaghan

Tel 047 - 82588 Fax 82291

and our Sister

The Lakeside Hotel

047 - 83599/83519

Backed by the Westenra Hotel, Monaghan's Michael Slowey holds off a challenge from Cavan defender Bernard Morris in the 1994 Ulster SFC.

FARRELL WALKS OUT!

Ulster SFC Semi-final, June 19
Down 0-14   Monaghan 0-8

Aidan Farrell came from nowhere to win an All Ireland Senior medal, yet for two weeks after the Ulster semi-final the full-forward turned his back on the panel. He walked out immediately after the Monaghan game, not even changing out of his playing gear, and didn't return until shortly before the final.

"I got a lot of stick for my performance against Monaghan, from our own supporters during the game and from the local press after it. It was difficult to take, especially as I was under pressure all year for my position from Peter Withnell. By the time I returned to the dressing-room I couldn't be bothered hanging around so I left, though it must have looked a bit odd, me walking through the crowd with my gear on after the game!"

Peter McGrath coaxed his fellow Rostrevor man back. Bigger names like McCartan, Blaney and Linden were getting all the attention yet the manager knew Farrell's return was vital to the smooth-running of the attacking unit. He didn't score much, but was adept at creating space for his team-mates and as a target man.

The forwards showed a few changes for the Monaghan game. An unfit Ross Carr was replaced by Gary Mason (returning from a year out with exams) and Ciaran McCabe was retained in the left corner. Mason top-scored with six points, five of them from free-kicks, but the Man of the Match was Greg Blaney.

A quick analysis of Blaney's performance tells much about his role on the Down team: He made twenty-one contributions during the game; he won break ball around the middle of the field ten times and picked up possession in the Down half five times; his delivery was first time on no fewer than nineteen occasions while five of his passes led directly to scores. In other words, Blaney was the linkman for Down, winning vital ball and putting it on a plate for his team-mates.

Blaney apart, it was a poor match. Players on both sides struggled in the wet, as the contest degenerated into a series of fouls and free-kicks. Referee Jim Curran awarded a total of 54 frees, with twenty of them going Down's way in an opening period played almost exclusively in the Monaghan half. However, Down also won the first half wides contest (eight-nil); it seemed on occasions that their forwards had too much time and lacked the decisive penetration of Celtic Park.

Goal hero Ciaran McCabe was guilty of a bad miss from eight yards, but even Mickey Linden was off-target a couple of times as Down

		Down	Monaghan
5 mins	Slowey		0-1
9 mins	G.McCartan	0-1	
10 mins	Hoey		0-2
11 mins	Mason	0-2	
14 mins	Mason (F)	0-3	
16 mins	Smyth (F)		0-3
17 mins	Linden	0-4	
32 mins	Mason (F)	0-5	
34 mins	Linden	0-6	
37 mins	Smyth (F)		0-4
HALF-TIME 37:00			
39 mins	Smyth		0-5
42 mins	Mason (F)	0-7	
43 mins	J.McCartan	0-8	
43 mins	C.Deegan	0-9	
46 mins	McShane		0-6
47 mins	Linden	0-10	
53 mins	Mason (F)	0-11	
56 mins	Mason (F)	0-12	
66 mins	Smyth (F)		0-7
67 mins	G.McCartan (F)	0-13	
68 mins	E.Burns	0-14	
70 mins	Hoey		0-8
FULL-TIME 73:00			

laboured to a half-time lead of 0-6 to 0-4. Monaghan made more of fewer chances with Slowey, Hoey and Declan Smyth (two frees) on the scoresheet.

Two minutes after the interval Smyth upped the tempo with a splendid point from distance but Down responded with six of the next seven scores. Conor Deegan took a grip at midfield, setting up James McCartan and then adding another point himself. Monaghan reacted by sending Davy Byrne into the action (in place of a still unfit Ray McCarron).

Farrell missed a goal chance but placed Linden for a point, and Mason tapped over three free-kicks for a 12-6 lead. Down were home and dry, even if two of the free-kick awards were deemed to be generous. Eamonn Burns wrapped things up by fisting over the bar after a good run.

At the final whistle, there were no wild celebrations on reaching the Ulster showdown at Clones. Foremost in people's minds was the previous evening's apalling massacre at O'Toole's Bar in Loughinisland. Greg Blaney spoke for everyone when he wrote in the Irish News.

"Loughinisland is one of those tiny rural clubs so typical of the GAA, but of course, the proximity of this particular atrocity really did hit hard at the emotions of the Mournes.

"In the hotel before Sunday's match, it was very noticeable that the usual banter and crack that our squad typically indulges in, was missing. In fact, there was a silence which reflected the sense of shock and numbness which everyone felt.

"The team took the field to nothing more than polite applause and the normal cheering and banter from the crowd was missing. I was told afterwards that the shouts of players could be heard quite clearly during the match, and with 14,000 in the crowd, that tells it's own story".

DOWN

		N.Collins		
M.Magill		B.Burns		P.Higgins
E.Burns 0-1		B.Breen		DJ Kane (c)
	G.McCartan 0-2		C.Deegan 0-1	
G.Mason 0-6		G.Blaney		J.McCartan 0-1
M.Linden 0-3		A.Farrell		C.McCabe

SUB: Gerard Deegan for McCabe (55).

MONAGHAN

		G.Murphy		
B.Murray		G.McGuirk (c)		D.Duffy
E.Murphy		D.Loughman		D.King
	F.McEneaney		P.McShane 0-1	
M.Slowey 0-1		R.McCarron		G.Hoey 0-2
D.Smyth 0-4		V.Martin		S.McGinnity

SUBS: N.Marron for Duffy (injrd 9 mins), D.Byrne for McCarron (44), G.Mone for Martin (49).

Referee: Jim Curran.
Linesmen: Mick McGrath (Donegal), Dessie Slater.
Bookings: James McCartan, Michael Magill, Frank McEneaney.
Man of the Match - Greg Blaney.

OUT WITH THE OLD, IN WITH THE NEW

Ulster SFC Semi-final, June 25
Tyrone 1-15   Donegal 0-10

Although Donegal people did not like to admit it at the time, this game marked the end of a golden era for their county. They may go on to win another All Ireland in the near future, but not with three of the men largely responsible for 1992. Manager Brian McEniff resigned after this defeat by Tyrone, former inspirational captain Anthony Molloy hung up his boots and current captain Martin McHugh later left to manage Cavan.

Donegal can expect a few more good years out of Matt Gallagher, Brian Murray and Joyce McMullan while John Joe Doherty, Barry McGowan and Tony Boyle are quality players who can certainly lead Donegal to further glories. What appears to be required is for these players to become leaders on and off the field, to replace McHugh and Molloy.

In the meantime, Tyrone could get there first. Led by Peter Canavan, their young lions looked hungry for success and well worth their place in what would be a first Ulster Final for thirteen of them. In direct contrast, thirteen of Donegal's team had started an All Ireland final, and taking the contrast even further, eight of this Tyrone team won All Ireland Under-21 medals just weeks before the Donegal Seniors' greatest moment in September, 1992.

Penalty? Donegal's Tony Boyle crashes to the ground under a challenge from Chris Lawn.

Tyrone burst out of the starting blocks with a Kilpatrick point after twelve seconds. McCaffrey added another on one minute and Loughran made it 3-0 in the third minute. Obviously Tyrone had not been affected by the start delay of eight minutes; both teams were in position after the parade and waiting for the national anthem when the delay was announced (to allow latecomers to arrive).

Donegal tried to work the ball out of their defence but were overwhelmed by swarms of white shirts; in the fourth minute Matt Gallagher found himself passing the ball back to his goalkeeper, while the first time Martin McHugh got the ball he was surrounded by three Tyrone men. Noel Hegarty also discovered that getting forward would not be as easy as it had appeared in the Antrim game.

Donegal scored only once in the opening 23 minutes, but with the benefit of hindsight Brian McEniff argues they should have had a penalty when Chris Lawn challenged Tony Boyle in the tenth minute. "Watching it again I think it was definitely a penalty". The former manager also has reason to rue wides by Declan Bonnar and Manus Boyle from scoreable free-kicks, while Martin McHugh's last appearance in a Donegal shirt ended in him being stretchered off the field after 25 minutes.

McHugh's exit was overshadowed by a brilliant second half solo show by Peter Canavan, who has the talent to become for Tyrone over the next ten years what McHugh has been for Donegal. He scored three wonderful points from play, two more from free-kicks and had time to hit the crossbar with a fisted effort as Tyrone took Donegal apart in the middle period of the half.

Pre-match talk had suggested Matt Gallagher would have problems in holding Canavan and that John Joe Doherty might be moved across. Only the first part of the theory was correct, as Canavan continually won good possession in front of his marker and made full use of it.

		Donegal	Tyrone
12 secs	Kilpatrick		0-1
1 min	McCaffrey		0-2
2 mins	Loughran		0-3
7 mins	M.Boyle (F)	0-1	
19 mins	Donaghy		0-4
22 mins	Canavan		0-5
23 mins	Bonnar (F)	0-2	
24 mins	J.McHugh	0-3	
36 mins	Bonnar (F)	0-4	
37 mins	Cush (F)		0-6
HALF-TIME 40:00			
41 mins	Canavan (F)		0-7
43 mins	Bonnar	0-5	
50 mins	Cush (F)		0-8
53 mins	Bonnar (F)	0-6	
55 mins	Cush		0-9
57 mins	Donaghy		0-10
59 mins	T.Boyle	0-7	
60 mins	Canavan		0-11
62 mins	Gormley		0-12
63 mins	S.Lawn		1-12
66 mins	Canavan		1-13
68 mins	Canavan		1-14
70 mins	J.McHugh	0-8	
71 mins	Canavan (F)		1-15
73 mins	T.Boyle	0-9	
76 mins	T.Boyle	0-10	
FULL-TIME 77:00			

Angry Art.
The Tyrone manager makes his point at half-time.

Out with the old, in with the new. Donegal's Martin McHugh makes a painful exit (below) while new Tyrone star Peter Canavan (right) is first to the ball.

That's what happened for the Tyrone's man's only score in the first half and again just after the break, when Canavan tapped over a simple free after Gallagher had fouled him.

His third point was one of the scores of the championship. Canavan got out in front, soloed twice, brushed off Mark Crossan, turned inside, took one bounce and with four defenders around him, still managed to kick the ball off the side of his boot and over the bar. Balance, strength and skill in equal abundance. Points four and five were almost identical, Canavan steadying himself before bending the ball over from the right side. That put Tyrone ten points clear, while his final score, a free-kick, was also his team's last of the match.

However, Tyrone did struggle during the early stages of the second half, as if they didn't believe they could go on and actually win the match. Donegal upped their game, displaying the flair and fight that had taken them to the verge of a sixth Ulster final in-a-row. They kept within two points of Tyrone until the fifteenth minute of the half, when Adrian Cush pointed after a superb eight-man move which had begun with goalkeeper Joe Cassidy. Two minutes later, the hard-working Plunkett Donaghy extended Tyrone's lead to four points when he again roamed free. Anthony Molloy's fantastic service as a Donegal senior player ended soon after, when he was replaced by Martin Gavigan.

Tyrone's goal came when substitute Brian Gormley reacted quickest to a breaking ball and sent a neat fist pass across the face of the Donegal square, to give Stephen Lawn a simple finish.

Brian McEniff announced his resignation after the game, stating that he was "tired and in need of a break. Also it's time for someone else to have a go". Reflecting some time later on Donegal's defeat in Breffni, McEniff felt a little aggrieved at a couple of decisions that went against his team, "particularly one call in the second half when there was only a couple of points it and Brian Murray was blown up for overcarrying. I would have said he was being fouled. But having said that, our attitude wasn't right on the day and Tyrone's will-to-win was impressive".

Brian McEniff congratulates Art McCrory and bids farewell to Donegal.

Referee: Pat McEneaney. Linesmen: Michael Cranney, PJ Quinn (Down).
Bookings: Chris Lawn, Stephen Lawn, Matt Gallagher. Man of the Match: Peter Canavan.

DOWN WALK TALL

Ulster SFC Final, July 17
Down 1-17 Tyrone 1-11

When both sets of players stepped onto the scales for the Ulster Final, not a single Down man weighed less than twelve and a half stone while Tyrone had four players as light as eleven stone. Three of their four lightest men were in the forwards who, as a unit, gave away an eleven and a half stone advantage to the Down defence.

And, as the players stood side-by-side at Clones for the National Anthem, Down found they had a height advantage in no fewer than twelve positions. Down had nine players of more than six foot, Tyrone had just four. The most striking difference was between the Down defence and the Tyrone forwards; Down had only one defender under six foot tall, Tyrone had five forwards between 5 '6 and 5 '10.

Eugene McKenna remembered a double bill at Croke Park several months previously. Tyrone came off the pitch after beating Wexford just as Down ran out to play Kerry. "We were like minors compared to Down's seniors. We were a small team then and still are". Many Tyrone supporters did not see this as a problem. They were confident the speed of their forwards would make up for the physical differences, and that Down would go the same way as Armagh and

Brian Gormley with Eugene McKenna.

Donegal. Art McCrory sounded a warning, "Down are at least ten points a better side than Donegal".

Down supporters quietly predicted a comfortable victory for their team, especially with Ross Carr fit again. They were to be proved right, though they were also to be outnumbered by Tyrone fans returning to St Tiernachs Park for the first time in five years. Like everyone else, they were suitably impressed by the new-look stadium which positively gleamed in the bright sunshine.

Centre of attraction was the Gerry Arthurs Stand, which sits opposite the Hill and houses the dressing-rooms. That means when the players now run out of the tunnel the first thing they see is the Hill. Tyrone's Aidan Morris will never forget the experience, "when we ran out the noise almost took the head of you! Thirteen of us were in our first final and never had a feeling like it before. I think we were a bit overawed at the start".

Down went to work right away, scoring in the first minute with a Gary Mason free-kick, awarded for a foul on Linden. DJ Kane had set up the move by bursting forward from half-back and finding Linden with an accurate pass. The move soon became familiar as the Down captain initiated numerous attacks throughout the half, and scored one point himself. Kane would also place Linden for two scores in the second half, on his way to taking the Man of the Match award.

Brian Burns gets to grips with Peter Canavan.

Tyrone looked to Peter Canavan for inspiration. He provided it in the sixth minute by pointing a free-kick, though the full-forward might have had a goal; Canavan looked like getting away from Brian Burns for a run at Neil Collins when he was fouled. Forty seconds later Stephen Lawn put Tyrone ahead after an excellent pass from Corr, and exactly forty seconds after that Linden scored at the other end. Clones braced itself for a possible classic when Brian Gormley popped up almost immediately for another Tyrone point after good work by Kilpatrick. Four scores in two minutes, 0-3 to 0-2 to Tyrone. However, the contest became one-sided during the rest of the half with Down out-scoring Tyrone by 0-7 to 0-2.

Down never lost the lead from the sixteenth minute when Carr pointed a free. And, when Mason punished another Tyrone indiscretion shortly after, the pattern was set. Fay Devlin admitted afterwards that Tyrone had played into Down's hands, "there was too much playing the man, not the ball. We handed Down a lot of simple frees and got punished for it. They were just too powerful for us and I think if we had stuck to playing football we might have fared much better".

Devlin himself was penalised in the 23rd minute for lifting the ball off the Tyrone goal-line

		Down	Tyrone
1 min	Mason (F)	0-1	
6 mins	Canavan (F)		0-1
7 mins	S.Lawn		0-2
7 mins	Linden	0-2	
8 mins	Gormley		0-3
10 mins	Mason (F)	0-3	
12 mins	Kane	0-4	
14 mins	Gormley		0-4
16 mins	Carr (F)	0-5	
18 mins	Mason (F)	0-6	
27 mins	Mason (45)	0-7	
29 mins	Carr	0-8	
30 mins	Canavan		0-5
31 mins	G.McCartan	0-9	
Half-Time 36:00			
40 mins	Mason	0-10	
43 mins	Carr	1-10	
47 mins	Higgins	1-11	
50 mins	Canavan (F)		0-6
52 mins	Canavan (F)		0-7
53 mins	Cush		1-7
56 mins	Linden	1-12	
57 mins	Blaney	1-13	
58 mins	Cush		1-8
58 mins	Linden	1-14	
63 mins	Carr (F)	1-15	
65 mins	Canavan (F)		1-9
68 mins	Carr (F)	1-16	
69 mins	E.Burns	1-17	
70 mins	Canavan (F)		1-10
73 mins	Canavan (F)		1-11
Full-Time 76:00			

after Blaney had been held up just short of the line. Linden had been successful with just three penalties of ten in training during the week, and contrived to side-foot this kick high and wide to the right. Tyrone fans enjoyed the moment, but Mason restored order with a 45 metre kick which cleared the crossbar by some distance. Carr increased the gap to four points with a brilliant long range kick.

Brian Burns and Peter Canavan were having their own private battle in a Down half which had been vacated by the rest of the Tyrone forwards. The plan seemed to be to isolate Canavan and hope that he benefitted from quick deliveries. It worked to perfection when Canavan lost Burns with a wonderful shimmy near the sideline, and cut inside to score on the half hour. However, Tyrone did not maintain the same quality of service to Canavan (Burns fared better under the high ball), and the other Tyrone forwards were largely ineffective outfield. Down had much more variety to their game, as highlighted by another superb long kick from Greg McCartan.

Paul Donnelly spent most of the first half niggling and jostling with James McCartan. The defender was booked before the break, ironically for one of his lesser crimes, and punished again when McCartan won a penalty early in the second half. The Down man lost a boot on his run towards goal; Donnelly's attempt to throw it into the crowd incurred the wrath of McCartan, Down fans, and most neutrals.

Peter McGrath wanted Mason to take the penalty but Ross Carr had already determined that he would assume responsibility. Carr drove the ball quite near the goalkeeper but with such power that Joe Cassidy had no chance of stopping it. Higgins added a marvellous point from all of 45 metres for a lead of 1-11 to 0-5.

Pascal Canavan's entrance marked a change in fortune for Tyrone as they made progress with their short game. Starting as far back as their own 21-yard line, Tyrone worked the ball through several players before winning successive free-kicks for Peter Canavan to convert. Better was to come, as the Canavan brothers and Kilpatrick ripped through the Down defence before Cush palmed a rebound of the crossbar into the net.

A revitalised Tyrone might have expected to capitalise on their goal, but Down stormed back to claim six of the next eight scores. Almost immediately, James McCartan was denied a goal by Cassidy, but Linden and Blaney (his first score of the championship) restored Down's superiorty. Kane picked out Linden for another, and the Mayobridge flyer was fouled twice more as Carr took his total to 1-4.

Tyrone's young lions left Clones utterly dejected, but they can take heart by the fact that they lost to the All Ireland champions. They have some quality forwards and if they can put this year's experience to good use, then a provincial title may not be beyond them. Down looked All Ireland material, with strong and skilful players all over the field. Many of them are comfortable kicking with either foot and they had eight different scorers, including a midfielder and three defenders.

CHAMPIONSHIP TOP SCORERS		
Peter Canavan (Tyrone)	1-17	(20)
Mickey Linden (Down)	0-12	(12)
Diarmuid Marsden (Armagh)	1-9	(12)
Gary Mason (Down)	0-11	(11)
Declan Smyth (Monaghan)	1-8	(11)
Declan Bonnar (Donegal)	0-9	(9)
Adrian Cush (Tyrone)	1-6	(9)
Greg McCartan (Down)	0-8	(8)
Conal Heatley (Antrim)	1-5	(8)

Note: Peter Canavan also won the BBC Player of the Championship Award.

DOWN

N.Collins

M.Magill   B.Burns   P.Higgins 0-1
E.Burns 0-1   B.Breen   DJ Kane (c) 0-1
          G.McCartan 0-1   C.Deegan
R.Carr 1-4   G.Blaney 0-1   J.McCartan
M.Linden 0-3   A.Farrell   G.Mason 0-5

SUB: P.Withnell for Farrell (69).

TYRONE

J.Cassidy

G.McGirr   C.Lawn   F.Devlin
P.Donnelly   F.Logan   A.Morris
          C.Corr (c)   P.Donaghy
A.Cush 1-1   A.Kilpatrick   S.Lawn 0-1
B.Gormley 0-2   Ptr.Canavan 0-7 C.Loughran

SUBS: Pl.Canavan for Loughran (44), P.Devlin for Fay Devlin (65), M.McGleenan for Gormley (68).

Referee: Tommy McDermott. Linesmen: Gerry McClorey, Damian Campbell.
Bookings: Gareth McGirr, Paul Donnelly, Brian Burns, Gregory McCartan.
Man of the Match: DJ Kane.

Above: Flower Power! Conor Deegan offers Greg McCartan a flower from Down's victory bouquet.

Right: DJ Kane with the Anglo-Celt Cup.

LAST TEN ULSTER FINALS

1985 - Monaghan 2-9	Derry 0-8
1986 - Tyrone 1-11	Down 0-10
1987 - Derry 0-11	Armagh 0-9
1988 - Monaghan 1-10	Tyrone 0-11
1989 - Tyrone 2-13	Donegal 0-7
1990 - Donegal 0-15	Armagh 0-14
1991 - Down 1-15	Donegal 0-10
1992 - Donegal 0-14	Derry 1-9
1993 - Derry 0-8	Donegal 0-6
1994 - Down 1-17	Tyrone 1-11

ROLL OF HONOUR

Cavan 37; Monaghan 14; Down 12; Antrim 10; Armagh 7;Derry, Tyrone 6; Donegal 5.

2

EASY FOR DOWN

All Ireland Semi-final, August 14
Down 1-13   Cork 0-11

In 1991, Down's semi-final victory over Kerry sent the mass of red and black supporters on Hill 16 into a tizzy of delight and emotion. The rest of Ulster rejoiced too, at a rare success in Croke Park. Peter Withnell's goals from that glorious, sunny day remain fresh in the memory, yet Down's 1994 semi-final defeat of Cork lacked any emotional high-points. Their win had been widely anticipated, and never really looked to be in doubt during the seventy minutes.

The main emotion at the finish was one of relief, as a more experienced Down team overcame a poor challenge from Cork. "It was a workmanlike performance", summed up '91 star Liam Austin. "Down lulled at times but were good overall. The forwards got good supply of the ball from outfield and that was the key".

Austin had identified a tactic that paid huge dividends for Down. With the half-forwards leaning back into midfield, Mickey Linden and Aidan Farrell were often left isolated, the only Down players within fifty yards of the Cork goal. All of a sudden, Conor Deegan or Barry Breen would spring a long ball into the less-populated half of the field and a Down score was almost sure to follow. It worked perfectly for Down's goal in the nineteenth minute, when Breen collected a breaking

Grounded! Cork's Anthony Davis, John Kerins and Down goalscorer Aidan Farrell, are on the floor as Mickey Linden celebrates.

		Down	Cork
20 secs	McGrath		0-1
7 mins	Farrell	0-1	
12 mins	Mason (F)	0-2	
13 mins	G.McCartan	0-3	
18 mins	Corkery (F)		0-2
19 mins	Farrell	1-3	
20 mins	Tompkins		0-3
24 mins	Linden	1-4	
26 mins	Deegan	1-5	
27 mins	Calnan		0-4
28 mins	Calnan		0-5
29 mins	Corkery (F)		0-6
32 mins	Mason	1-6	
33 mins	Corkery (F)		0-7
Half-Time	38:00		
42 mins	Mason (F)	1-7	
45 mins	Mason (45)	1-8	
47 mins	Mason (F)	1-9	
50 mins	Carr (F)	1-10	
53 mins	Farrell	1-11	
55 mins	Mason (F)	1-12	
56 mins	Corkery (F)		0-8
59 mins	G.McCartan (F)	1-13	
61 mins	Corkery (F)		0-9
62 mins	Corkery (F)		0-10
74 mins	Corkery		0-11
Full-Time	75:00		

ball and, a la 1991, drove it deep into the danger zone. Linden won the race and set up the inrushing Farrell for a simple finish from six yards.

Down in fact played a total of twelve passes towards Linden in the first half, with nine of them getting through and a goal and four points coming off him. Farrell was Linden's perfect ally as he made space, linked defence with attack and scored 1-2 on what was his championship debut in Croke Park. The 21-year-old was to Down in 1994 what Peter Withnell had been in 1991.

The most intriguing and telling part of the contest was the third quarter. Down won it by six points to nil, yet Cork had plenty of possession and some glorious chances to score. Teddy McCarthy (on for Fahy) helped win a few balls around midfield, but in the opening exchanges Honohan blazed wide from under the posts and Tompkins just missed the target. Down immediately swooped upfield to score when O'Brien fouled Blaney. Gary Mason's precision kicking from dead balls reaped another breakaway score from a 45 on seven minutes,

Barry Breen soloes away from Larry Tompkins.

and again from a free when Ross Carr was fouled. Three points in six minutes, 1-9 to 0-7.

Carr punished Cork again from a free-kick in the twelfth minute, Farrell fisted a point after the "Route One" tactic worked again (Deegan to Linden who left Cahalane in his wake) and Mason once more from a free put Down eight points clear. DJ Kane noticed "a number of Cork heads beginning to drop" and when Cork finally replied, on 18 minutes, Corkery's free-kick was greeted only with polite applause. Corkery, who was well marked by Paul Higgins, tagged on three more points (two frees) as the Down support, three times that of Cork, waited for the formality of the final whistle and another All Ireland final.

The accuracy of Down's free-takers played a major part in this victory, emphasised in the 21st minute when Greg McCartan showed that he could do what Mason and Carr had done earlier. Down missed just one free in the game.

Cork had stayed with Down in the first half. Paul McGrath (after 22 seconds), Tompkins and Calnan all had fine scores while a slip by Neil Collins almost presented them with a goal in the opening minutes. Down's first score took seven minutes to arrive, Farrell taking a pass from Linden and wisely fisting over the bar even though a goal was on, "it was important to get a score on the board to settle us". James McCartan, Mason and Carr had registered wides.

Down lost Eamonn Burns after ten minutes when he turned ackwardly chasing a breaking ball, but they had a ready-made replacement in John Kelly. Cork soon had casualties of their own after a clash of heads between Danny Culloty and Don Davis, the former having to go off while Davis soldiered on with a large, white bandage around his head.

After Farrell's goal, Down extended their lead to five points but faded for a period in which Cork scored three times and had three other chances (two wide and one saved). "We went to sleep for a few minutes and it cost us dearly. We have to keep concentrating", said the manager as he walked to the dressing-room.

Peter McGrath was much happier when he made the same journey at the end of the game, "Cork were poor and our experience showed". His 1991 players had indeed performed well. Conor Deegan's fielding was impressive, Breen had been masterful in his new position and Linden was Linden. The new boys also came up trumps - Brian Burns, Michael Magill, and Man of the Match Aidan Farrell who outplayed three markers, including Cahalane who "nearly pulled the jersey of me". James McCartan recognised the contributions of Burns and Magill. "A lot of uncomplimentary things were said about our full-back line in the run-up to the game, but it was our defenders who won us the match today. I thought Brian Burns was outstanding". McCartan was otherwise engaged in filming his own amateur video of the dressing-room scenes, with camera in hand and adding his own commentary as he focussed on team-mates, "and now Mickey Linden goes past Niall Cahalane again..."

Eamonn Burns was too sore to smile for James, fearing broken bones in his foot, while Neil Collins was of the opinion that the work they had done since "knuckling down in February" had paid off. The goalkeeper felt it had provided the necessary fitness and generated the right spirit in the camp.

DOWN

N.Collins

M.Magill   B.Burns   P.Higgins
E.Burns   B.Breen   DJ Kane (c)

G.McCartan 0-2   C.Deegan 0-1

R.Carr 0-1   G.Blaney   J.McCartan
M.Linden 0-1   A. Farrell 1-2   G.Mason 0-6

SUB: J. Kelly for E. Burns (10).

CORK

J.Kerins

M.Farr   M.O'Connor   N.Cahalane
B.Corcoran   S.O'Brien (c)   T.Davis

S.Fahy   D.Culloty

S.Calnan 0-2   L. Tompkins 0-1   D.Davis
C.Corkery 0-7   J.Kavanagh   P.McGrath 0-1

SUBS: L.Honohan for Culloty (15), T.McCarthy for Fahy (half-time),
J.O'Driscoll for D.Davis (50).

Referee: Brian White (Wexford).
Booked: Paul Higgins, Mark Farr, Stephen O'Brien, Barry Breen.

The Down team stand to attention before their supporters.

3

"WE IN DOWN DON'T KNOW HOW TO LOSE ALL IRELANDS"

All Ireland Final, September 18
Down 1-12 Dublin 0-13

Michael Magill: "a weak link", Greg Blaney: "doesn't have too much left to give", James McCartan: "not scoring enough", Gary Mason: "a better player in 1991", and Barry Breen: "Vinny Murphy will trouble him".

Larry Tompkins views on the Down players were contained in an article titled "Dublin to lift Sam" in the Sunday Press. He assessed and marked each player, with Dublin totalling 127 to Down's 121.

Another former All Ireland winner, Liam Hayes agreed. "It should be no real contest. Dublin to win by three points", he told the Irish News. The Meathman also told UTV that Dublin "deserved to win this All Ireland" and that "Down don't know what it takes to win an All Ireland".

Over at the Sunday Tribune, Colm O'Rourke gave Down a little more credit, "Down have been able to coast to this final. Whenever they have had to produce high quality football they have done so", yet he came down on the side of Dublin as he warned, "Down should fear a big day from Charlie".

Peter McGrath and his players turned the comments of the experts to their advantage. Liam Hayes' interview was replayed at the Country Club in Portmarnock where DJ Kane addressed his team a few hours before the game; afterwards the Down captain said it was "the best thing we could ever have seen".

Down went into the game with a steely determination, and with confidence in their own ability. "Eleven of them have been here before. so I'm sure the occasion won't pass us by", assured McGrath on the team bus as it journeyed South. "Also, I watched the 1991 video the other day, and told the boys to recall the expressions of the Meath faces at the end of the game".

Like 1991, Down were unchanged from the semi-final, which meant John Kelly returning to the bench as Eamonn

Men behind the wire. Ross Carr watches the Minor Final.

Burns made a late recovery from injury. The Dubs were concerned about Mickey Linden, especially when corner-back Ciaran Walsh was injured in a club match. "The way Linden left Niall Cahalane for dead over fifteen yards in the semi-final was alarming" commented Dublin captain John O'Leary. His manager Pat O'Neill decided Paul Curran was the man for the job, even though he was a recognised half-back.

Curran might have taken the advice of a clever banner beside a Toyota advertisement at the Canal End, "The man in front is Mickey Linden!" (See colour section). Supporters from Castlewellan joined in the mood with another slogan borrowed from a television ad, "Did it, Done it, Liked it, Loved it, Doing it again!"

ALL-IRELAND FINAL		
FIRST HALF		
	Down	Dublin
2 mins G.McCartan	0-1	
4 mins Clarke		0-1
6 mins Redmond (45)		0-2
7 mins Linden	0-2	
9 mins Carr (45)	0-3	
12 mins Carr (F)	0-4	
13 mins Carr (F)	0-5	
14 mins Sheedy		0-3
18 mins J.McCartan	1-5	
19 mins A.Farrell	1-6	
23 mins Murphy		0-4
27 mins Guiden		0-5
27 mins Mason	1-7	
28 mins Linden	1-8	
29 mins Stynes		0-6
32 mins Sheedy		0-7
Half-Time 36:00		

Red and black flags covered the Canal End as Down emerged from the tunnel. DJ strode out purposefully, Michael Magill burst past Neil Collins and Aidan Farrell glanced up at Hill 16 (from where he had watched the '91 final) while James McCartan strolled out with an almost casual indifference to the whole occasion. Ross Carr was last man out. DJ Kane won the toss and played into the Hill, as the three previous All Ireland winning captains had done.

Dublin looked sharp in the opening exchanges but Down scored first, Greg McCartan absorbing two strong challenges before dropping his kick over the bar. Paul Clarke equalised sixty seconds later when he ran unchallenged from half-back to take a pass from Dessie Farrell. Players on both sides were having difficulty with the wet conditions, DJ Kane accepted a new pair of boots at the sideline from Pat O'Hare.

Redmond put the Dubs ahead from a 45, but only briefly. Greg McCartan collected a kick-out from Collins and worked the ball through Farrell, Blaney and Linden who slipped inside Curran to score. James McCartan was unlucky twice inside sixty seconds. First, his high kick came off a post and then O'Leary made a spectacular reflex save when James tried to flick a superb long pass from Breen to the net. Carr put the resulting 45 on target.

Carr's next score was one of those moments you get in finals which capture the mood and ask searching questions of the protagonists. Just before, the whole of Hill 16 had roared with delight as Carr's close-in free-kick was blocked down by a Dublin defender. Tommy Sugrue waved away Down protests (the defender was barely ten yards away from the ball) but he did penalise Keith Barr for overcarrying and so present Carr with another free-kick. This time it was much further out and directly under the Hill. Carr stepped back slowly, in his usual fashion, and paused in a still, upright position, taking aim at the posts. At that moment, the din from the Hill became louder, as if the Dublin support was inviting Carr to take them on.

"That score was the sweetest of the three I got, though funny enough the noise from the Hill didn't bother me that much. It was actually louder when we played here in the league in February because there was less people in the stadium, and that helped."

Down struck another blow to Dublin's heart with a goal fashioned by Linden and scored by James McCartan. Greg McCartan began the move with a line-ball from under the Hogan Stand, aimed at Gary Mason. The corner-forward was second favourite, but flung himself in front his marker to deflect the ball towards Linden. Suddenly, the Dublin defence was split apart and Linden and James McCartan were in a two-on-one situation with John O'Leary. "At first I felt I had the beating of John and could take the goal myself", recalls Linden, "but then I thought to myself that this was an All Ireland final and it was no time to be selfish or foolish. I spotted James out of the side of my eye and gave him the pass and once he got it into his hands I knew the ball was in the back of the net".

The goal came in Down's most productive period, between the seventh and 19th minutes, when they scored 1-5 to Dublin's 0-1.

The last score in this spell, a point from Farrell, typified one of the best features of Down's performances this year, forwards putting defenders under serious pressure. James McCartan blocked an attempted clearance, then Sheedy was closed down and forced to kick the ball straight to Blaney who gave it to Farrell. Down might have emphasised their superiorty with more scores in this period but for another controversial block from a Mason free-kick (even closer than before) and a shot from Deegan which screwed just wide.

Dublin rallied briefly with a long range point from Murphy and a close-in fisted score from Guiden. The latter had run straight at the Down goal but was forced to opt for a point when Neil Collins narrowed the angle. Within a minute, Gary Mason kicked a wonderful point of his left-foot and Linden made it 1-8 to 0-5 after another solo run.

Stynes and Sheedy reduced the gap to four points in the closing minutes of the half though Down had another concern. Dr Martin Walsh was already in the dressing-room preparing a pain-killing injection for DJ Kane who had kept quiet a calf muscle injury received in training ten days earlier. "I had a lot of treatment with John Martin and Brian Strain (Portadown soccer player) in Belfast but the injury came back at me towards the end of the first half and I was caught for speed a few times. The half-time injection did it's job until near the end".

Down won the crucial period at the start of the second half, partly because of their work rate and partly because of Dublin's old failings. Sheedy blazed wide after two minutes at one end while Down were handed easy frees at the other. James McCartan was fouled for the first, Greg Blaney for the second. Then, Brian Stynes appeared to be in no danger as he fetched a 45 in front of his own goal, but wee James came from behind to knock the ball out of his hands. Blaney crossed to Farrell who slipped and skied a pass to Linden who fisted over the bar. 1-11 to 0-8 after twelve minutes.

SECOND HALF		Down	Dublin
43 mins	Mason (F)	1-9	
45 mins	D.Farrell		0-8
46 mins	Mason (F)	1-10	
48 mins	Linden	1-11	
49 mins	Curran		0-9
51 mins	Linden	1-12	
53 mins	Redmond (F)		0-10
57 mins	Redmond (F)		0-11
60 mins	Cahill		0-12
72 mins	Redmond		0-13
Full-Time	73:00		

Referee Tommy Sugrue signals another point by Mickey Linden.

Dublin got one thing right. They finally released Paul Curran to his natural attacking half-back role from where he prospered for the rest of the game, starting with a quick point. James McCartan explained later why Curran had found so much room in which to manoeuvre, "Pete told me to go over to the middle and try to get hold of the ball, but every time I looked round Paul was away!" Ross Carr spotted the problem and covered brilliantly, chasing back seventy yards to catch and dispossess Curran on one occasion.

Down's last score of the game came fifteen minutes into the second half and 22 minutes from the final whistle. Blaney got a vital hand in to flick the ball out of Keith Barr's grasp and into the path of Linden who took a simple point. Down's last three points had come directly from Blaney. A week later his manager praised Blaney at the Carryduff club in Belfast when he begged the question, "can you remember Keith Barr doing anything of consequence in the match?"

But if the Down forwards had put their team in the driving seat, then it was the defence and goalkeeper who kept them there, as Dublin came with a grandstand finish. Michael Magill limited dangerman Charlie Redmond to one score from play (in the last minute), the same player and Kane made vital blocks and Neil Collins wrote himself into the history books with a penalty save.

Dublin had begun to take control when substitutes Paul Bealin and Sean Cahill arrived in the middle of the field. A clean catch by Bealin led to a goal chance for Redmond on nineteen minutes, but Magill got in the way. Redmond did score from the next attack, from a free-kick after Cahill had won the kick-out and Guiden was fouled by Brian Burns.

Redmond apart, Dublin wasted excellent opportunities in the closing stages. Only Cahill added to the Dublin tally while the likes of Mick Deegan and Bealin appeared to suffer from stage fright. The latter found acres of space in the right-half-forward position yet, as if intimidated by Hill 16, he skied his kick aimlessly to the left of the posts. "The occasion seemed to get to the Dublin players, they looked frightened and took the wrong options", observed Liam Austin.

Curran and Sheedy added weight to Austin's argument by kicking bad wides before Cahill narrowed the gap to three points going into the last ten minutes. In Dublin's next attack, a high ball from Curran broke between Redmond and Magill to substitute Johnny Barr who drove into the Down square. Surrounded by defenders, he slipped the ball to Farrell who fell to the ground under a tackle from Brian Burns. PENALTY!

Charlie Redmond, "darling" of the Hill, had one kick to level the scores and put to rest all of Dublin's disappointments and failures of the previous decade. Neil Collins knew a save would almost certainly win the All Ireland for his county, but the odds were stacked against him as he prepared to face the championship's top scorer (4-29 to date) and with the Hill breathing down his neck.

As Redmond placed the ball, Greg Blaney turned away, DJ Kane thought "oh no, I'm going to captain the first Down team to lose an All Ireland", and up in the Hogan Stand Mrs Loretta Collins buried her head in her hands.

Redmond kicked to his left, Collins guessed right and pushed the ball back into play. Johnny Barr, DJ Kane and Redmond raced to the rebound. Barr might well have scored if he had not slipped, but it was Kane who got a vital boot in to nudge the ball wide of the far post. Considering the captain's injury, it was a tremendous interception which saved the day as much as Collins' save.

James McCartan leapt into his goalkeeper's arms, tears were shed in the Hogan Stand and Down were still three points ahead. "I was always going to dive to the right", revealed the hero of the moment, "it was an educated guess because Tom Potter (coach) and I had done our homework on Charlie. We studied videos and saw that he missed one to the other side in the '92 All Ireland final, and then scored one against Kildare to the keeper's right this year, so there was no question of me going to the left. I had to get down low to the right and behind the ball, though if he had put it to my other side then it was a goal".

Opinions were divided on whether the missed penalty cost Dublin the match. "Down were in poor shape, we would have gone on to win by a few points" offered Barney Rock. Pat O'Neill and Greg Blaney agreed, but John O'Leary disagreed, "we had other chances to win and didn't take them". Michael Magill argued "Dublin were lucky to get the penalty" while Ross Carr gave the credit to his goalkeeper, "Dublin shouldn't blame Charlie, he was up against the best keeper in the country. Surely Neil will get an All Star now" (Collins was unlucky to miss out in 1991).

After the penalty, Down were pinned in their own half. Magill cleared his lines twice, but Dublin kept coming. The corner-back looked up at the clock as he heard Paul Higgins shouting across, "No more goals and we have Sam". Outfield, Ross Carr called to Greg McCartan to "do more clean catching" to relieve the pressure. The midfielder did what he was told, and although the subsequent attack ended with Carr kicking the ball wide, it was as good as a score.

Down were on their last legs: "Those last ten minutes were the longest of my life", Barry Breen admitted, "I can't ever remember feeling so tired". DJ's leg began to hurt again, Blaney was obviously drained and Eamonn Burns looked to the line

Going forward with Down!

Ulster Bank

Sponsors of

DOWN GAA

to come off. Peter Withnell and John Kelly were bursting to get on to gee up an ailing team yet Peter McGrath, as in 1991, refused to make changes (until the injured Conor Deegan had to be replaced). The manager's philosophy in both finals was, "why make changes when new players need time to adjust to both the conditions and the pace of the game?"

Dublin meanwhile, were at panic stations and couldn't score. Johnny Barr went for a goal when a point was on, Redmond put a 45 wide and then had a soccer-style snapshot blocked by Kane. Ross Carr cleared the rebound. Dublin's ace card also tried to get through with a brilliant fetch, dummy and pass to Curran but Breen stood firm and won a free out. Redmond finally got the ball over the bar, but time was nearly up. The last opportunity fell to Stynes but his effort was badly wide.

Greg Blaney forgot his tiredness when Tommy Sugrue blew the final whistle, as he jumped for joy and made a quick dash for the dressing-room. "I made the mistake three years ago of staying out on the pitch and got caught in the crowds."

DJ Kane proudly held the Sam Maguire Cup aloft for a full seventeen seconds and was full of emotion when he returned to the winner's base. "There's great tradition in our family for gaelic football, going right back to the sixties. I met my brother Val (1968 panellist) on the way in here and it's just great to win. A dream since I was a boy".

Less then twelve months previous, Kane's dream looked to be no more than that. The story goes that DJ was in the mood for following Blaney and McCartan into self-imposed exile when he was called back at a training night, and announced as new team captain.

DJ was also delighted to prove a few media people wrong. "We had all the motivation we needed from what others said about us after the Cork game. Self-appointed experts made some personal comments, but I think we proved that '91 was no fluke. We played extremely well for forty minutes, then lay down. If there had been another five minutes they might have caught us, but then again, All Ireland finals are only seventy minutes long".

Peter McGrath paid tribute to the fitness of his players. "We had 129 training sessions since last September, including a gruelling schedule in January under new trainer Pat O'Hare. We needed something new at the time and Pat brought fresh ideas with him. Fitness counted today as the rain got heavier in the second half and the conditions worsened. The game tightened up and we couldn't get play opened up as well as we had in the first half".

"We showed flair in 1991 but this All Ireland was won more by guts and determination", concluded James McCartan as Conor Deegan was carried into the dressing-room by Eamonn Connolly and Gareth Bailie. After a quick injection, Deegan was able to rejoin the celebrations by popping open a bottle of champagne, though there was not quite the same wild euphoria of '91. Down PRO Fintan Mussen summed up the mood after his county had equalled Cavan's haul of five All Ireland titles, "we are not arrogant, just quietly jubilant".

Ross Carr was finally at peace with himself. "The win in '91 was great for everyone in the county and in the province, it was a public thing, but this was a more personal thing. We celebrated with people after '91 who turned on us after that. Because of the last two years we had become a flash-in-the-pan team, but we've come back and shown we're a solid team, a good team. I cried after losing to Derry in 1993, I remember every single one of their eleven points, but when Derry won the All Ireland I said there's no way I'm going to leave Derry finish my career".

Carr warranted a mention as the "Man of the Match" awards were handed out to Michael Magill (from the Ulster Bank) and to Mickey Linden from Colm O'Rourke on RTE that evening.

And what of the losers? Dublin had failed once again on the big day but were offered plenty of sympathy votes. Greg Blaney came close to agreeing with Liam Hayes, "I don't mean to be patronising but if there's a team other than Down I'd like to see win an All Ireland it has to be Dublin. They're entitled to win one at this stage". Pat O'Neill owned up to the mistake of playing Curran on Linden and leaving him there too long. Perhaps Bealin should also have played from the start and Tommy Carr should have come on? Vinny Murphy suggested the Dubs were afraid of making mistakes because they tend to over-analyse their performances on video and on the training ground at Parnell Park.

The final word goes to the man from Rostrevor who has now led Down to two All Irelands in four years, Peter McGrath. His achievement is a mighty one, yet his reign appeared to be in jeopardy last winter before the return of Greg Blaney and James McCartan. McGrath insisted he was always one hundred per cent certain the players would come back, "I have known them a long time and have known that they were committed and passionate about Down football. I knew also that common sense and mutual trust and respect would prevail".

In 1991, McGrath devised the slogan "We're the team that beat the team that couldn't be beaten". This year, he addressed thousands of Down supporters in Newry the day after the final, "one well-known journalist said on television the other night that Down don't know what it takes to win an All Ireland. We in Down say..... We don't know how to *lose* an All Ireland!"

DOWN

	N.Collins	
M.Magill	B.Burns	P.Higgins
E.Burns	B.Breen	DJ Kane (c)
G.McCartan 0-1		C.Deegan
R.Carr 0-3	G.Blaney	J.McCartan 1-0
M.Linden 0-4	A.Farrell 0-1	G.Mason 0-3

SUB: G.Colgan for Deegan (71)

DUBLIN

	J.O'Leary (c)	
P.Moran	D.Deasy	P.Curran 0-1
P.Clarke 0-1	K.Barr	M.Deegan
B.Stynes 0-1		J.Sheedy 0-2
P.Gilroy	V.Murphy 0-1	N.Guiden 0-1
C.Redmond 0-4	M.Galvin	D.Farrell 0-1

SUBS: P.Bealin for Gilroy (39), S.Cahill 0-1 for Galvin (53), J.Barr for Guiden (60).

Referee: Tommy Sugrue (Kerry).
Booked: Niall Guiden, Gary Mason, Dermot Deasy.
Man of the Match: Mickey Linden.
Attendance: 58,864

DOWN 1991

	Games	Mins	Scores
Ross Carr	6	420	0-30
Neil Collins	6	420	—
DJ Kane	6	420	0-3
John Kelly	6	420	—
James McCartan	6	420	—
Conor Deegan	6	419	—
Mickey Linden	6	415	2-8
Eamonn Burns	6	409	0-2
Barry Breen	6	404	1-1
Brendan McKernan	6	401	—
Greg Blaney	6	400	0-6
Peter Withnell	6	393	2-3
Gary Mason	6	385	0-12
Paddy O'Rourke	6	385	—
Paul Higgins	6	315	0-1
Liam Austin	4	167	0-1
Mark McCartan	2	25	—
Paul McCartan	1	25	0-1
Cathal Murray	1	10	—
Ambrose Rodgers	2	7	—
Michael Quinn	2	4	—

DOWN 1994

	Games	Mins	Scores
Greg Blaney	5	371	0-1
Barry Breen	5	371	—
Brian Burns	5	371	—
Neil Collins	5	371	—
DJ Kane	5	371	0-1
Mickey Linden	5	371	0-17
Michael Magill	5	371	—
Gregory McCartan	5	371	0-11
James McCartan	5	371	1-3
Conor Deegan	5	369	0-2
Aidan Farrell	5	364	1-4
Paul Higgins	5	350	0-1
Gary Mason	4	297	0-20
Ross Carr	4	277	1-8
John Kelly	2	86	—
Gerard Deegan	2	81	—
Ciaran McCabe	2	66	1-0
Peter Withnell	2	28	—
Gerard Colgan	1	2	—

RESULTS

LEINSTER

Wicklow 0-14	Offaly 3-11 (R: 0-12 1-9)
Westmeath 1-9	Louth 0-13
Laois 4-15	Longford 2-4
Offaly 0-8	Wexford 0-10
Meath 0-20	Laois 2-10
Louth 3-19	Carlow 0-11
Dublin 1-14	Kildare 1-9 (R: 0-11 0-11)
Meath 4-14	Wexford 2-6
Dublin 1-15	Louth 1-8
Dublin 1-9	Meath 1-8

CONNACHT

London 0-6	Galway 2-21
Roscommon 0-12	Leitrim 1-10
Mayo 2-18	Sligo 1-5
Galway 0-10	Leitrim 0-11 (R: 1-6 0-9)
Leitrim 0-12	Mayo 2-4

ULSTER

Armagh 1-6	Fermanagh 0-6
Cavan 1-12	Monaghan 3-10
Derry 1-12	Down 1-14
Antrim 1-9	Donegal 1-12
Tyrone 3-10	Armagh 1-10
Down 0-14	Monaghan 0-8
Tyrone 1-15	Donegal 0-10
Down 1-17	Tyrone 1-11

MUNSTER

Clare 0-13	Tipperary 2-8
Kerry 2-19	Limerick 0-8
Cork 1-13	Kerry 2-8
Tipperary 5-14	Waterford 0-15
Cork 2-19	Tipperary 3-9

ALL IRELAND SEMI-FINALS

Down 1-13	Cork 0-11
Dublin 3-15	Leitrim 1-9

ALL IRELAND FINAL

Down 1-12	Dublin 0-13

ULSTER'S ALL IRELAND CHAMPIONS

1933 - Cavan 2-5	Galway 1-4
1935 - Cavan 3-6	Kildare 2-5
1947 - Cavan 2-11	Kerry 2-7
1948 - Cavan 4-5	Mayo 4-4
1952 - Cavan 0-9	Meath 0-5
1960 - Down 2-10	Kerry 0-8
1961 - Down 3-6	Offaly 2-8
1968 - Down 2-12	Kerry 1-13
1991 - Down 1-16	Meath 1-14
1992 - Donegal 0-18	Dublin 0-14
1993 - Derry 1-14	Cork 2-7
1994 - Down 1-12	Dublin 0-13

ROLL OF HONOUR.

Kerry 30; Dublin 21; Galway 7; Cork 6;
Cavan, Down, Meath, Wexford 5; Kildare,
Tipperary 4; Louth, Mayo, Offaly 3;
Limerick, Roscommon 2; Derry, Donegal 1.

4

PLAYER OF THE YEAR -
MICKEY LINDEN, DOWN.

"Mickey can certainly do a few tricks with the ball. In fact, I swear I've seen him make it talk to him in training!", James McCartan joining the Mickey Linden fan club before the All Ireland final.

Defenders up and down the country will know what James means, after years of trailing in the wake of the Mayobridge flyer, though it is not so much Linden's speed that beats them as much as his anticipation.

"Got it in one. It's knowing when to move and when to stay, knowing when the ball coming in will bounce in front of you or be hit long". There was a perfect example in the third minute of the final when Ross Carr struck a long ball from his own half towards the right corner. Paul Curran, so anxious to win the first contest, dashed forward to meet it but Linden held his position. The ball skidded off the greasy surface, over Curran's head and into the Down man's arms. He duly slipped the ball inside to Gregory McCartan for his team's first score. First blood to Linden.

During Down's second attack Linden drifted across the full-forward line, accepted a pass from Greg Blaney, rounded his marker and scored a point. In the twelfth minute, Linden turned Curran again, only to be fouled by Jack Sheedy. Carr converted the free-kick. Then the goal. Many players would have taken the glory of what would have been a simple goal in an All Ireland final, but Linden unselfishly set it on a plate for James McCartan.

So, after eighteen minutes Down led 1-5 to 0-3 with Linden directly or indirectly responsible for 1-3. He went on to score three more points and deservedly take the Man of the Match Award, and plaudits from all sides, including one from a manager who had watched him develop from a very good player into a great one.

"Mickey has succeeded in varying his game", analysed Peter McGrath after the final. "In 1991 he was all pace, energy and drive but in 1994 he is much more subtle and uses the ball better. He has worked at his game and is a true model for all young players".

Taking the comparison further, Linden's scoring total for the 1991 championship was 2-8, for 1994 it was 0-17. The latter correctly suggests a more consistent contribution.

LINDEN'S 1994 CONTRIBUTION			
Opponents	Scored	Set up	Fouled for
Derry	0-6	1-1	—
Monaghan	0-3	0-1	0-3
Tyrone	0-3	0-2	0-3
Cork	0-1	1-2	0-1
Dublin	0-4	1-1	0-1
Totals	0-17	3-9	0-8

Seventeen points scored, three goals and nine points set up in one way or another, and eight points coming from fouls on him, making an incredible grand total of 3-34. Consider also that he does not take free-kicks, so although Peter Canavan ended the Ulster Championship as top scorer on 1-17, to Linden's 0-12, the Down man actually scored more from play, 0-12 to Canavan's 0-8. Consider also that Linden missed a penalty in the Ulster final, the only blot on his copybook all year.

It is also interesting to note that Linden turned 31 years of age in July. Just like Linford Christie, he seems to get faster as the years go by! His talents are not confined to football, for at the traditional All Ireland final winners banquet at the Burlington Hotel, live on RTE television, the same Mickey Linden sang a beautiful rendition of the "Cliffs of Duneen". So well was this received that the following lunchtime he was again called to the microphone at the Monday reception for the All Ireland winners and losers. This time Mickey sang a love song for his wife Louisa while Dublin defender Ciaran Walsh drew a standing ovation for his version of the "Rare Ould Times". They certainly are, for Mickey Linden, for Down and for Ulster football!

Mickey Linden outfoxes Niall Cahalane.

5

BRIAN McENIFF'S 1994
ALL STARS

Neil Collins
(Down)

Paddy Moran	Seamus Quinn	Fay Devlin
(Dublin)	*(Leitrim)*	*(Tyrone)*
Stephen O'Brien	Barry Breen	DJ Kane
(Cork)	*(Down)*	*(Down)*

Conor Deegan   Danny Culloty
(Down)   *(Cork)*

Trevor Giles	Greg Blaney	James McCartan
(Meath)	*(Down)*	*(Down)*
Mickey Linden	Peter Canavan	Charlie Redmond
(Down)	*(Tyrone)*	*(Dublin)*

Greg Blaney got his first in 1983, James McCartan hasn't won one since 1990 and Mickey Linden surprisingly has never won one, but former Donegal manager Brian McEniff tips all three Down forwards to become All Stars this year.

"Blaney's best game was in that epic at Celtic Park, and he was very good against Monaghan though he tailed off a little bit towards the end of the championship. James also started brilliantly and wasn't consistent throughout, but I'm a big fan and he did score the goal in the final. As for Mickey, he should win Footballer of the Year".

McEniff travelled to see championship matches in all the other provinces after resigning from Donegal in June. "I saw a lot more than ever before", he reveals, before making one important clarification, "My selection is the one I think will be named, not necessarily the one I would like to see".

He gives Down seven All Stars, the same as allocated to Donegal and Derry in the last two years. Tyrone get two votes and McEniff has no qualms about giving the same to All Ireland finalists Dublin. "That's why they didn't win the thing. Paul Curran was unlucky and John O'Leary is a close call for goalkeeper - the best around for the last dozen years - but Brian Stynes didn't deliver in the final and Jack Sheedy is consistently inconsistent. Where is his best position? Charlie Redmond will be remembered for the wrong reason but he carried Dublin to the final.

"Neil Collins' save from Redmond put the lid on a very good championship for the Down man, so he should be an All Star. In front of him, Paddy Moran was Dublin's most consistent defender while Seamus Quinn was outstanding for Leitrim. Down's Brian Burns looked an unwilling full-back at first but then improved with every game. Fay Devlin had a good league and championship and was unlucky to be injured after doing well on Linden in the Ulster final.

"There's only the toss of a coin between Stephen O'Brien and Barry Breen so I'd put both in, though Graham Geraghty will run them very close. Breen got better as the year went on at centre-half-back where his anticipation and use of the ball was excellent. DJ Kane was the All Ireland winning captain and he is a winner, a great competitor who played consistently.

"To be frank, there isn't a lot of competition for the midfield places. Stynes and Pat Donoghue of Leitrim did well up to a point, while Danny Culloty was unlucky to be injured at the end of a good year. Conor Deegan emerged as a midfielder who can compete with the best.

"Peter Lambert very nearly got a vote from me after scoring freely for Nemo Rangers and Tipperary, while league champions Meath are represented by Trevor Giles who showed very well. They could nearly have Tommy Dowd as well but Peter Canavan should win full-forward for his all-round class and super performances all year. One other forward who deserves a mention is Ross Carr who, along with Linden, was Down's best forward in the All Ireland final".

ULSTER'S RECENT ALL STARS
1991 - Conor Deegan, Barry Breen, Ross Carr, Greg Blaney (Down).
1992 - Gary Walsh, Matt Gallagher, Martin Gavigan, Anthony Molloy, Martin McHugh, James McHugh, Tony Boyle (Donegal), Tony Scullion, Anthony Tohill, Enda Gormley (Derry).
1993 - John Joe Doherty (Donegal), Tony Scullion, John McGurk, Henry Downey, Gary Coleman, Brian McGilligan, Anthony Tohill (Derry), Ger Houlahan (Armagh), Enda Gormley (Derry).
1994 - ?

ROLL OF HONOUR.
Kerry 74; Dublin 56; Cork 42; Offaly 29; Meath 26; Galway 18; Derry 17; Roscommon 14; Donegal, Down, Mayo 12; Tyrone 8; Armagh 7; Monaghan 6; Kildare, Laois, Sligo 2; Antrim, Cavan, Clare, Fermanagh, Leitrim, Wicklow 1.

Barry Breen fends off Henry Downey.

6

DOWN'S FINEST...

A personal selection by Dr. Maurice Hayes.

Dressing-rooms are busy places after matches, but none can be busier than the one belonging to the winning team on All Ireland day. 1994 was no different; the full panel of Down players joined by journalists taking notes, television cameras recording the scenes as the Sam Maguire Cup arrived with DJ Kane and numerous visitors (such as 1991 captain Paddy O'Rourke) showering congratulations.

Among the mayhem one figure quietly milling around in the background, almost unnoticed, caught my eye. It was Dr.Maurice Hayes, the man credited with inspiring Down to their first All Ireland in 1960. If the same television cameras had been present in his day then his face would be as well-known as that of Peter McGrath. The thought occurred to me that this man was a link between all five of Down's All Ireland victories. I wondered what he made of it all.

A few weeks later I contacted Maurice to see if he was interested in selecting his "best Down fifteen from the five All Ireland teams". By coincidence, he told me that he had in fact spent part of the evening of the latest All Ireland win discussing and debating the very same subject with sixties star Paddy Doherty. Dr.Hayes also admitted, just a little sheepishly, that the pair of them had found room for only one player (Mickey Linden) from the 1994 champions! They had dismissed many of the current crop on the basis of Down's second-half performance against Dublin, but with the passing weeks Maurice was prepared to give them more credit.

"Down frustrated me a little this year because they tended to let opponents back into matches before realising they had to lift the tempo again. They allowed Dublin back into it, just as they had against Tyrone and Cork.

"However, I was terribly proud of them in Celtic Park when they beat Derry. With ten minutes to go I didn't know who was going to win that match and to be honest I didn't care who won because it had been such a tremendous sporting game of football. The fact that Down won and went on to take a second All Ireland in three years means that they deserve to be up there with the sixties champions. Indeed, I feel there is a third All Ireland in them".

Maurice has accommodated five of the nineties Down double-winners on his team, two more who played only in the 1968 final and eight players from the 1960-61 trend-setters.

MAURICE HAYES' FINEST DOWN ALL IRELAND TEAM

Neil Collins

| Patsy O'Hagan | Leo Murphy | Tom O'Hare |
| Kevin Mussen | Dan McCartan | DJ Kane |

Colm McAlarney   Joe Lennon

| Greg Blaney | James McCartan Snr | Paddy Doherty |
| Mickey Linden | Sean O'Neill | James McCartan Jnr |

"The 1960 team has to remain my favourite, because it was the first and because it was a very good team. They had six excellent forwards, any two of whom could win a game on any day. My only regret is that they did not win a third All Ireland in 1963".

Four of the 1960-61 champions did go on to complete a hat-trick of medals on a 1968 team which Maurice Hayes views as the least impressive of the five All Ireland winning teams. "The experienced men were still there but apart from the likes of Tom O'Hare, Colm McAlarney and Peter Rooney there were a lot of youngfellas on the team who we never heard of again".

Maurice's reasons: "Neil Collins was an easy choice for goalkeeper. He's big, has a good kick-out and narrows the angle well as he did on one important occasion in the first half against Dublin to prevent a goal chance.

At number two, Michael Magill is promising but I had to fit Patsy O'Hagan into my selection. He was a better half-back but was also a utility player. I don't hesitate in naming Leo Murphy at full-back. He played well in finals and had an enormous kick-out which enabled us to almost dispense with the midfield. His kick was like a hurling puck going straight to the half-forwards. At left-corner-back, Tom O'Hare was consistent, stylish, never flustered and had a great final in '68.

Kevin Mussen's service to Down simply must be recognised. He played through the fifties when it was unfashionable to talk about winning All Irelands, and so was nearing the end of his career when he captained the 1960 team. He was

Greg Blaney, All Star 1994?

also a classy player. Dan McCartan proved to be a great success when we moved him from the forwards to centre-half-back, just as James McCartan Senior switched in the opposite direction. One outstanding memory of Dan is from the '61 final when he stopped an Offaly attack at one end of the field and cleared the ball to start a Down attack at the other end. At number seven I have DJ Kane. He epitomised the spirit of the '94 team, a true captain and a big-hearted half-back who can go forward and take scores.

Colm McAlarney was the classiest, natural and most sporting midfielder I have seen. He was very young in '68 and, like Tom O'Hare, unlucky not to win more All Irelands. I've placed Joe Lennon alongside Colm although he played in the half-backs when he captained the '68 team. Joe thought a lot about the game and was a very constructive player.

I was tempted to keep the famous 1960 half-forward line of O'Neill, McCartan and Doherty together, but Sean played his best football at full-forward and I had to get Greg Blaney on the team. Greg was the "Man of the '91 team", and contributed so much again this year as the playmaker, outside maybe the final. Mickey Linden was without doubt the Player of the Year but it was Blaney's intelligent play that brought him into the action so often.

James McCartan Senior epitomised the 1960-61 team, a strong electrifying forward who could always get you a score when you needed it. People still talk about his goal against Offaly, when he fielded a ball and thumped it to the net as he landed on the ground, almost in one movement. A buzz of expectancy would go round the crowd whenever he got the ball. At number 12, Paddy Doherty was simply an all-time great, a natural and instinctive footballer, like Christy Ring in hurling. You could give him three balls and he would give you two scores.

The Down '94 style of play developed in such a way that it brought out the best in Mickey Linden. When his team-mates left room in the attack and sent him a decent ball, they knew Mickey would win any race over the first three or four yards. He blossomed this year and was outstanding in every game, it didn't matter who was put on him. Sean O'Neill is another of the greats. He had tremendous class and intelligence throughout a long career, while James McCartan Junior was like his dad in some ways but not in others. He has more skill and close control as opposed to his father's greater strength, yet they share(d) the ability to electrify a crowd and to get a score when needed. Compare James Senior's goal against Offaly with James Junior's point in the second-half against Derry in Celtic Park this year, a score that tilted the balance towards Down at a time when it could easily have drifted away from them. It was the best score I have seen in years.

I would have liked to have had room for many others on my selection, such as George Lavery, Peter Rooney, Tony Hadden, Brian Morgan and the unobtrusive Barry Breen, who gave the appearance of being slow this year yet his positional sense was very good. He also held Vinny Murphy to a point, and did well on the likes of Larry Tompkins and Dermot McNicholl. Then there's Paddy O'Rourke, another number six and a really great captain, while Conor Deegan could win a place in my midfield after a few more years in the position".

Note: Only Kerry have won more All Ireland titles than Down since 1960.

7

JAMES, PETER AND THE FIVE IN-A-ROW

1994 Railway Cup Final, February 27
Ulster 1-6 Munster 1-4

James McCartan sent a note to Brian McEniff before the All Ireland final in September. The Down man was about to complete an amazing comeback from his much-publicised exile from football over the winter to win a second All Ireland medal, yet he took the time and trouble to remember the Ulster manager who had shown him a way back.

That was on the 13th of February, a week after McCartan had watched impatiently from the terraces at the Marshes as his county lost to Derry in the National League. He knew in himself that he wanted back, that he wanted to play again. McEniff threw McCartan a lifeline, despite his lack of match fitness, by playing him in a Railway Cup semi-final against Leinster at Armagh.

Early in the game the corner-forward took a pass on the run from Ross Carr and fired over a typical point. McCartan spent the rest of the match torturing the life out of Robbie O'Malley, and generally repaying McEniff's faith by helping keep alive the Donegal man's dream of a first ever five in-a-row of Railway Cups for Ulster.

However, the hero of the final was another young forward, Peter Canavan. He's different in style to McCartan, but equally exciting to watch and just as committed to the game. Indeed, Canavan could easily have been excused for not turning up for the final, as it came the day after his Errigal Ciaran club had lost an All Ireland club semi-final to Nemo Rangers in Newbridge, after extra-time. That evening, the dejected team captain travelled back to Tyrone, but he still turned up the next afternoon in Ennis for Railway Cup duty, as a substitute.

A tense Ulster team played poorly, giving Brian McEniff the concern that Munster might deny them the record. That's when he gambled on the fitness of Peter Canavan and sent him into the play. Soon after, John Joe Doherty picked up possession on his own goal-line. The ball was worked out to Ross Carr in the left-half-back position, from where he delivered a long, direct pass towards Ger Houlahan. The Armagh man flicked the ball above his head into the path of James McCartan who in turn gave it to the inrunning Anthony Tohill. He could have gone on alone but, seeing Canavan out of the corner of his eye, the Derryman laid the ball off.

"It was a poor pass", recalls McEniff. "it bobbled towards Peter as their goalkeeper came racing out. Still, Peter got there first and kicked it soccer-style over the goalie and into the net for a vital score". "However, what I remember most about that last fifteen minutes was a free-kick Peter struck with the outside of his right boot. It was taken from the right side of the field, thirty yards out and into the wind. He put it straight over the black spot for a brilliant point."

Canavan helped seal McEniff's seventh title as manager and Ulster's twenty-second in all, so drawing level with Leinster at the top of the Railway Cup Roll of Honour. "There was great excitement despite the wet evening and the great distance we were from home, which once again makes me wonder about the timing of this special competition on the GAA calendar", reflects McEniff who was as usual assisted by Art McCrory.

Ulster captain Brian McGilligan proudly took the Railway Cup home that night, (see Back Cover) along with his fourth winners' medal. Tony Scullion and Martin McQuillan, both previous captains, have the distinction of playing in all five finals.

ULSTER

D.McCusker
(Derry)

JJ Doherty	M.Gallagher	T.Scullion
(Donegal)	(Donegal)	(Derry)
M.McQuillan 0-1	D.Loughman	DJ Kane
(Armagh)	(Monaghan)	Down)

B.McGilligan
(Derry) (c)

A.Tohill 0-2
(Derry)

J.McHugh	N.Smyth	R.Carr
(Donegal)	(Armagh)	(Down)
G.Houlahan	D.Heaney	J.McCartan 0-2
(Armagh)	(Derry)	(Down)

SUBS: Henry Downey (Derry) for Loughman, Peter Canavan 1-1 (Tyrone) for McHugh, Brian Murray, (Donegal) for Heaney.

Referee: P.O'Toole (Longford).

1994 SEMI-FINALS

Ulster 0-9	Leinster 1-5
Connacht 0-10	Munster 1-15

FINAL

Ulster 1-6	Munster 1-4

ULSTER'S FIVE-IN-A-ROW

1989 - Ulster 1-11	Munster 1-8
1991 - Ulster 1-11	Munster 1-8
1992 - Ulster 2-7	Munster 0-8
1993 - Ulster 1-12	Leinster 0-12
1994 - Ulster 1-6	Munster 1-4

Brian McEniff smiles as captian Martin McQuillan holds the Railway Cup in 1992. They are joined by Ronan Carolan, Stephen King, Martin McHugh and Neil Collins.

FIVE IN-A-ROW TEAMS

1989: Paddy Linden (Monaghan), Ciaran Hamill (Antrim), Gene Sherry (Monaghan), Tony Scullion (Derry), Martin McQuillan (Armagh), Declan Loughman (Monaghan), Jim Reilly (Cavan) (c), Plunkett Donaghy (Tyrone), Mark Grimley (Armagh), Martin McHugh (Donegal), Eugene McKenna (Tyrone), Greg Blaney (Down), Joyce McMullan (Donegal), Damien O'Hagan (Tyrone), Jim McConville (Armagh). Subs: Paul McErlean (Antrim) for McMullan, Anthony Molloy (Donegal) for Donaghy.

1991: Gary Walsh, John Joe Doherty (Donegal), Conor Deegan (Down), T.Scullion (c), M.McQuillan, D.Loughman, Martin Shovlin (Donegal), Brian McGilligan (Derry), P.Donaghy, Adrian Cush (Tyrone), Neil Smyth (Armagh), Declan Bonnar (Donegal), Peter Canavan (Tyrone), G.Blaney, James McCartan (Down). Subs: Dermot McNicholl (Derry) for Cush, Enda Kilpatrick (Tyrone) for Deegan, Ciaran McGurk (Armagh) for Bonnar.

1992: Neil Collins (Down), Matt Gallagher (Donegal), C.Deegan, T.Scullion, M.McQuillan (c), E.Kilpatrick, Barry Breen (Down), Stephen King (Cavan), Pauric Brogan (Donegal), Ross Carr (Down), N.Smyth, A.Cush, Mickey Linden (Down), Tony Boyle (Donegal) Ronan Carolan (Cavan). Subs: B.McGilligan for Brogan, M.McHugh for Cush.

1993: Damien McCusker (Derry), Kieran McKeever (Derry), M.Gallagher, T.Scullion, M.McQuillan, Noel Hegarty (Donegal), DJ Kane (Down), Anthony Tohill (Derry), B.McGilligan, Dermot Heaney (Derry), M.McHugh (c), N.Smyth, J.McCartan, Ger Houlahan (Armagh), Enda Gormley (Derry). Subs: Fintan Cahill (Cavan) for McHugh, Fay Devlin (Tyrone) for McQuillan.

1994: D.McCusker, JJ Doherty, M.Gallagher, T.Scullion, M.McQuillan, D.Loughman, DJ Kane, B.McGilligan, A.Tohill, James McHugh (Donegal), N.Smyth, R.Carr, G.Houlahan, D.Heaney, J.McCartan. Subs: Henry Downey (Derry) for Loughman, P.Canavan for McHugh, Brian Murray (Donegal) for Heaney.

APPEARANCES:
5 - Martin McQuillan, Tony Scullion
4 - Brian McGilligan, Martin McHugh, Neil Smyth
3 - Matt Gallagher, Declan Loughman, James McCartan

Note 1: Greg Blaney and Martin McHugh also have winners medals from 1983-84. McHugh therefore has a total of six medals which brings him level on the All-time list with Ray Carolan. Sean O'Neill is out in front with eight winners medals.

Note 2: In the five in-a-row finals, Brian McEniff used thirteen different players from Donegal, nine from Derry, eight from Down, seven from Tyrone, six from Armagh, four from Cavan, three from Monaghan, two from Antrim and none from Fermanagh (though Collie Curran played in the semi-finals this year). But, just in case you were thinking of accusing the Donegal manager of bias, please note that of the thirteen players used from his own county, only three of them played in more than one final!

8

TRIBUTE TO GERRY ARTHURS

Dr McKenna Cup Final, September 25
Armagh 3-9 Down 1-14

Gerry Arthurs was an institution in the GAA in Ulster. For close on four decades he was Secretary of the Ulster Council, and when he passed away three years ago he was President of the Armagh County Board. It was fitting then that the magnificent new stand erected at St Tiernachs Park in Clones should bear his name, and that Armagh should win the McKenna Cup on the day the Gerry Arthurs Stand was officially declared open.

GAA President Jack Boothman performed the ceremony before a crowd of 4,500 on September 25, exactly one week after he had presented the Sam Maguire Cup to DJ Kane in Croke Park. This time DJ was absent as Down started with only six of their All Ireland winners, though Greg McCartan and goalkeeping hero Neil Collins came on as substitutes. Collins actually replaced the injured James McCartan, with reserve keeper Eamonn Connolly moving outfield.

Armagh substituted Jim McConville with his younger brother Oisin who took his chance with both hands, scoring 1-2 and helping his team into a six-point lead with only three minutes of ordinary time left. Rory Sharvin goaled for Down and points followed from Greg Blaney and Gary Mason but they had left it too late. It was Armagh's ninth successful McKenna Cup campaign though few will have taken as long to complete; their Preliminary Round game against Monaghan was played on March 20.

1994 RESULTS			
Monaghan	1-8	Armagh	1-14
Cavan	0-7	Fermanagh	2-4
Derry	0-12	Donegal	2-10
Down	2-13	Antrim	0-8
Armagh	3-8	Tyrone	0-14
Fermanagh	1-7	Down	3-8
Donegal	2-9	Armagh	4-9
FINAL			
Armagh	3-9	Down	1-14

LAST TEN FINALS			
1985 - Donegal 0-13	Cavan		0-8
1986 - Armagh 3-7	Antrim		1-8
1987 - Down 2-9	Cavan		1-10
1988 - Cavan 0-14	Derry		1-8
1989 - Down 3-9	Derry		1-11
1990 - Armagh 1-11	Tyrone		0-13
1991 - Donegal 0-11	Tyrone		1-6
1992 - Down 1-11	Cavan		0-7
1993 - Derry 2-6	Down		0-7

ARMAGH: B.Tierney, J.Rafferty, G.Reid, D.Horisk, K.McGeeney, J.Grimley (c), M.McQuillan, P.McGrane, J.Burns, D.Marsden 0-1, D.Mackin 1-2, C.O'Rourke 0-2, J.McConville, F.Harney 1-0, B.O'Hagan 0-2.
Subs: M.Hanratty for McQuillan, O.McConville 1-2 for J.McConville, D.Clarke for Rafferty.

DOWN: E.Connolly, B.Hynes, S.McMahon, R.Starkey 0-1, M.Magill, J.Kelly, P.Higgins, R.Sharvin 1-0, G.Bailie, R.Carr 0-7, G.Blaney 0-1, J.McCartan, G.Murdock, P.Withnell 0-2, G.Mason 0-2.
Subs: G.McCartan for Kelly, N.Collins for J.McCartan. Ref: G.McClorey (Antrim).

9

FERMANAGH WIN ULSTER TITLE

Ulster Under-21 Final, May 1
Fermanagh 2-8   Derry 0-8

They say Peter McGinnity is Mr.Football in Fermanagh. It's a crown he wears reluctantly, but the facts speak for themselves. In 1970, he played at left-corner-forward on the first Fermanagh team to win the Ulster Under-21 title. In 1977, he was on their McKenna Cup winning side, and this year no fewer than seven of his 1992 MacRory Cup winners from St Michaels, Enniskillen, played on the Fermanagh team that won the Ulster Under-21 Championship.

As a player and coach, McGinnity has had a hand in most good things in Fermanagh football. Probably the latter achievements will have been the most satisfying, with a new crop of good young players reinstating Fermanagh on the Ulster map at school and under-age levels. The Under-21 title was in fact the first provincial competition won by the county since 1977.

Another man with Fermanagh football in his blood is Jim Carty, who managed the Under-21's to victories over Donegal and Tyrone on the way to the final. Raymond Gallagher scored seven points in the first round, Mark O'Donnell 1-1 in the semi-final, yet Fermanagh were underdogs going into the final against Derry at Omagh on the first of May. That suited Fermanagh just fine.

Raymond Gallagher kicks a point for Fermanagh.

After thirty-five seconds O'Donnell had the ball in the Derry net. Fifteen minutes later Fermanagh led by 1-5 to 0-1, and with another goal from Brian Maguire, they were ahead at the break by 2-5 to 0-4. Gallagher ended up with five points, and O'Donnell 1-2, as the Irish News Cup returned to the Erne county for the first time in twenty-three years.

Fermanagh had won the Under-21 Championship in both 1970 and 1971, and on both occasions they had progressed to the All Ireland final. But in 1994, the gap between the Ulster final and the All Ireland semi-final (May 1 to August 6) did not help Fermanagh's cause. "The fitness level wasn't as good as before, the captain John Hanna had an injury and a few others had been in America", recalls Tommy Mohan, who was called up to the panel after scoring four goals in a club championship game.

"Still, we had good chances in the first ten minutes against Mayo when Mark O'Donnell shot over instead of under the bar, and Brian Maguire put one wide". Mayo took their points and led by four when Fermanagh came with a late charge. Raymond Gallagher goaled from a penalty and Shane King got another in injury time, but the Connacht side replied with a goal to hold out for a two-point win.

FERMANAGH TEAM IN ULSTER FINAL

Dermot Smyth
(Enniskillen)

Tony Leonard	Paddy McGuinness	Neil Cox
(Belcoo)	(Devenish)	(Enniskillen)
Ciaran Gallagher	Tony Collins	Pearse Collins
(Devenish)	(Lisnaskea)	(Lisnaskea)

John Hanna   Martin Greene
(Brookeboro)(c)   (Derrygonnelly)

Shane King 1-4	Raymond Gallagher 1-3	Oisin Quinn
(Lisnaskea)	(Erne Gaels)	(Teemore)
Kevin Cassidy 0-1	Mark O'Donnell 0-1	Brian Maguire 0-1
(Derrygonnelly)	(Lisnaskea)	(Derrylin)

SUBS: Ciaran Woods (Lisnaskea), Michael McCaffrey (Brookeboro).

Referee: Pat Casserly (Westmeath).

UNDER-21 RESULTS			
Monaghan	0-10	Tyrone	1-8
Fermanagh	0-11	Donegal	1-7
Cavan	1-6	Armagh	1-8
Derry	0-9	Antrim	1-4
Tyrone	0-9	Down	0-6
Armagh	1-9	Derry	1-12
Tyron	0-10	Fermanagh	1-8
Fermanagh	2-8	Derry	0-8

ALL IRELAND SEMI-FINAL

Fermanagh	2-10	Mayo	1-15

TOP SCORERS

Gerard Cavlan (Tyrone)	0-17
Raymond Gallagher (Fermanagh)	0-16
Mark O'Donnell (Fermanagh)	2-3
Oisin McConville (Armagh)	0-7
B.O'Hagan (Armagh), E.Cassidy (Derry), O.McCluskey (Derry)	0-6

Notes: Gerard Cavlan was also fifth Top Scorer in the Minor Championship and runner-up in the Tyrone Championship. Shane King added 1-4 against Mayo but Raymond Gallagher ended the campaign as Fermanagh's top marksman with 1-19.

TRACEY

CONCRETE

REINFORCED MANHOLE RINGS, COVER SLABS, ROAD GULLIES,
CATTLE SLATS, DRAINAGE PIPES, HYD. COMP. FLAGS & KERBS,
POSTS AND OTHER GENERAL PRECAST

Patsy Tracey presents Jerseys for the Fermanagh Senior Football Team.

Official Sponsors of the Fermanagh Senior Football Team

10

THE LATE, LATE SHOW WITH ARMAGH MINORS!

Ulster Minor Football Championship

Gay Byrne would be proud of Armagh's late shows on the way to winning the Ulster Minor Championship. Against Tyrone, they came from four points down to level; in the replay a dramatic late goal by substitute Barry Hughes decided the tie, and in the Ulster Final they scored three late goals in the last ten minutes.

Hughes was the outstanding character of Armagh's five-game run to the title. Not picked for the Preliminary Round defeat of Fermanagh, and taken off in Omagh, the Keady teenager did not appear to have a major role to play. He then came off the bench to become the hero in the replay, scored another goal to effectively end Donegal's challenge in the semi-final, and then rolled the ball into the Down net three minutes from the end at Clones. Appropriately, the supersub's last score was also the last of the championship.

Armagh's more consistent performers were Ronan Harte, Barry Duffy, team captain Kieran Rafferty and Davy Wilson, who had an excellent final. Rafferty's proud father Kevin played in the 1977 All Ireland Senior Final for Armagh.

Sons of well-known fathers also figured early in the championship. Kevin

Winston, son of Joe, who played for Donegal in the 1972/74 Ulster Senior Finals, scored 1-5 in the defeat of Antrim at Casement Park. Damien Keaney, son of Cavan County Chairman Brendan Keaney, scored nine of his team's ten points against Monaghan, while Cavan corner-back Martin Cusack is a son of Johnny Cusack who played on the county's 1952 All Ireland winning team. John Murphy from Down is another former All Ireland winner (from 1968) and his son Gavin played for Down Minors in Celtic Park, though a hand injury kept him out of the final.

Favourites Derry had seven of Maghera's MacRory Cup winning side against Down yet couldn't translate possession into scores, and were rocked by two fine Brian Dougherty goals. Down captain, Paul McShane from Clonduff, added five points from midfield.

Tyrone captain Colin Holmes drives through.

Gerard Cavlan went one better with six points from midfield for reigning champions Tyrone in their First Round game with Armagh. His team led 0-10 to 0-6, but in the end were lucky to survive at 0-10 to 0-10 as Armagh finished strongly. Tyrone made three changes to their forwards for the replay, and gave a debut to 16-year-old Brian McGuckin. The changes seemed to work as another four points from Cavlan had Tyrone in control at 0-9 to 0-7, but with just three minutes left two Armagh substitutes turned the game on it's head. Anthony Bennett dispossessed a Tyrone defender and lobbed a high hopeful ball towards the edge of the square, where Barry Hughes was waiting unmarked to gleefully palm the ball into the net.

Gary Donnelly added an Armagh point for 1-8 to 0-9 before Tyrone frantically tried to save the game. Sean Corr kicked one point but Damien Woods missed another chance as the referee blew the final whistle. Cavlan and several other

		DOWN	ARMAGH
30 secs	Dougherty	1-0	
4 mins	Rafferty		0-1
8 mins	D.Wilson (F)		0-2
10 mins	S.O'Hare		0-3
13 mins	Daly	1-1	
14 mins	T.McEntee		0-4
18 mins	O'Hagan (F)		0-5
19 mins	D.Wilson		0-6
20 mins	Quinn	1-2	
24 mins	Daly	1-3	
32 mins	O'Hagan (F)		0-7
33 mins	O'Reilly		0-8
Half-Time 34:00			
36 mins	O'Hagan		0-9
40 mins	Rafferty		0-10
45 mins	D.McConville	1-4	
45 mins	D.Wilson		0-11
49 mins	Cunningham	1-5	
50 mins	Daly	1-6	
52 mins	O'Hagan (F)		0-12
53 mins	Byrne		0-13
54 mins	D.Wilson		1-13
57 mins	Duffy		2-13
62 mins	Daly	1-7	
66 mins	Hughes		3-13
Full-Time 67:00			

Tyrone players fell to the ground in disbelief, the scenes ironically reminiscent of Armagh's All Ireland final defeat by Meath in 1992.

Armagh ran out clear winners against Donegal in the semi-final after Barry Hughes' goal twelve minutes into the second half. There had been only three points between them (0-10 to 0-7) but Armagh went to win by 1-15 to 0-8.

Down staged a remarkable recovery in their semi-final at Casement Park. They appeared helpless as Monaghan fired over five unanswered points in the third quarter for a 0-14 to 0-3 lead, but within a minute Brian Dougherty and Conor Daly both had the ball in the Monaghan net. Another goal from Shane Mulholland and six points earned Down an improbable victory, by 3-9 to 0-15.

In the final at Clones, Brian Dougherty stunned Armagh with his fourth goal of the championship after just thirty seconds, palming the ball in at the far post after a cross from Paul Cunningham. However, Down's lead was cancelled within fourteen minutes, and by half-time Armagh led by 0-8 to 1-3. Down were unfortunate to lose centre-half-back Sean Ward early on, and to see David McConville's shot come back off the crossbar in the 22nd minute. Midway through the second half, the difference was still two points (0-11 to 1-6), but then Armagh went on a scoring spree. Barry Duffy's long ball set Davy Wilson up for a goal, Duffy added a second himself three minutes later after a pass from Paul O'Hagan, and a third goal arrived when Wilson's drive came off the crossbar into the path of Hughes. Armagh won by twelve points, Kieran Rafferty raised the Murray Cup.

Armagh manager Brother Laurence Ennis knew the All Ireland semi-final with Kerry would be a step-up in class, "Kerry are one of the best minor teams I've seen in quite a while". They had indeed looked impressive in winning the Munster title with full-forward Jack Ferriter scoring 2-3 on a team looked after by all-time greats Charlie Nelligan and Mike Sheehy.

All six Kerry forwards scored against Armagh in a 2-10 to 0-9 victory. They led by six at the break with goals by Mike Russell and Gerry Murphy, and although James Byrne struck the crossbar late in the second half, Armagh were always chasing the game. Davy Wilson, star of the Ulster Final, was replaced after getting little change out of Barry O'Shea. The winners went on to beat Galway in the All Ireland final by six points, 0-16 to 1-7.

ULSTER MFC PRELIMINARY ROUND - May 15, Armagh 1-8 Fermanagh 1-5

ARMAGH
Mark Campbell
(Silverbridge)

Conor Grimes	Aidan O'Rourke	Enda McNulty
(Harps)	(Dromintee)	(Mullabawn)
Kevin O'Reilly	Tony McEntee	Ronan Harte
(C'cruppin)	(Crossmaglen)	(Pearse Og)

Barry Duffy   James Byrne 1-0
(Killeavey)   (Clann Eireann)

Paul O'Hagan 0-2	Kieran Rafferty	Anthony Bennett
(Clan na Gael)	(Maghery) (c)	(C'cruppin)
Davy Wilson 0-3	John McEntee	Paul Dynes 0-3
(St Peters)	(Crossmaglen)	(Harps)

SUBS: Sean O'Hare (St Patricks) for Bennett, Jason McGahan (Tullysarron) for Rafferty.

FERMANAGH
Peter Baird
(St Josephs)

Clive Fitzpatrick	Rory McEnhill	Paul Connolly
(Newtownbutler)	(Enniskillen)	(Lisnaskea)
Barry Morris	Peter Quinn	Raymond Johnston
(St Josephs)	(Teemore)	(N'butler)

Liam McBarron   Sean McBrien
(Kinawley)   (N'butler)

Brendan McKenna	Ciaran Donnelly 0-1	Johnathan McCaffrey
(Roslea)	(Brookeboro) (c)	(Lisnaskea)
Rory Gallagher 1-3	Tom Brewster 0-1	Niall Monaghan
(Erne Gaels)	(Enniskillen)	(St Josephs)

SUBS: Niall Rooney (Brookeboro) for Monaghan.
Referee: Jarlath O'Donnell (Antrim).
Linesmen: Raymond Doon (Antrim), Noel O'Brien (Antrim).

FIRST ROUND - May 22, Cavan 0-10 Monaghan 1-8

CAVAN
Aaron Donohoe
(Belturbet)

Philip Galligan	Adrian Oates	Martin Cusack
(Mullahoran)	(Laragh United)	(Lavey)
Ciaran McGovern	Brian Donohoe	Michael Reilly
(Denn)	(Ballymachugh)	(Knockbride)

Dermot McCabe   Brian McHugh
(Gowna)   (Maghera)

Anthony Forde	Sean Donnelly 0-1	Conor Walsh
(Killygarry)	(Arva)	(Belturbet)
Damian Keaney 0-9	Ian Reilly	Brian Clarke
(Killygarry)	(Drumgoon)	(Killinkere)

SUBS: Thomas Reilly (Mullahoran) for Forde, Fergus Reilly (Killinkere) for McHugh, Brian Mulvey (Castlerahan) for Walsh.

MONAGHAN

Barry Kerr
(Castleblayney)

Ronan Sheehan   James McKiernan   Fergal McFarland
(Emyvale)   (Clones)   (Clones)

Adrian Campbell   Cyril Ronaghan   Colm Donnelly
(Killanny)   (Tyholland)   (Castleblayney)

Dermot McArdle   Fabian Greenan
(Castleblayney)   (Killeevan)

Colin Malone 0-1   Mark Daly 0-1   Gary Meehan 0-2
(Ballybay)   (Drumhowan)   (Truagh)

Rory Mone 0-3   Ciaran McKenna   Alan Duffy 1-0
(Clontibret)   (Eire Og)   (Aughnamullen)

SUBS: Damien Woods (Drumhowan) for Ronaghan, Darren Swift (Monaghan Harps) 0-1 for
Meehan, Dessie McGarry (Monaghan Harps) for McFarland.

Ref: Brendan Gorman (Armagh).
Linesmen: Eamonn McPartland (Fermanagh), Gerry McElroy (Tyrone).

FIRST ROUND - May 29, Derry 0-9 Down 2-10

DERRY

Padraig McKeague
(Slaughtneil)

Sean Doherty   Johnny McBride 0-1   John McVeigh
(Bellaghy)   (Loup)   (Loup)

Cathal Diamond   Sean Lockhart   Eugene Lynch 0-1
(Bellaghy)   (Banagher) (c)   (Dungiven)

Garrett O'Neill   Mark Diamond
(Greenlough)   (Bellaghy)

Gary Biggs 0-1   Sean McGuckin 0-4   Adrian McGuckin
(Banagher)   (Swatragh)   (Ballinderry)

Gareth Dougherty 0-1   Kevin Heaney 0-1   Enda McQuillan
(Bellaghy)   (Castledawson)   (Loup)

SUBS: G.Devlin for McVeigh, D.O'Neill for M.Diamond.

DOWN

Martin Doyle
(Burren)

Kieran O'Hare   John Morgan   Damien McCrickard
(Kilcoo)   (Clonduff)   (Leitrim)

Gavin Murphy   Sean Ward   Simon Poland
(Shamrocks)   (Burren)   (Bryansford)

Paul McShane 0-5   Eoghan Woods
(Clonduff) (c)   (Mayobridge)

Aidan Quinn 0-3   Shane Mulholland   Paul Cunningham
(Newry Bosco)   (Ballyholland)   (Ballymartin)

Conor Daly 0-1   Brian Dougherty 2-1   Chris Burden
(Rostrevor)   (Castlewellan)   (Longstone)

SUBS: Kieran Doran for Burden, Cathal McConville for McCrickard.

Referee: Liam Brown (Donegal).
Linesmen: Rory Robinson (Armagh), Raymond Doone (Armagh).

FIRST ROUND - June 5, Antrim 0-7 Donegal 1-14

ANTRIM

Paddy Murray
(St Galls)

Alister McDonnell	Aaron Cushley	Ciaran Hartley
(Portglenone)	(Aghagallon)	(St Pauls)
Adrian Campbell	Kevin Burns	Kieran Clarke
(Aghagallon)	(St Pauls)	(Sarsfields)

Niall Quinn Adrian Gallagher
(Ballymena) (St Pauls) (c)

Kevin Madden 0-1	Sean McCartan	Kevin Doyle 0-2
(Portglenone)	(St Pauls)	(Cargin)
Enda McKenna 0-1	Joe Quinn 0-1	Barry McMullan 0-2
(St Johns)	(St Pauls)	(Rasharkin)

SUBS: David Reynolds (St Johns) for McCartan, Brian McFaul (St Johns) for Madden, Paul Hasson (Rasharkin) for Cushley.

DONEGAL

Gerard Crossan
(Carndonagh)

Damien Daly	Niall O'Donnell	Sean McDaid
(St Eunans)	(Ardara)	(Urris)
Martin McMenamin	Shaun White	Conal Cunningham
(Robert Emmets)	(Ardara)	(Naomh Columba) (c)

James Cullen Shane Carr
(Termon) (Four Masters)

Kevin Winston 1-5	Adrian Sweeney 0-3	Shane Bradley 0-4
(St Eunans)	(Dungloe)	(MacCumhaills)
Brian McLaughlin 0-1	John Haran 0-1	Brendan McGee
(St Michaels)	(St Eunans)	(Dungloe)

SUBS: Shane McArt (Burt) for McLaughlin, Dermot McColgan (Muff) for Carr.

Referee: Martin McBrien (Fermanagh).
Linesmen: Liam Kealey (Derry), A.R. O'Neill (Derry).

FIRST ROUND - June 12, Tyrone 0-10 Armagh 0-10

TYRONE

Stephen McCarron
(Aghaloo)

Conor McCarron	Sean Corr	Brian Meenan
(Aghaloo)	(Clonoe)	(Killyclogher)
Ciaran Devlin	Colin Holmes	Justin Murray
(Ardboe)	(Moy) (c)	(Moy)

Paddy McGuirk Gerard Cavlan 0-6
(Kildress) (Dungannon)

Noel Woods	Niall McSorley 0-1	Barry O'Hare
(Coalisland)	(Omagh)	(Cookstown)
Sean Douglas 0-2	Cathal McNamee	Damien Woods
(Aghaloo)	(Eskra)	(Coalisland).

SUBS: Cathal Loughran (Dungannon) 0-1 for McSorley, Patrick McGuckin (Edendork) for McGuirk, Damien Teague (Clonoe) for Devlin.

Tyrone Minor squad at Omagh.

ARMAGH: M.Campbell, C.Grimes, A.O'Rourke, E.McNulty, K.O'Reilly, T.McEntee, R.Harte, B.Duffy, J.McEntee, P.O'Hagan 0-3, P.Dynes 0-1, K.Rafferty 0-1 (c), D.Wilson 0-3, Barry Hughes 0-1, Gary Donnelly. Subs: J.Byrne 0-1 for Hughes, J.McGahan for O'Hagan, S.O'Hare for O'Reilly. Referee: Brian Crowe (Cavan). Linesmen: Martin Brady, Des Kearney.

REPLAY - June 19, Armagh 1-8 Tyrone 0-10
ARMAGH: M.Campbell, C.Grimes, A.O'Rourke, E.McNulty, R.Harte, T.McEntee, J.McEntee, B.Duffy 0-1, C.Coleman, P.O'Hagan, K.Rafferty 0-2 (c), P.Dynes 0-1, D.Wilson, J.Byrne 0-2, G.Donnelly 0-2.
Subs: A.Bennett for O'Hagan, B.Hughes 1-0 for J.McEntee, S.O'Hare for Grimes.
TYRONE: S.McCarron, C.McCarron, D.Teague, B.Meenan, C.Devlin, C.Holmes (c), J.Murray, P.McGuirk 0-1, G.Cavlan 0-4, N.Woods 0-1, S.Corr 0-1, B.O'Hare 0-1, S.Douglas 0-2, C.Loughran, B.McGuckin.
Subs: N.McSorley for O'Hare, D.Woods for Loughran. Ref: Brian Crowe. Linesmen: Martin Brady, Des Kearney

SEMI-FINAL - June 26, Armagh 1-15 Donegal 0-8
ARMAGH: M.Campbell, C.Grimes, A.O'Rourke 0-1, E.McNulty, K.O'Reilly, J.McEntee, R.Harte, B.Duffy, C.Coleman, P.Dynes 0-4, T.McEntee 0-4, K.Rafferty 0-2 (c), D.Wilson, B.Hughes 1-0, G.Donnelly 0-2.
Subs: P.O'Hagan 0-2 for Wilson, J.Byrne for Coleman, A.Bennett for Hughes.
DONEGAL: G.Crossan, D.Daly, N.O'Donnell, S.McDaid, M.McMenamin, S.White, C.Cunningham, J.Cullen, J.Haran, K.Winston 0-3, A.Sweeney 0-1, S.Bradley 0-2, B.McLaughlin 0-1, C.Doherty 0-2, B.McGee.
Subs: D.McColgan for Haran, N.McGinley for McMenamin.
Referee: Martin McBrien (Fermanagh). Linesmen: Eamonn McPartland (Fermanagh), Martin Brady.

SEMI-FINAL - July 3, Down 3-9 Monaghan 0-15
DOWN: M.Doyle, K.O'Hare, J.Morgan, D.McCrickard, E.O'Hagan, S.Ward, S.Poland, P.McShane (c), E.Woods, A.Quinn 0-2, P.Cunningham, S.Mulholland 1-1, C.Daly 1-4, B.Dougherty 1-1, C.McConville.
Subs: D.McConville for McCrickard, S.Caulfield 0-1 for Woods, B.Kerr for Doyle.
MONAGHAN: F.Greenan, F.McFarland, J.McKiernan, S.McGeough, A.Campbell, C.Ronaghan, R.Sheehan, D.McArdle, J.Kerley, C.Malone 0-2, M.Daly 0-2, D.Swift, R.Mone 0-7, A.Duffy 0-2, G.Meehan 0-2.
Subs: C.Sherry for McFarland, C.McKenna for Meehan. Referee: Brendan Gorman (Armagh).

FINAL - July 17, Armagh 3-13 Down 1-7
DOWN: M.Doyle, K.O'Hare, J.Morgan, S.Poland, E.O'Hagan, S.Ward, C.McConville, P.McShane (c), E.Woods, P.Cunningham 0-1, D.McConville 0-1, S.Mulholland, C.Daly 0-4, B.Dougherty 1-0, A.Quinn 0-1.
Subs: H.Greene for O'Hagan, K.Doran for Sean Ward, S.Caulfield for Woods.
ARMAGH: M.Campbell, C.Grimes, A.O'Rourke, E.McNulty, K.O'Reilly 0-1, J.McEntee, R.Harte, S.O'Hare 0-1, B.Duffy 1-0, P.Dynes, T.McEntee 0-1, K.Rafferty 0-2 (c), P.O'Hagan 0-4, D.Wilson 1-3, G.Donnelly.
Subs: J.Byrne 0-1 for McNulty, A.Bennett for Dynes, B.Hughes 1-0 for O'Reilly.
Referee: Liam Brown (Donegal). Booked: C.Grimes, K.O'Hare, E.Woods, K.Doran.

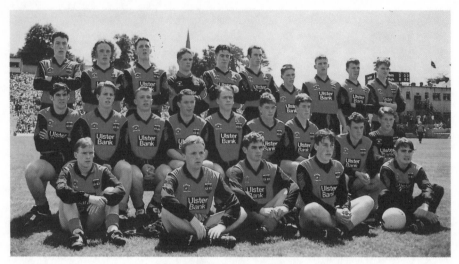

Down Minor squad at Clones..

ULSTER MINOR CHAMPIONSHIP TOP SCORERS					
Brian Dougherty (Down)	4-2	(14)	Barry Hughes (Armagh)	3-1	(10)
Conor Daly (Down)	1-9	(12)	Damien Keaney (Cavan)	0-9	(9)
Davy Wilson (Armagh)	1-9	(12)	Paul Dynes (Armagh)	0-9	(9)
Paul O'Hagan (Armagh)	0-11	(11)			
Gerard Cavlan (Tyrone)	0-10	(10)	**ALL IRELAND SEMI-FINALS**		
Rory Mone (Monaghan)	0-10	(10)	Galway 1-12	Dublin 0-12	
Kevin Winston (Donegal)	1-7	(10)	Kerry 2-10	Armagh 0-9	
			FINAL		
			Kerry 0-16	Galway 1-7	

ARMAGH V KERRY: M.Campbell, S.O'Hare, A.O'Rourke, E.McNulty, K.O'Reilly, J.McEntee, R.Harte, B.Duffy 0-1, C.Coleman, P.Dynes, T.McEntee 0-1, K.Rafferty (c), P.O'Hagan 0-6, D.Wilson 0-1, G.Donnelly. Subs: C.Grimes for Coleman, J.Byrne for Donnelly, B.Hughes for Wilson. Ref: M.Curley (Galway).

Armagh, Ulster Minor Champions, in Croke Park.

11

MAGHERA AGAIN

1994 Bank of Ireland MacRory Cup Final
St. Pats Armagh 0-7   St. Pats Maghera 0-11

Picture the scene. A cool, crisp St Patricks Day morning in the cathedral city of Armagh. The traditional parade would later make it's way through the streets, but over at the Athletic Grounds, St Pats Armagh were about to contest their first MacRory Cup final in 27 years. The throw-in was midday and with home advantage, the scene was perfectly set for a first Armagh victory since 1953.

St Pats Maghera had not read the script, for within twenty-five seconds of the start, most romantic notions of a return to the glories of yesteryear were dashed by the modern-day kings of college football. Armagh may have won the first MacRory final in 1917, and twelve more up to 1953, but Adrian McGuckin's Maghera were in an incredible sixteenth final since 1976.

Winning possession from Tommy McDermott's throw-in, seven swift hand-passes worked the ball to Sean McGuckin in enough space to kick a simple point.

The score set the pattern for the rest of the contest. Maghera's well-rehearsed short, running game was to prove more successful than Armagh's direct, long ball tactic. Adrian McGuckin had taken note of the home side's strength in central positions in previous games and reasoned on countering it. Maghera's keep-ball, running game would pull Armagh across the park, while full-forward Ronan McGuckin and centre-half-forward Sean McGuckin would play vital roles. Ronan dragged his marker away from the danger area while Sean put in a Man of the Match performance to keep Armagh centre-half-back Colin Holmes fully occupied.

Indeed, it was a beautifully floated free-kick from out on the sideline by Sean McGuckin which gave him and Maghera a second point after only three minutes. Barry Hughes replied soon after for Armagh, but it was one of only two scores from them in the entire half and the only one from play.

Maghera captain Ronan McGuckin raises the MacRory Cup in Armagh.

Action from the 1994 MacRory Cup Final.

In the seventh minute, Enda McQuillan flighted over a lovely left-footed kick, Fintan Martin scored another and Michael McCormick converted a 45 to put Maghera firmly in control. Armagh were less accurate from distance, Paul Dynes shooting wide twice, while Barry Hughes missed a goal chance when he sliced a low shot across the face of goal and wide. Oisin McConville had been Armagh's most accurate score-taker on the way to the final (4-29), but Adrian McGuckin Junior kept a close reign on him, while the supply of ball into the corner was poor and infrequent. Maghera ended the half as they started it, with McQuillan pointing after an eight-man move initiated by full-back Sean Lockhart.

		Maghera	Armagh
25 secs	S.McGuckin	0-1	
3 mins	S.McGuckin (F)	0-2	
5 mins	Hughes		0-1
7 mins	McQuillan	0-3	
10 mins	Martin	0-4	
16 mins	S.McGuckin (F)	0-5	
17 mins	McCormick	0-6	
22 mins	O'Hagan (F)		0-2
30 mins	McQuillan	0-7	
Half-Time 31:00			
33 mins	O'Hagan		0-3
35 mins	Gribben	0-8	
39 mins	McConville (F)		0-4
40 mins	O'Hagan (F)		0-5
42 mins	Harte		0-6
44 mins	S.McGuckin (F)	0-9	
50 mins	McCormick (F)	0-10	
53 mins	Dougherty	0-11	
59 mins	McConville (F)		0-7
Full-Time 62:00			

Armagh had chances to get back into the contest early in the second half. Paul Dynes should have scored within twenty seconds of the re-start but was denied by a brilliant block from Gareth Dougherty. David Gormley squandered another opportunity in the eighth minute though two points from Eugene O'Hagan, Armagh's hero from the semi-final defeat of Dungannon, still hinted at a comeback. Ronan Harte confirmed as much with a good score from play to reduce the deficit to two points.

However, that's as near as Armagh got, for Maghera stretched their lead once again with frees from Sean McGuckin, McCormick, and a high dropping ball from Dougherty which was allowed to bounce over the crossbar. Three points in nine minutes and Maghera were champions for the ninth time.

"This is sweeter than any of them", beamed manager and proud dad Adrian McGuckin. Two of his sons played on the winning side, Adrian Junior and team captain Ronan, who followed in the footsteps of former Maghera skippers like Martin Tully, Dermot McNicholl, Danny Quinn and Eamonn Burns.

The Hogan Cup however was a different story. Maghera did beat St Brendan's Killarney in the semi-finals, with Anthony Tohill's brother Brian scoring one of two goals, but St Jarlaths, Tuam ran away with the final. Maghera can point to the fact that they lost midfielder Michael McCormick because of the different age rule for the Hogan Cup, and they were disappointed when the final was originally postponed minutes before it was due to start, but Tuam were eleven points better on the day and therefore worthy All Ireland champions.

Earlier in the MacRory Cup, holders St Colmans Newry had gone out to St Patricks Academy, Dungannon in the quarter-finals. Abbey CBS defeated Omagh with a last-minute goal and a dramatic penalty save, while Enniskillen had been pipped at the post by Armagh in a thrilling finish at Scotstown. Leading by 1-7 to 1-5 at the end of normal time, thanks to a late Ciaran Donnelly goal, Oisin McConville scrambled a goal and a point in injury time to send Armagh through. In the semi-finals they had a comfortable victory over Dungannon, while Maghera defeated Abbey CBS.

MacRORY CUP FINAL TEAMS

MAGHERA

Padraig McKaigue
(Slaughtneil)

Adrian McGuckin	Sean Lockhart	John Heaney
(Ballinderry)	(Banagher)	(Glenullin)
Conleth Murphy	David O'Neill	Gareth Dougherty 0-1
(Glen)	(Bellaghy)	(Bellaghy)

Mark Diamond   Michael McCormick 0-2
(Bellaghy)   (Lavey)

Brian Tohill	Sean McGuckin 0-4	Michael Gribben 0-1
(Swatragh)	(Swatragh)	(Castledawson)
Enda McQuillan 0-2	Ronan McGuckin (c)	Fintan Martin 0-1
(Loup)	(Ballinderry)	(Loup)

SUB: Garry Doyle (Lavey) for Tohill.

ARMAGH

Niall Douglas
(Sarsfields)

Sean O'Hare	Seamus Duffy	Aidan Lloyd
(Cullyhanna)	(Cullyhanna)	(Cullyhanna)
Conor Grimes	Colin Holmes	Ronan Harte 0-1
(Harps)	(Moy, Tyrone) (c)	(Pearse Og)

Paul Dynes   Eugene O'Hagan 0-3
(Harps)   (Pearse Og)

Brian McGeary	Barry Hughes 0-1	Shane Connolly
(Collegeland)	(Keady)	(Keady)
Jason McGahan	Conor McGurgan	Oisin McConville 0-2
(Tullysarron)	(Harps)	(Crossmaglen)

SUBS: David Gormley (Desertmartin, Derry) for Connolly,
Stephen Tiffney (Tir na nOg) for McGahon.

Referee: Tommy McDermott (Cavan). Bookings: Oisin McConville, Conor Grimes.
Man of the Match - Sean McGuckin.

Ronan McGuckin clutches his dad, Adrian, and the match ball.

MAGHERA v KILLARNEY: P.McKaigue, A.McGuckin, S.Lockhart, J.Heaney, C.Murphy, D.O'Neill 0-1, G.Doherty, M.Diamond 0-2, G.Doyle, R.McGuckin 0-1, S.McGuckin 1-3, M.Gribben 0-1, E.McQuillan 0-3, B.Tohill 1-0, F.Martin 0-3. Subs: Brendan Kearney for Tohill, Paul Diamond 0-1 for M.Diamond, Aengus Murphy for McQuillan. Referee: Pat Casserly (Westmeath).
MAGHERA v TUAM: P.McKaigue, A.McGuckin, S.Lockhart, J.Heaney,C.Murphy, D.O'Neill, G.Doherty, M.Diamond, G.Doyle, R.McGuckin, S.McGuckin, M.Gribben, E.McQuillan, B.Tohill, F.Martin. Subs: B.Kearney for Doyle, A.Murphy for Gribben.

THE MAGHERA PHENOMENON

St Pats, Maghera's amazing run of success in the MacRory Cup began in 1976 when they reached their first final. It was only their third year in the competition and they lost to St Colmans, Newry who would become their closest rivals in the fightfor supremacy in colleges senior football. Adrian McGuckin's team returned in 1977 to lift the cup for the first time. They went on participate in no fewer than eleven successive finals, winning six of them.

From 1982-85 a Dermot McNicholl-inspired Maghera won four MacRory Cups in-a-row. Incredibly, McNicholl played in five finals from 1980-84 (twice winning captain) and was assisted along the way by other future All Ireland stars such as Henry and Seamus Downey, Danny Quinn, Damien McCusker and Damien Cassidy.

This year Maghera, contested their sixteenth final, which means they have missed out on just three deciders since the 1976 breakthrough. They have been champions nine times and Hogan Cup winners twice, in 1989 and 1990. Anthony Tohill, Karl Diamond, Eamonn Burns and Brian McCormack played significant parts in those years.

So, what is the secret behind the Maghera phenomenon? One answer is the fact that Adrian McGuckin took his first training session with his 1994-95 squad on October 18th, a full five months ahead of another possible final. Another is that the catchment area includes most of South Derry, a strong gaelic football region with a good club base, and it does not have a competitor next door, like St Colmans and the Abbey in Newry. The last reason, but certainly not the least, is their devoted coach Adrian McGuckin who has been an ever-present at the school. The fact that fourteen of the 1993 Derry All Ireland panel brought the Sam Maguire to the school the Wednesday after the final shows the respect with which he is held.

MacRORY CUP FINALS 1976-94		
1976 - St Colmans, Newry 1-4	St Pats, Maghera 0-4	
1977 - St Pats, Maghera 1-7	Abbey CBS 0-8	
1978 - St Colmans, Newry 1-10	St Pats, Maghera 1-3	
1979 - St Colmans, Newry 0-7	St Pats, Maghera 0-5	
1980 - St Pats, Maghera 3-9	Abbey CBS 3-6	
1981 - St Colmans, Newry 1-3	St Pats, Maghera 0-4	
1982 - St Pats, Maghera 1-7	Abbey CBS 1-6	
1983 - St Pats, Maghera 2-10	Abbey CBS 0-8	
1984 - St Pats, Maghera 1-9	St Marys CBS, Belfast 0-6	
1985 - St Pats, Maghera 2-9	St Michaels, Lurgan 1-1	
1986 - St Marys CBS, Belfast 1-8	St Pats, Maghera 0-6.	
1987 - Abbey CBS 2-6	St Colmans, Newry 0-8	
1988 - St Colmans, Newry 3-5	St Pats, Maghera 1-9	
	(Rs: 0-5 0-5; 2-7 2-7)	
1989 - St Pats Maghera 4-10	St Colmans Newry 4-9	
1990 - St Pats Maghera 3-6	St Colmans, Newry 1-5	
	(R: 0-6 0-6)	
1991 - St Pats, Dungannon 2-7	St Colmans, Newry 1-9	
1992 - St Michaels, Enniskillen 1-8	St Pats, Dungannon 0-9	
1993 - St Colmans, Newry 0-10	St Pats, Maghera 1-5	
1994 - St Pats Maghera 0-11	St Pats, Armagh 0-7	

TEAMS IN FINALS:

1976 - ST COLMANS: Pat Donnan, Adrian McAulfield, Patrick McGivern, Michael Sands, Jim McCartan, Declan McConville, Cathal Strain, John McCartan, Sean McNulty, Noel Rodgers, Tom Connell, Damien Digney, Tom Bradley. Sub: Peter Walshe for McNulty.
MAGHERA: Raymond McLaughlin, Seamus Doyle, Eunan Brolly, Terence Laverty, Sean Conway, Tom McCann, Peter McCloy, Larry Cudden, Sean McAuley, Cathal Faulkner, Hugh Martin McGurk, Kevin McWilliams, Sean McCrystal.

1977 - MAGHERA: Raymond McLaughlin, Seamus Doyle, Pat Mulholland, Liam Bradley, Eugene Donnelly, Terence Laverty, Paddy Boyle, Peter McCloy, Brian Murphy, Kevin McWilliams, HM McGurk, Sean McCrystal, Gerry Monaghan, Sean McAuley, Joe Boyle.
ABBEY: Michael O'Neill, Joe Murphy, Peter Grant, Shane Brunker, Colm McAteer, Brian Canavan, Michael McParland, Liam Austin, Eamonn Larkin, Dermot Dowling, John McAleavey, Jarlath Digney, Brian Campbell, Brendan Loughran, Eddie Curtis.

1978 - ST COLMANS: Pat Donnan (c), Seamus Fegan, Oliver Short, Brian Lambe, Paul Skelton, Peter Donnan, Declan Strain, John McCartan, Sean McElroy, Ray Tumilty, Seamus Carr, Greg Blaney, Pat O'Neill, Dermot Russell, Paul Walsh.
MAGHERA: Fergal Kelly, Sean McKenna, Sean McKillen, Joe Boardman, Pat Hagan, Seamus Doyle, Paddy Mackle, Eugene Donnelly (c), Thomas Close, Eugene Murphy, Sean McCrystal, Mick McGuckin, Thomas Mullan. Subs: Olcan McAteer for McKenna, Martin McGilligan for T.Mullan, Kevin McPeake for Murphy.

1979 - ST COLMANS: Edward Gallagher, Paul Hazzard, Pat Maginn, Eugene McNulty, Paul Skelton, Peter Donnan (c), John O'Hagan, Declan Strain, Greg Blaney, Damien Leonard, Seamus Carr, Martin Rodgers, Pat O'Neill, Frank McClorey, Paul Walsh. Sub: Stephen French for Leonard.
MAGHERA: Colin McKenna, Thomas Mullan, Liam McElhinney, Joe Boardman (c), Paddy Mackle, Pat Hagan, Sean McKenna, Mick McGuckin, Eugene Murphy, Brendan Henry, Peter McCloskey, Paul McKiernan, Martin McGilligan, Tom Cassidy, Kieran Kelly. Subs: Terence Keenan for McGilligan, Joe Beattie for Murphy.

1980 - MAGHERA: Colin McKenna, Martin Tully, Brendan McPeake, Sean McKenna, Paul McKiernan, Paddy Mackle (c), Damien-McCloskey, Danny O'Kane, Eugene Murphy, Michael McGurk, Peter McCloskey, Brendan Henry, Eamonn Reilly, Joe Beattie, Dermot McNicholl. Subs: Martin McGilligan for Reilly, Liam McElhinney for McGurk.
ABBEY: Paul Crimmins, Vincent Toner, Brendan Carroll, Francis Digney, Kieran Shields, Martin Magennis, PJ Gallagher, Martin McKevitt (c), James Murray, Martin Durkin, Jim McGreevy, Kieran Dinsmore, Jim Smyth, Brian Doran, Kieran Goss.

1981 - ST COLMANS: Brian Quinn, Paul Hazzard, Mickey Doyle, Gerard Dillon, Ciaran Hamill, Martin Rodgers, John Gorman, Donard King, Paul Skelton, Brian Walsh, Greg Blaney, Dominic O'Hanlon, Eamonn O'Hare, Sean McKay, Tommy Sands.

MAGHERA: Cathal Glass, Paul McCann, Cathal Kelly, Ephrim Bradley, Martin Tully (c), Brendan McPeake, Declan McLaughlin, Danny O'Kane, Liam McElhinney, Cathal McNicholl, Mick McGurk, Eunan Rafferty, Eamonn Reilly, Paul McCormack, Dermot McNicholl. Subs: Gabriel O'Kane for C.McNicholl, Sean McElhennon for Rafferty.

1982 - MAGHERA: Don Kelly, Peter McGrellis, James McGrath, Martin Tully (c), Mick McGurk, Brendan McPeake, Eamonn Reilly, Dermot McNicholl, Danny O'Kane, Seamus McNabb, Cathal McNicholl, Mark Mellon, Damien Cassidy, Kieran Barton, Eamonn Tohill. Subs: Gabriel O'Kane for Barton, Paul McCann for Tohill.

ABBEY: Paul Crimmins, Stephen McVeigh, Pauric O'Neill, Pat Savage, Ronan Carroll, Aidan Murdock, Malachy Murdock, Brendan Carroll, Donal Durkin, Brian Conlon, Michael Burns, Kevin McGurk, Damien Kane, Lee O'Loughlin, Kieran Ruddy.

1983 - MAGHERA: Don Kelly, Danny Quinn, James McGrath, Peter McGrellis, Vincent McNicholl, Paul McCann, Niall Mullan, Dermot McNicholl (c), Damien Dougan, Gabriel O'Kane, Cathal McNicholl, John McGurk, Colm Rafferty, Damien Cassidy, Rory Scullion. Sub: Dermot Mackle for Quinn.

ABBEY: Damien McCorry, Aidan McGuinness, Pauric O'Neill, Brian Irwin, Ronan Carroll, Ciaran McShane, Jim Carville, Brian Conlon, Redmond O'Neill, Derek Kearney, Damien Kane, Kevin McGurk, Arthur Ruddy, Ciaran Rankin, Mickey McEvoy. Sub: Adrian Toner for Rankin

1984 - MAGHERA: Damien McCusker, Danny Quinn, Eamonn Burke, Peter McGrellis, Collie McGurk, Niall Mullan, Stephen Walls, Dermot McNicholl (c), Damien Dougan, Enda Gormley, Cathal McNicholl, John McGurk, Colm Rafferty, Damien Cassidy, Don Mulholland.

ST MARYS, BELFAST: Ciaran Ferran, Terry McCrudden, Dan Crummey, Ciaran Austin, Brendan Byrne, Jim Hughes (c), Sean Smart, Gerard Kelly, Sean Mahon, Mark McCrory, Tony McKernan, Mark O'Doherty, Conal Heatley, Tony Austin, Brendan Austin. Subs: Dermot McAneny for Kelly, Kelly for B.Austin.

1985 - MAGHERA: Damien McCusker, Francis Dillon, Eamonn Burke, Paddy Cassidy, Collie McGurk, Henry Downey, Seamus McKenna, Danny Quinn (c), Paddy McErlean, Mark Cassidy, John Darragh, Don Mulholland, Gary McGill, Paddy Barton, Seamus Downey.

ST MICHAELS, LURGAN: Colin Loughran, Francis Doran, Colm Walsh, Sean Heaney, Brendan Headley, Donal Harte, Damian Lavery, Greg O'Reilly, Gary Catney, Mark McGuinness, Laurence Ward (c), Stephen Mallon, Philip Smith, Stuart Corey, Niall Morrow.

St Pats, Maghera, 1984. Ten of the squad won All Ireland Senior medals in 1993: Collie and John McGurk, *Back Row, second and fifth from left;* Damien McCusker and Colm Rafferty, *Middle Row;* Danny Quinn, Dermot McNicholl, Damien Cassidy, Enda Gormley and Henry Downey, *Front, first fifth, sixth, eighth and ninth from left.* Seamus Downey is missing from the photograph.

1986 - ST MARYS, BELFAST: John McCullough, Enda McGurk, Patrick Weir, Paddy Nicholl, Mark Keenan, Paul Fox, Liam Donnelly, Gerard Kelly, Ciaran Devlin, Joe Kennedy, Eamonn Blaney, Terry Parkes, Simon O'Doherty, Conal Heatley (c), Sean Connors. Sub: Emmett McCorry for O'Doherty.

MAGHERA: Danny Norton, Kevin Strathern, Gregory McCloskey, Seamus McKenna, Eamonn Higgins, Francis Dillon (c), Niall Lynn, Mark Cassidy, Paddy McErlean, Ciaran O'Neill, Paddy Barton, Declan Cassidy, Fergal McCusker, Seamus Downey, Raymond Tracey. Sub: Eamonn Convery.

1987 - ABBEY: John Kearns, Rowan Lyons, Gary Lyons, Tony Kearney, Gary Fearon, John Markey, Gary Miller, Colm Burns, Eddie O'Neill, Ronan Stokes, Tony McMahon (c), Barry Forshaw, Tony O'Hare, Ciaran Lynch, Terence McCreesh.
Sub: Eoin Hamill for Lynch.
ST COLMANS: Benny Tierney, Mark Rooney, Shane O'Neill, Mark Matthews, Peter Morgan, Larry Duggan, Mark McNeill, Brian McCartan, Ian Hall (c), Martin Burns, Olly Reel, Cathal Murray, Paul McCartan, Tom Fegan, James McCartan.

1988 - ST COLMANS: (First game) Eamonn Connolly, Barry Hynes, Larry Duggan, Barry Fearon, Donal O'Neill, Mark McNeill, Mark Matthews, Brian McCartan, Eamonn McKay, Paul McCartan, Tom Fegan, Paddy Tinnelly, Bernard Connolly, Ger Reid, James McCartan. Subs: Paul O'Hare for Tinnelly, Martin Morgan for Connolly.
MAGHERA: Michael McKeefry, Terry Bradley, Paddy McAllister, Dermot O'Neill, Damien Heavern, F.McCusker (c), Roderick Skelly, Declan Cassidy, G.McCloskey, John Quinn, Joe McCullough, Hugh Tohill, Brian McCormack, D.Norton, Declan Higgins. Subs: Anthony Tohill for Higgins, Terry McGilligan for Tohill, Brian Murphy (in replay).

1989 - MAGHERA: Barry McGonigle, Gregory Simpson, Paddy McAllister, Dermot O'Neill, Damien Heavern, Terry Bradley, Seamus Mulholland, Roderick Skelly, Joe McCullough, Eamonn Burns, Brian McCormack, Karl Diamond, Brian Murphy, Anthony Tohill, Eunan O'Kane.
ST COLMANS: Eamonn Connolly, Brian Clarke, Barry Hynes, Brian Grant, Peter Casey, Paddy Tinnelly, Martin McEvoy, James French, Eamonn McKay, Gareth McCaugherty, Paul O'Hare, Bernard Connolly, Michael Hall, James McCartan, Martin Morgan.

1990 - MAGHERA: John Murtagh, Kevin Bateson, Ronan McCloskey, Gregory Simpson, Martin McGonigle, Barry McGonigle, Paddy McEldowney, Brian McCormack, Hugh Mullan, Eamonn Burns, Dermot Dougan, Ryan Murphy, Eunan O'Kane,

Geoffrey McGonigle, Karl Diamond. Subs: Brian McElhennon for O'Kane, Paddy McAllister (c) (in replay).
ST COLMANS: Patrick Farrell, Martin Gorman, Barry Hynes (c), Garnet McFerran, Brian Clarke, Martin McEvoy, Conor Lavery, Aidan Farrell, Michael Hall, Gareth McCaugherty, Mark McCrory, Martin Bardon, Martin Morgan, James French, Paul Laverty.

1991 - ST PATS, DUNGANNON: Christopher Rafferty, TP Sheehy, Patrick McCartan, Rory McGarrity, JJ Kavanagh, Kieran Hughes, Darren McNally, Damien O'Neill, Don Sonner, Marcus Mulgrew, Brendan Mallon, Jimmy McAllister, John Coyle, BJ McCann, Pat Muldoon. Subs: Jeremy Quinn for McAllister, Marty Morgan for McGarrity.
ST COLMANS: Colm Gilmore, Sean Cunningham, Kieran Doyle, Ronan Hamill, Patrick Farrell, Conor Lavery, Garnet McFerran, Martin McEvoy, Aidan Farrell, Paul McGovern, Paul McGrane, Charlie Pat McCartan, P.Lavery, Dermot O'Neill, Michael Cole. Sub: Diarmuid Marsden for P.Lavery.

1992 - ST MICHAELS, ENNISKILLEN: Dermot Smyth, Kieran Murphy, Declan O'Brien (c), Lorcan Sherry, Tony Collins, Michael Farry, Sean Monaghan, Martin Greene, Edwin Breen, Brian Maguire, John Hanna, Paul McCaffrey, Raymond Gallagher, Sean Moohan, Mark O'Donnell. Subs: Niall Corry for McCaffrey, Shane King for Breen.
ST PATS, DUNGANNON: Damien Harvey, TP Sheehy, Darren McNally, Damien Teague, Brendan Sheehy, Brendan Mallon, Kieran Hughes, Bosco Lyons, Don Sonner, Marcus Mulgrew, Jimmy McAllister, Niall Corry, Marty Morgan, Rory McGarrity, Mark Rodgers. Subs: JJ Kavanagh for Corry, Brendan Kelly for Morgan.

1993 - ST COLMANS: Martin Doyle, Kevin O'Reilly, Ronan Hamill (c), Sean Cunningham, Finbar Caulfield, Mark Rowland, Gary Farrell, CP McCartan, Paul McShane, Aidan McGivern, Diarmuid Marsden, Declan Toner, Michael McVerry, Tony Fearon, James Byrne.
MAGHERA: Padraig McKaigue, Sean Lockhart, Sean McGuckin, Eamonn Turner, Aidan McPeake, Peter Diamond, Ronan McGuckin, Mark Diamond, Conor Gribben, Enda McQuillan, Kevin Ryan, Ronan Rocks, Michael McCormick, Colin McEldowney, Damien Hasson. Sub: Conleth Murphy for McQuillan.

Notes: Yes, the Kieran Goss at left-corner-forward on the losing Abbey CBS team in 1980 is the singer, and the Jim Carville at left-half-back on the 1983 Abbey team is the well-known golfer! Carville however may not like to be reminded that he was sent off in the final! UTV's Frank Mitchell (McClorey) has two winners medals from his time at St Colmans. He also played in the 1978 Hogan final. Northern Ireland soccer international Jim Magilton excelled in the early rounds of the 1986 MacRory Cup for St Marys, Belfast, before signing for Liverpool. Brothers Ciaran and Ronan Hamill both played in finals for St Colmans, Ciaran in 1981 while Ronan was team captain twelve years later. Greg and Eamonn Blaney also played in different finals, but for different schools, Greg with St Colmans in 1978/79/81 and Eamonn with St Marys in 1986. Their father, Sean Blaney, captained the first two St Colmans' teams to win the MacRory Cup in 1949/50.

A hero returns. Derry Captain Henry Downey shows the Sam Maguire to pupils at St. Pat, Maghera in 1993.

1994-1995 MANAGERS
Abbey CBS - Val Kane; *Omagh CBS* - Brendan Harkin; *St Colmans, Newry* - Ray Morgan, Pete McGrath; *St Michaels, Enniskillen* - Peter McGinnity, Dominic Corrigan; *St Pats, Armagh* - Brother Ennis, Brendan McGeary, Ciaran Connor; *St Pats, Cavan* - JJ O'Reilly; *St Pats, Dungannon* - Martin O'Farrell, Peter Herron, Jody Kelly; *St Pats, Maghera* - Adrian McGuckin

1993-94 BANK OF IRELAND ULSTER COLLEGES ALL STAR FOOTBALLERS

Padraig McKaigue
(Maghera)

Paul Tierney	Seamus Duffy	Aidan Lloyd
(Omagh CBS)	(Armagh)	(Armagh)
Tony McEntee	Colin Holmes	Damien Teague
(Abbey CBS)	(Armagh)	(Dungannon)

Eugene O'Hagan   Mark Diamond
(Armagh)   (Maghera)

Alan Duffy	Michael McCormick	James Byrne
(Monaghan)	(Maghera)	(St Colmans)
Paul Cunningham	Shane Mulholland	Oisin McConville
(Abbey CBS)	(Abbey CBS)	(Armagh)

ALL STAR HURLERS

Ciaran Cunningham
(La Salle, Belfast)

PJ Ward	Robert Stitt	Sean Harvey
(Maghera)	(La Salle)	(G'Tower)
Kieran Kelly	Sean Lockhart	Eamon Matthews
(Ballycastle)	(Maghera)	(G'Tower)

Declan Toland
(La Salle)

Neil Fox
(St Marys CBS, Belfast)

Kieran Killyleagh	Aidan McCloskey	Daryl Connolly
(La Salle)	(B'castle)	(B'castle)
Gerard McAuley	John McKay	Ronan Harte
(B'castle)	(B'castle)	(Armagh)

ULSTER COLLEGES ROLL OF HONOUR 1994
"A" Football

MacRory Cup - St Patricks, Maghera   bt   St Patricks, Armagh
Rannafast Cup - St Patricks, Maghera   bt   St Michaels, Enniskillen
Corn na nOg - St Colmans, Newry   bt   St Patricks, Downpatrick
Dalton Cup - Abbey CBS   bt   St Colmans, Newry

HIGHER EDUCATION COLLEGES FOOTBALL

SIGERSON CUP		WINNING SIGERSON CAPTAINS
UU.Coleraine 0-5	Cork RTC 0-6	1959 - Hugh O'Kane (Antrim)
QUARTER-FINALS		1964 - Des Sharkey (Antrim)
Queens 1-16	Trinity 3-7	1971 - Paddy Park (Tyrone)
Athlone RTC 1-4	UUJ 1-9	1982 - Seamus Boyd (Antrim)
Univ. Limerick 2-18	St Marys 0-7	1986 - Colin Harney (Armagh)
SEMI-FINALS		1987 - DJ Kane (Down)
Queens bt	Limerick AET	1989 - John Reihill (Fermanagh)
UCC bt	UUJ	1990 - Fergal Logan (Tyrone)
FINAL		1991 - Noel Donnelly (Tyrone)
UCC 1-9	Queens 2-5	1993 - Paul Brewster (Fermanagh)

QUEENS TEAM IN SIGERSON FINAL

Conor O'Neill
(Down)

Ronan Hamill	Paddy McGuinness	Gareth McGirr
(Antrim)	(Fermanagh)	(Tyrone)
Andy McCann	Paul Brewster	Conor Wilson
(Armagh)	(Fermanagh) (c)	(Armagh)

Anthony Tohill   Mark McRory
(Derry)   (Armagh)

Paul Greene	Cathal O'Rourke	JJ Kavanagh
(Fermanagh)	(Armagh)	(Tyrone)
Tom Rodgers	Eamonn Burns	Diarmuid Marsden
(Armagh)	(Derry)	(Armagh)

Subs: Paul McGrane for Greene, Barry Hughes for Rodgers,
Terry McGivern for Wilson, Donal Mulholland.

SIGERSON MANAGERS: Queens - Dermot Dowling, UUJ - Eugene Young
St Marys - Peter Finn.
1994 RYAN CUP FINAL Queens 3-8   UCC 2-9

MACKIE
INTERNATIONAL

MACKIE INTERNATIONAL LIMITED.
385 Springfield Road, Belfast, BT12 7DG. N.Ireland

HURLING

12

SAMBO'S FINAL

Ulster Senior Final, July 3
Antrim 1-19   Down 1-13

There is no sight more distinctive and natural to Antrim hurling than Terence "Sambo" McNaughton striding onto the field. However, when he was announced over the tannoy at the Ulster Final as "Antrim substitute, number 24" the reception from the crowd was anything but natural. Antrim supporters roared with approval, Down fans jeered with derision.

The story behind McNaughton's dramatic entrance dates back to September 1993, when the Cushendall man struck a Ballycastle opponent in the Antrim county final. He was suspended for eighteen months, but the ban was reduced to twelve on appeal and eventually lifted completely on Monday, June 27th, 1994 - just five days before the Ulster final.

Sambo McNaughton on a determined run.

It is understood that moves had been made to lift the suspension earlier in the year, in the form of a personal appeal, after a recommendation from a Review body in Antrim. When this was sent back by the GAA's Management/Reinstatement Committee, it appears that a county bye-law, allowing a player to apply for reinstatement if he has served more than nine months, was applied. Antrim clubs had also to vote on the issue. I understand that a number of hurling clubs objected to lifting the ban but they were narrowly out-voted. Sambo was available to Jim Nelson.

Down did not protest in the run-up to the final, but after McNaughton had played a part in Antrim's victory, Down manager Sean McGuinness cried foul. "The game of hurling is not straight. I am very disappointed in the shannanigans that went on before to make sure Sambo played. He's a very good friend of mine, but everybody should ahere to the same rules. Last year one of my boys, Chris Mageean, was given three months by the same Antrim Board for very little, there was no chance of him getting back (for the Ulster final)".

Sambo himself later commented: "I've paid all my dues. I made a mistake and I paid for it. What happened that day (the1993 County Final) was the lowest point of my career, I'm sorry it happened but it's something that occurred in the heat of the moment".

		Antrim	Down
2 mins	Jennings (F)	0-1	
4 mins	Elliott	0-2	
5 mins	O'Prey (F)		0-1
7 mins	Connolly	0-3	
9 mins	O'Prey (F)		0-2
9 mins	Walsh	0-4	
10 mins	Walsh	0-5	
12 mins	Gilmore		0-3
13 mins	Elliott	0-6	
16 mins	Connolly	0-7	
17 mins	Gilmore		0-4
21 mins	Walsh	0-8	
22 mins	Ggy O'Kane	0-9	
27 mins	Ggy O'Kane (F)	0-10	
29 mins	O'Prey (F)		0-5
30 mins	McKillen	0-11	
31 mins	Hughes		0-6
33 mins	B.Coulter		0-7
35 mins	Connolly	0-12	
36 mins	Jennings (F)	0-13	
Half-Time 36:30			
38 mins	Elliott	0-14	
44 mins	K.Coulter (45)		0-8
45 mins	Mageean		1-8
48 mins	O'Prey (F)		1-9
49 mins	Gilmore		1-10
52 mins	Jennings	0-15	
53 mins	Walsh	0-16	
55 mins	Elliott	0-17	
57 mins	O'Prey (F)		1-11
59 mins	Elliott	0-18	
62 mins	Carson (F)	0-19	
64 mins	O'Prey (F)		1-12
64 mins	McCambridge	1-19	
70 mins	Sands		1-13
Full-Time 72:30			

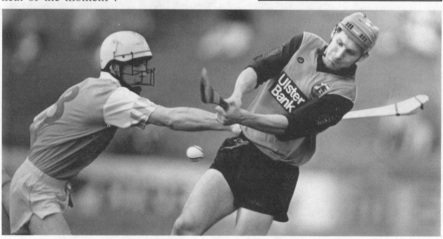

Down's Danny Hughes clears from Antrim's Paul McKillen.

McNaughton's influence as a substitute in the 1994 Ulster Final was significant. When he came on, ten minutes into the second half, Down had just scored a goal to close within three points, and were building up a head of steam in a crucial period.

The goal came when Chris Mageean doubled on a dropping ball from John McCarthy, and followed a 65 from Kevin Coulter. Antrim were down to fourteen men with the dismissal of Jim Connolly for a reckless pull on Dermot Woods early in the second half, and they had to thank goalkeeper Brendan Prenter for keeping out a Noel Sands shot.

Down's momentum remained unchecked in the minutes after McNaughton's introduction, as a free from Dermot O'Prey and a superb effort from near the sideline by Hugh Gilmore narrowed the gap further, to 0-14 to 1-10 for Antrim. But then Sambo went to work, featuring in two vital, relieving scores. First, he was involved in the move leading to a Paul Jennings point and ninety seconds later he set-up Paddy Walsh with a lovely lay-back.

Down never got back into the game after that, managing just one point in the next fifteen minutes and three more scores before the end. Antrim ran out comfortable winners with McNaughton involved twice more. First, he won a free for Jackie Carson to point, and then he intercepted Kevin Coulter racing out of the Down defence. Alastair Elliott slipped the loose ball to Conor McCambridge, who drilled it clinically past Noel Keith for an Antrim goal.

Dominic McKinley collected the Liam Harvey Cup for the third time as Antrim captain and gave reasons outside the "Sambo factor" for the latest success. "The character of the team pulled us through. We were sharper in most of the vital areas, the forwards scored some super points".

Antrim, Ulster Champions, 1994.

Indeed, Paddy Walsh and Jim Connolly stretched an experienced Down defence with three flamboyant scores each; Paul Jennings added two magnificent long-distance frees in the first half. Down, in contrast, had eleven wides in the second half. Noel Sands drew a blank from four goal chances, denied by the crossbar and Man of the Match Brendan Prenter. How they missed 1992 All Star Gerard McGrattan (damaged cruciate ligament) and other injured players, Martin "Spike" Bailie and '93 top scorer Jerome McCrickard.

Both sides had key men Stateside - Gary Savage and Stephen McAree from Down, Ronan Donnelly and Jim Close from Antrim. In fact, Jim Nelson had fielded with only eight of his 1993 Ulster Final team.

ANTRIM

Brendan Prenter
(St Endas)

Seamus McMullan	Dominic McKinley	Frankie McMullan
(Dunloy)	(Loughgiel) (c)	(Dunloy)
Sean Paul McKillop	Paul Jennings 0-3	Joe McCaffrey
(Loughgiel)	(Ballycastle)	(Rossa)

Paul McKillen 0-1   Jim Connolly 0-3
(Ballycastle)   (Rossa)

Jackie Carson 0-1	Gary O'Kane	Paddy Walsh 0-4
(Cushendall)	(Dunloy)	(Cushendall)
Conor McCambridge 1-0	Gregory O'Kane 0-2	Alastair Elliott 0-5
(Cushendall)	(Dunloy)	(Dunloy)

SUBS: Terence McNaughton (Cushendall) for Gary O'Kane (47), Aidan McAteer (Cushendall) for McCaffrey (50), Brendan McGarry (Loughgiel) for Gregory O'Kane (54).

DOWN

Noel Keith
(Ballycran)

Kevin Coulter 0-1	Ger Coulter	Paddy Branniff
(Ballygalget)	(Ballygalget)	(Ballygalget)
Marty Mallon	Paul McMullan	Dermot Woods
(Portaferry)	(Portaferry)	(Ballycran)

Danny Hughes 0-1   John McCarthy
(Ballycran)   (Ballycran)

Barry Coulter 0-1	Chris Mageean 1-0	Dermot O'Prey 0-6
(Ballygalget)	(Portaferry)	(Ballycran)
Paul Coulter	Hugh Gilmore 0-3	Noel Sands 0-1
(Ballygalget)	(Ballycran)	(Portaferry)

SUB: Philbin Savage (Ballygalget) for P.Coulter.

Referee: Pat Horan (Offaly). Sending-off: Jim Connolly (39 mins).
Booked: Gregory O'Kane, Paddy Branniff, Seamus McMullan, Paul Jennings.
Man of the Match - Brendan Prenter.

ULSTER FINALS					WINNING CAPTAINS
(for the Liam Harvey Cup)					
1989 - Antrim	2-16	Down	0-9		1989 - Ciaran Barr
1990 - Antrim	4-11	Down	2-11		1990 - Dominic McKinley
1991 - Antrim	3-14	Down	3-10		1991 - Dominic McKinley
1992 - Down	2-16	Antrim	0-11		1992 - Noel Sands
1993 - Antrim	0-24	Down	0-11		1993 - Dominic McMullan
1994 - Antrim	1-19	Down	1-13		1994 - Dominic McKinley

13

ANTRIM HUMBLED

All Ireland Semi-final, August 7
Antrim 0-11   Limerick 2-23

After eight years as Antrim manager, Jim Nelson's last game was the one he will most wish to forget. "We were a disgrace", he admitted after his team lost by eighteen points for the second year in-a-row at Croke Park, on August 7th.

"On behalf of the team, all I can do is apologise to Antrim people for that disastrous, gutless and outlandish performance. It's an absolute embarrassment to Antrim and hurling in general to put that sort of performance together. There's no point trying to cover it up or make excuses".

A month later Nelson resigned, to be replaced by 34-year-old team captain Dominic McKinley, who also faced the media after the Limerick mauling. "I don't know what went wrong. We had high expectations and prepared as well as ever but Limerick won 95 per cent of the field. It's a sad day, I've played my last game here". The Loughgiel man played on the Antrim team in the 1989 All Ireland final, the highlight of a 14-year senior county career, but his aim now is to return as Antrim manager in 1995. (McKinley applied for and won the position on September 22. The only other applicant was Rab Coyles).

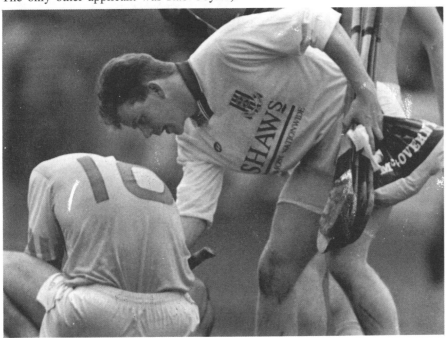

Limerick goalkeeper Joe Quaid has a word of comfort for Antrim's John Carson after the final whistle

McKinley's main task will be to identify the reason(s) for inept back-to-back performances in Croke Park, and to restore confidence in Antrim's ability to compete on the All Ireland stage. Nelson appeared to have tried everything, even employing Craig Mahoney, the Australian sports physchologist who worked with the Derry footballers in 1993.

Perhaps some of the current Antrim panel have a fear of playing before the large crowd on All Ireland semi-final day though their opponents from Limerick had not, ironically, played on the same stage since 1980. On paper this looked like one-up for the Ulster Champions, but that would have been to overlook the passion and style with which Limerick had shown in emerging from a most competitive Munster Championship. Indeed, the testing campaign worked to Limerick's advantage in the semi-final.

A mere 35 seconds were on the clock when Mike Houlihan began the onslaught. After 35 minutes Limerick led by 2-12 to 0-5. Every forward wearing green scored in that first half, though their half-forward line must be singled out. Frankie Carroll struck five magnificent points from all sorts of impossible angles, while Mike Galligan and Gary Kirby scored a goal apiece. Galligan's came after nine minutes, a low sweetly-struck shot into the far corner of the net, and Kirby's arrived five minutes later when he powered an unstoppable ground shot past a bemused Brendan Prenter for 2-5 to 0-2.

Paul Jennings converted a 65 and Conor McCambridge added another Antrim point to hint at a revival, but the next score re-emphasised the difference in the quality of finishing. An Antrim free dropped short of it's target and into the hands of Limerick goalkeeper Joe Quaid, who cleared long and accurately to the unmarked Frankie Carroll. The half-forward turned and almost in one movement struck the ball cleanly over the Antrim crossbar. Easy!

Antrim sent on Aidan McAteer in an attempt to bolster an overrun defence but there were problems all over the pitch. Midfield belonged to Ciaran Carey and Mike Houlihan, while the Antrim forwards managed only two scores between them in the entire first half, the second from a Carson free in the 35th minute. Heads had dropped minutes earlier when both Carson and McCambridge missed straightforward frees; Limerick won almost every race to the breaking ball and piled on the agony with every point.

		Antrim	Limerick
35 secs	Houlihan		0-1
3 mins	Carroll		0-2
4 mins	McKillen	0-1	
5 mins	Ryan		0-3
6 mins	Jennings (65)	0-2	
9 mins	Galligan		1-3
11 mins	Carroll		1-4
13 mins	Carroll		1-5
14 mins	Kirby		2-5
16 mins	Jennings (65)	0-3	
17 mins	Cr McCambridge	0-4	
20 mins	Carroll		2-6
22 mins	Quigley		2-7
23 mins	L.O'Connor		2-8
28 mins	Carroll		2-9
32 mins	Houlihan		2-10
34 mins	Quigley		2-11
35 mins	Carson (F)	0-5	
36 mins	Galligan (F)		2-12
Half-Time 37:00			
40 mins	Kirby (F)		2-13
41 mins	Carson (F)	0-6	
45 mins	Kirby		2-14
46 mins	Kirby (F)		2-15
47 mins	McKillen	0-7	
49 mins	Kirby (F)		2-16
53 mins	Carroll		2-17
55 mins	Kirby (F)		2-18
56 mins	Ggy O'Kane	0-8	
57 mins	Houlihan		2-19
58 mins	Carey		2-20
59 mins	Carson	0-9	
60 mins	Carroll		2-21
62 mins	Hegarty		2-22
64 mins	S.McMullan (F)	0-10	
67 mins	Kirby		2-23
69 mins	Carson (F)	0-11	
Full-Time 73:00			

The second half brought little solace to Antrim fans. After only five seconds Jim Connolly was booked and substituted after a wild pull. Gary Kirby, wearing a head bandage after suffering a gruesome cut in the first-half, went to town with six points, the first a masterful effort from the sideline. Carroll, now on his third marker, added another two. On the rare occasions Antrim ventured upfield, they went for goals but first Elliott missed, then Carson's shot went over the bar and finally a well-placed McGarry took his eye off the ball at the vital moment. Somehow, that summed up Antrim's day.

Inevitably, but understandably after this latest defeat, observers questioned Antrim's worthiness to appearing on the second most important day in the hurling calendar. It was the province's tenth defeat in eleven attempts since the current system began in 1984.

If Antrim or Down cannot close the gap of the last two years in particular, then the calls will become louder for a restructuring of the All Ireland series which may mean Ulster losing their place on the glamour semi-finals day. One suggestion is that the Ulster Championship be scrapped and Antrim and Down be entered into the Leinster Championship, another is for the Ulster Champions to play-off with Galway for a place in the semi-finals. Dominic McKinley has another idea, "I think an open draw would benefit hurling in general. If anything, it would help us rather than hinder us and I would think Galway look upon it in the same way. Maybe we need more competitive action before going into an All Ireland semi-final".

ULSTER'S ALL IRELAND RECORD 1984-94				
1984	-	Antrim	2-5	Cork	3-26
1985	-	Antrim	0-12	Offaly	3-17
1986	-	Antrim	1-24	Cork	7-11
1987	-	Antrim	2-11	Kilkenny	2-18
1988	-	Antrim	2-10	Tipperary	3-15
1989	-	Antrim	4-15	Offaly	1-15
FINAL	-	Antrim	3-9	Tipperary	4-24
1990	-	Antrim	1-13	Cork	2-20
1991	-	Antrim	1-19	Kilkenny	2-18
1992	-	Down	1-11	Cork	2-17
1993	-	Antrim	1-9	Kilkenny	4-18
1994	-	Antrim	0-11	Limerick	2-23

Ulster ears might prefer not to hear such suggestions, though as McKinley admitted a few months after the Limerick debacle. "The general public is not going to keep on accepting it".

Now, with the focus and pressure more than ever on Ulster performances, the task for Sean McGuinness and McKinley as the new Antrim boss to ensure that it doesn't happen again. "We have to put a lot of thought into it. We must demand a lot of honesty from our players, some of them felt guilty after the Limerick game, they hadn't given one hundred per cent. They didn't do it intentionally but it just happened".

Those same Antrim players had come under the scrutiny of Clare hurler Anthony Daly after their league quarter-final. "We beat Antrim fairly comfortably (2-17 to 0-10, they just don't seem to have the calibre of players they had a few years back". However, it is worth remembering that many of the 1989 All Ireland final team had been around for years, that the likes of Dessie Donnelly, Niall Patterson and McKinley spent ten years on the county circuit before they made an impact.

New, young players, who have been coming through in recent years, will also require patience and support to make the grade. That's why top-class games in Division One of the National League, as Jim Nelson consistently emphasises, is vital to the future of Antrim hurling. Ironically, Antrim's league form in 1993-94 was their best ever. They even beat Limerick.

Nelson is once-removed from the scene now, though he still kept a promise made when he resigned, to support Antrim from the terraces. Leaving his Belfast home at 8 O'Clock on Sunday morning, October 7th, the former boss arrived in Thurles in time for Antrim's first game in the 1994-95 National League against Tipperary. With dedication like that, Antrim and Ulster hurling will survive.

ANTRIM: B.Prenter, S.McMullan 0-1, D.McKinley (c), F.McMullan, SP McKillop, P.Jennings 0-2, Ciaran McCambridge, P.McKillen 0-2, J.Connolly, J.Carson 0-4, Gary O'Kane, P.Walsh, Conor McCambridge 0-1, T.McNaughton, A.Elliott. Subs: A.McAteer for McKillop (25), Gregory O'Kane 0-1 for Walsh (h-t), B.McGarry for Connolly (38).

LIMERICK: Joe Quaid, Stephen McDonagh, Michael Nash, Joe O'Connor, Dave Clarke, Ger Hegarty 0-1, Declan Nash, Ciaran Carey 0-1, Mike Houlihan 0-3, Frankie Carroll 0-7, Gary Kirby 1-6, Mike Galligan 1-1, TJ Ryan 0-1, Leo O'Connor 0-1, Damien Quigley 0-2.

Ref: Dickie Murphy (Wexford). Bookings: J.Connolly, S.McMullan. Attendance: 45,053

1994 RESULTS

LEINSTER		MUNSTER	
Carlow 1-10	Meath 1-12	Clare 2-11	Tipperary 0-13
Wexford 3-22	Dublin 1-11	Limerick 4-14	Cork 4-11
(R: 3-13 2-16)		Clare 2-16	Kerry 1-8
Kilkenny 1-19	Meath 1-8	Limerick 2-14	Waterford 2-12
Offaly 2-16	Kilkenny 3-9	Limerick 0-25	Clare 2-10
Wexford 4-14	Laois 4-6	ULSTER	
Offaly 1-18	Wexford 0-14	Antrim 1-19	Down 1-13

ALL IRELAND SEMI-FINALS		ALL IRELAND FINAL	
Limerick 2-23	Antrim 0-11	Offaly 3-16	Limerick 2-13
Offaly 2-13	Galway 1-10		

New Antrim manager Dominic McKinley "on the ball" in the Ulster Final.

14

N0 MORE HEROES

Railway Cup Semi-final, February 6
Leinster 2-17 Ulster 0-8

After the euphoria of a first ever defeat of Munster in the 1993 semi-finals, Ulster came thudding down to earth with a fifteen-point reverse by Leinster at Nowlan Park in Kilkenny on February 6th.

Only a few months earlier Casement Park had drooled over a superb display of point-scoring by Ulster in reaching only their third final. No fewer than twenty-one times did Sean McGuinness's team split the posts, which is why the manager had high hopes of carrying on the momentum. Leinster had beaten Ulster in the final, but 1-15 to 2-6 wasn't too bad.

Nobody is keener than McGuinness to forward the cause of Ulster hurling, so he naturally regarded this as a setback, and, put in the context of Antrim's poor showing in the All Ireland semi-finals and heavy defeats for the province's Minor and Under-21 representatives on the same stage, he's right. Like Antrim, the team just didn't function on the day, with only four players scoring and only one of them managing more than a single score.

Still, while newspaper hacks spent the evening of the Antrim defeat in August analysing Ulster's All Ireland semi-final record over the past decade, it's interesting to note the progress of Ulster in the Railway Cup in the nineties. Two finals in-a-row (the only other final reached was in 1945) and beaten by five points in one semi-final, until this year.

ULSTER'S RAILWAY CUP RECORD		
(Semi-final except where marked)		
1985	- Ulster 2-6	Munster 3-16
1986	- Ulster 0-11	Munster 1-19
1987	- Ulster 0-15	Connacht 5-13
1988	- Ulster 1-8	Leinster 1-13
1989	- Ulster 1-22	Munster 3-31
1991	- Ulster 1-6	Connacht 1-11
1992	- Ulster 2-6	Connacht 0-7
FINAL	- Ulster 1-8	Munster 3-12
1993	- Ulster 0-21	Munster 0-18
FINAL	- Ulster 2-6	Leinster 1-15
1994	- Ulster 0-8	Leinster 2-17

Note: Connacht won the 1994 final, 1-10 to 0-9 over Munster.

ULSTER
Noel Keith
(Down)

Seamus McMullan	Ger Coulter	Paddy Braniff
(Antrim)	(Down)	(Down)
Martin Mallon	Dominic McKinley	Paul McMullan
(Down)	(Antrim) (c)	(Down)

Paul McKillen   Jim Connolly 0-1
(Antrim)   (Antrim)

Dermot O'Prey	Gary O'Kane 0-1	Jackie Carson 0-5
(Down)	(Antrim)	(Antrim)
Alastair Elliott	Sean Paul McKillop 0-1	Noel Sands
(Antrim)	(Antrim)	(Down)

SUBS: Barry Coulter (Down) for McKillen, Conor McCambridge (Antrim) for Elliott.

Referee: P.O'Connor (Limerick).

15

DOWN'S MINOR MIRACLE

Ulster Minor Final, July 3
Antrim 3-10 Down 3-11

If Armagh footballers provided the comeback of the year in 1993, when they beat Fermanagh, then Down's Minor hurlers take the honours for 1994 after their incredible victory in the Ulster final. Trailing by six points and with a minute of normal time left on the clock, they somehow schemed to take the title by a single point, though they had to wait a few agonising seconds to get confirmation of the result.

Such had been the pace of play in those frantic closing minutes that the scoreboard operators at Casement Park had neglected to register a Down point scored in injury time. Even the television cameras failed to record the score as they were still showing a replay of Aidan McCloskey's point for Antrim when a quick puck-out was caught and immediately rifled over the bar at the opposite end by Johnny McGrattan.

The scoreboard therefore had the teams level at 3-10 each at the finish, but the mistake became evident to a stunned crowd when Down players jumped for joy after consulting referee Pat Aherne. A bizarre end to a brilliant comeback.

The first-half had not hinted at anything exceptional, as a McGrattan-inspired Down sneaked into a 5-4 lead after Antrim had been reduced to fourteen men when Michael Conway was sent off. The only other incident of note was a fine save by Down goalkeeper Stephen Kelly from a McCloskey penalty.

McCloskey made amends eight minutes into the second half with a brilliant individual goal, by which time Antrim had raced into an seven-point lead. They were ahead 2-9 to 0-7 going into the last quarter, which is when Down made their move. McGrattan tapped over his fourth free of the match and Fergal Bell goaled after Antrim goalkeeper Mickey McCloskey fumbled a high ball.

Down closed to within two points as Antrim appeared to panic, Molloy and Delargy missing glorious chances to stem the tide before Loughgiel's ever-reliable Aidan McCloskey

		Antrim	Down
7 mins	McCloskey	0-1	
10 mins	Matthews		0-1
17 mins	McCloskey	0-2	
17 mins	McQuillan	0-3	
18 mins	Pucci (F)		0-2
20 mins	J.McGrattan (F)		0-3
21 mins	J.McGrattan (F)		0-4
23 mins	J.McGrattan (F)		0-5
28 mins	Molloy	0-4	
Half-Time	33:00		
34 mins	Kelly	0-5	
35 mins	McQuillan	0-6	
36 mins	Molloy	1-6	
37 mins	Rogan (F)		0-6
40 mins	McFaul (F)	1-7	
41 mins	McCloskey	2-7	
42 mins	McCormick	2-8	
43 mins	J.McGrattan		0-7
45 mins	Kelly	2-9	
49 mins	J.McGrattan (F)		0-8
50 mins	Bell		1-8
56 mins	J.McGrattan (F)		1-9
59 mins	Murray		1-10
60 mins	McQuillan	3-9	
62 mins	McCloskey	3-10	
62 mins	J.McGrattan		1-11
63 mins	Murray		2-11
65 mins	Murray (Pen)		3-11
Full-Time	67:00		

calmed things down. First, he set up Ruari McQuillan for a goal and then he added a superb long-range point to send Antrim into a lead of 3-10 to 1-10 in the 29th minute of the half.

Down looked beaten for a second time, but then came McGrattan's quick-as-a-flash reply (catching out the scoreboard and the cameras) and two terrific goals in a minute from midfielder Stephen Murray. Portaferry's Darren O'Neill did the spade work to set up the first goal, then Murray himself lashed a glorious penalty off the goalkeeper's stick and into the Antrim net. In the hectic sixty seconds between the goals, the home side raided quickly upfield only for Malachy Molloy's shot to bobble across the Down goal-line and wide. The penalty was awarded after a high ball into the Antrim square by Down's Peter Mallon had caused utter confusion. Referee Pat Aherne signalled for a penalty amid the rash swinging of hurls by Antrim defenders attempting to clear.

You had to feel sorry for the losers and their mentors Olcan McFetridge and Mickey McCallin, who face a difficult and important job. Antrim have won only one of the last six Ulster Minor titles, a worrying statistic for a great hurling county.

Down meanwhile looked forward to an All Ireland semi-final with Jimmy Barry Murphy's Cork on August 14th in Croke Park. Sean McGuinness assisted in the preparations but there was to be no heroics this time as the Ulster Champions were simply outskilled by a physically bigger team. The margin at half-time was twelve points, with Down only managing a goal from Barry Coleman and a point from David Rogan. In the second half, Johnny McGrattan slammed to the net when the Cork goalie mishandled a long free from Rogan, but it was to be Down's only scoring contribution of the second period as they lost by nineteen points. Cork lost the final to Galway by 2-10 to 1-11.

1994 RESULTS

ULSTER - SEMI-FINAL: Down 3-10 Derry 1-8   FINAL: Down 3-11 Antrim 3-10
ALL IRELAND - SEMI-FINAL: Down 2-1 Cork 2-20

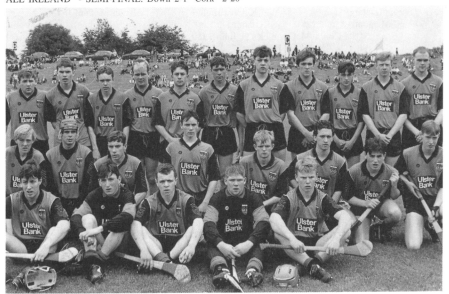

Down, Ulster Minor Champions 1994.

Antrin, beaten Minor Finalists.

ANTRIM

Mickey McCloskey
(Rossa)

Raymond McMullan	Sean Harvey	Paul McClelland
(Ballycastle)	(Glenariffe)	(Gort na Mona) (c)
Adrian Gallagher	Stephen McGarry	Paul Coyles
(St Pauls)	(Loughgiel)	(Ballycastle)

Ciaran Kelly 0-2   Malachy Molloy 1-1
(Ballycastle)   (Dunloy)

Ruari McQuillan 1-2	Aidan McCloskey 1-3	Michael Conway
(Emmetts)	(Loughgiel)	(Ballycastle)
Aidan Delargy	Kevin Elliott	Brian McFaul 0-1
(Cushendall)	(Lamh Dhearg)	(St Johns)

SUB: Conor McCormick (St Johns) 0-1 for Elliott (half-time).

DOWN

Stephen Kelly
(Ballycran)

Liam Clarke	John O'Connor	Gerard Murray
(Ballygalget)	(Ballygalget)	(Darragh Cross)
Eugene McGrattan	Michael Pucci 0-1	David Rogan 0-1
(Ballycran)	(Ballygalget) (c)	(Ballycran)

Stephen Murray 2-1   Chris Young
(Portaferry)   (Portaferry)

Gary Gordon	Padraig Matthews 0-2	Feargal Bell 1-0
(Ballycran)	(Clonduff)	(Ballycran)
Gary Smyth	Johnny McGrattan 0-6	Darren O'Neill
(Portaferry)	(Ballygalget)	(Portaferry)

SUB: Peter Mallon (Portaferry) for Young, Barry Coleman (P'ferry) for Bell,
Philip Mageean (P'ferry) for E.McGrattan.

Referee: Pat Aherne (Carlow).

DOWN TEAM v CORK:

S.Kelly, L.Clarke, J.O'Connor, J.Murray, E.McGrattan, M.Pucci, D.Rogan 0-1, B.Coleman 1-0, P.Brown, S.Murray, P.Matthews, G.Gordon, F.Bell, J.McGrattan 1-0, P.Mallon. Subs: C.Young for Bell, D.O'Neill for Matthews, G.Smyth for J.McGrattan. Ref: A.MacSuibhne (Dublin).

ANTRIM'S WOE

Ulster Under-21 Final, June
Antrim 1-20 Down 1-4

Antrim lifted the Costello Cup at the end of the Ulster Under-21 Hurling Championship final, but by the time they played Galway in the All Ireland semi-finals, they had a different manager! Therein lies another tale of woe for Antrim, at Parnell Park on Saturday, August 13th (the seniors lost to Limerick six days before).

Rab Coyles was in charge for the comprehensive defeat of Down in the Ulster final, but following a war of words with the County Board, he was sacked. His replacement, Jim McClean from Dunloy, had just a few weeks to get the team ready for Galway but with Jim Connolly unavailable because of suspension and Conor McCambridge injured, the new manager's first job was to find a new midfield. The reshuffle meant that only three outfield players stayed in the same position from the provincial final.

ULSTER Under-21 FINAL TEAMS

ANTRIM

Gary Agnew
(Lamh Dhearg)

Brendan Hill	Paul McDonnell	Anto Finnegan
(Ballycastle)	(Rossa)	(Lamh Dhearg)
Barry O'Hara 0-1	Frankie McMullan 0-1	John Hamill
(Cushendun)	(Dunloy)	(Rossa)

Jim Connolly 0-4   Conor McCambridge
(Rossa)   (Cushendall)

Colin Roddy 0-3	Paul Montgomery 0-1	Seamus Shannon 0-5
(Ballycastle)	(St Johns)	(Rossa)
Mark McConnon 1-0	Darren Connolly 0-1	Donal O'Hara 0-2
(Ballycastle)	(Cushendall)	(Lamh Dhearg)

SUBS: Aidan Mort (Cushendun) 0-1 for D.O'Hara,
Declan McGreevy (Rossa) 0-1 for Connolly, Ciaran McDonnell (Rossa) for B.O'Hare.

DOWN

Terence Masterson
(Ballycran)

Stephen Murray	Liam Coulter	Neil McGrattan
(Portaferry)	(Ballygalget)	(Ballycran)
Hugh O'Prey	Conor Mallon	Graham Clarke 0-1
(Ballycran)	(Ballycran) (c)	(Ballygalget)

Cormac McGrattan   Barry Milligan
(Ballygalget)   (Portaferry)

Brian Braniff	James Crawford 1-0	Sean Masterson 0-1
(Portaferry)	(Ballygalget)	(Ballycran)
Martin Coulter	Dominic McKenna 0-2	Paul Rogers
(Ballygalget)	(Ballygalget)	(Portaferry)

SUB: Johnny McGrattan (Ballygalget) for Rogers.

Last-minute preparations didn't go too well either for Cyril Farrell's Galway team as they arrived late at the Dublin venue, but with nine of their 1993 All Ireland winning team on board, they soon fell into a comfortable stride. Antrim did score five times in the first half, three from Cushendun's Aidan Mort, but only Martin McClafferty found the target after the break. The difference at the finish was fifteen points, but the cards had obviously been stacked against a young Antrim team. Most of them will be available again next year.

1994 UNDER-21 RESULTS	
Fermanagh 1-7	Tyrone 5-10
Armagh 3-6	Donegal 3-4
SEMI-FINALS	
Antrim 4-18	Tyrone 0-10
Down w/o	Derry
FINAL	
Antrim 1-20	Down 1-4
ALL IRELAND SEMI-FINAL	
Antrim 0-6	Galway 1-18

LAST TEN UNDER-21 FINALS	
1985 - Down 1-12	Antrim 1-10
1986 - Derry 3-9	Down 1-2
1987 - Derry 2-7	Antrim 0-9
1988 - Antrim 6-11	Down 1-4
1989 - Antrim 4-18	Down 0-4
1990 - Down 2-9	Antrim 2-6
1991 - Antrim 2-19	Down 2-6
1992 - Antrim 3-11	Down 3-4
1993 - Derry 2-13	Antrim 1-8
1994 - Antrim 1-20	Down 1-4

ANTRIM V GALWAY: G.Agnew, J.Hamill, S.Ramsey, C.McCloskey, B.O'Hara, F.McMullan, B.McNaughton, A.Finnegan, C.McGuckian, C.Roddy, A.Mort 0-3, M.McClafferty 0-2, P.McAuley, M.McConnon, P.Montgomery 0-1. Subs: M.O'Kane for Roddy, D.Connolly for McConnon, S.Shannon for Montgomery. Ref: Pat Aherne (Carlow).

JOE'S GLORY DAY
All Ireland Special Junior Final, July 3
Fermanagh 3-13 London 2-11

Joe McGoldrick is Mr.Hurling in Fermanagh. He first played for the county "somewhere around 1975" but won precious little until July of this year when Fermanagh landed the All Ireland Special Junior title at Ruislip.

"I'll never forget the final. It was a blistering hot summer's day and we beat London by five points. We'd been beaten in that many finals that we never believed we could win one, until then".

Full-forward McGoldrick led from the front, scoring seven points to add to nine he got in the Ulster final defeat of Cavan (4-20) to 3-2). What's more, he came in for "special" treatment from London. "My marker was spoken to after the first ball came in. He was later sent off and followed by a team-mate as they went down to thirteen men. I ended up sore all over but I have never been sent off in my life and I just kept knocking the frees over the bar".

Fermanagh trailed at half-time, 1-8 to 0-9, before taking control of the contest. The second half was only two minutes old when Jimmy Donovan from Belcoo latched onto a 65 from McGoldrick and sent it to the London net. Adrian Phillips powered a super second ten minutes from time, before young Shane O'Donnell (who scored two goals in the Ulster final) put the icing on the cake with a third.

PLAYER OF THE YEAR, 1994!
Above: Hero of the fans.
Below: Mickey Linden too fast for Niall Calahane.

Above: **The Down team keen to get started!**

Below: Down on tour

Above: **The Penalty Save, by Neil Collins**

Below: **James McCartan makes his point to referee Tommy Sugrue.**

Above: Tyrone's Adrian Kilpatrick bursts forward against Armagh.

Right: Armagh forward Jim McConville surrounded by Meath defenders in the NFL final.

Below: Brian McGilligan under pressure against Down.

Above: Confusion at Casement, Antrim and Donegal players search for the ball!

Below: "You won't get away next time!", Gerry Sheridan gets to grips with Declan Smyth.

Above Left: Ballycran captain Paddy Dorrian, (left), with the Down Hurling Championship Cup and Man of the Match John McCarthy.

Above Right: Eamonn Coleman in happier times.

Ulster, Railway Cup winners, 1994.
Back, Left to Right: Brian McEniff, Art McCrory, Ronan Carolan, Declan Loughman, Brian Murray, Gary Walsh, Damien McCusker, Anthony Tohill, Dermot Heaney, Tony Scullion, Paul Brewster, Pauric McShea, Michael Feeney.
Middle: Martin McHugh, Ross Carr, Collie Curran, Neil Smyth, Brian McGilligan, Henry Downey, Martin McQuillan, DJ Kane, Peter Canavan, Fay Devlin.
Front: Ger Houlahan, Matt Gallagher, James McHugh, John Joe Doherty.

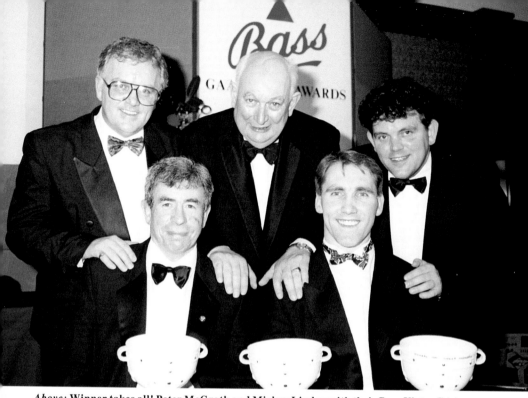

Above: **Winner takes all! Peter McGrath and Mickey Linden with their Bass Ulster GAA Writers trophies at the 1994 Banquet in Monaghan. Standing are,** *from left:* **Brian Houston, Bass PR Manager, GAA President Jack Boothman, and UGAAWA Chairman Adrian Logan.**

Below: **Antrim captain Dominic McKinley swings into action in the Ulster SHC Final.**

COUNTY CHAMPIONS
Above: Clontibret, Monaghan.   *Below:* Lisnaskea, Fermanagh.

Dan McCartan of the Games Administration Committee of the GAA presented the Cup to Fermanagh captain Sean Duffy. McCartan praised Fermanagh's persistence and singled out their manager Sean Donegan and his backroom team.

Persistence was a good choice of word; this was the first thing Fermanagh hurling had won since the game was resurrected in the county in 1971, and the first All Ireland title to come to Fermanagh since the Junior Footballers in 1959. That title was also won in London, at New Eltham Park, on October 11, 1959, just a month before Joe McGoldrick was born!

No-one is enjoying Fermanagh hurling's new-found status more than the 34-year-old, from being introduced to the crowd at half-time in the county football final, to being honoured by Fermanagh District Council, though he has one remaining ambition. "I'd love to win a National League medal for winning Division Four. For years we've plodded along on the bottom rung of the ladder but this year most of the team have stuck around after the All Ireland so it could be my best chance. If we get out of the fourth Division then I'll die happy!"

FERMANAGH IN ALL-IRELAND FINAL

Stephen Hanna
(Lisbellaw)

Seamus McCusker	Donal McShea	John McCusker
(Lisbellaw)	(Lisbellaw)	(Lisbellaw)
Rory O'Donnell	Kevin McKeogh	Seamus Breslin
(Lisbellaw)	(St Johns)	(Clondalkin, Dublin)

Sean Duffy
(Lisbellaw) (c)

Paulinus Leonard 0-1
(Donagh)

Paul McManus 0-2	Adrian Phillips 1-0	Jimmy O'Donovan 1-2
(Lisnaskea)	(Lisbellaw)	(Belcoo)
Jason McManus	Joe McGoldrick 0-7	Shane O'Donnell 1-1
(Lisnaskea)	(St Marys)	(Lisbellaw)

SUBS: Paul Cogan for S.McCusker, Paul Jackman for Leonard.
Note: St Marys is an amalgamation of Irvinestown and Ederney.

London re-visited. Fermanagh are All Ireland Champions once again.

16

CLUBS

1994 Senior Football & Hurling Championships

Antrim

ANTRIM SFC

Holders - St. Galls
Name of Cup - McNamee Cup

FIRST ROUND

Glenavy 3-7	Dunloy 1-13
Ballymena 1-6	Davitts 0-12
Rossa 1-10	Tir na nOg 2-6
St Galls 2-14	Rasharkin 1-7
Cargin 1-8	St Johns 0-8
McDermotts 2-3	Glenravel 1-15
Lamh Dhearg 1-12	St Endas 0-9
St Pauls 1-10	St Teresas 1-1

QUARTER-FINALS

Lamh Dhearg 0-15	St Galls 1-10
Cargin 2-8	Glenravel 0-7
St Pauls 2-9	Davitts 0-4
Dunloy 1-12	Rossa 1-6

SEMI-FINALS

St Pauls 2-7	Lamh Dhearg 0-2
Cargin 2-13	Dunloy 1-3

FINAL

St Pauls 0-14	Cargin 1-7

"Battle of the Bridesmaids" was the unofficial title for the Antrim football final between three-timer losers St Pauls (1985/86/91) and four-time losers Cargin (1987/89/90/93). Something had to give and late in the game it did, as the city side finally turned on the style to win by four points.

"At the final whistle I could almost feel the tension lifting around Casement Park", recalls midfielder Paul McErlean."We've only been in senior football for fourteen years but in that time we have had the potential to win the county title without ever making the all-important breakthrough, until now".

St Pauls still managed to torment their supporters a little bit longer as they threatened to collapse once again on the big day. Their forwards contributed just one point in the first half, McErlean added two more and Adrian Craig netted for Cargin to give them a lead of 1-4 to 0-3.

Fergus Donnelly quickly made an impression as a second half substitute, with an early point. John McManus and Joe Kennedy also helped to haul St Pauls back into the contest. Cargin still pulled away to lead by

Aidan and Fergus Donnelly celebrate St. Pauls victory with their sister Anne Marie

three points, before young McManus again came to the rescue with three scores in as many minutes.

Dermot McPeake swung this topsy-turvy encounter towards Cargin with a point, but it was to be their last score. Kennedy set up Chris Murphy for the equaliser and then scored three more himself, the last two from free-kicks as St Pauls went on the rampage.

Team trainer Peter Finn must take credit for disciplining the squad and for the high fitness level which stood to St Pauls in the latter stages. Finn prepared the Antrim hurlers in 1989 and the St Marys Sigerson Cup of the same year. Cargin also worked very hard this year in winning the league and sailing through to the championship final with little fuss, but they fell away in the second half and will rue the fact that their captain, Martin McAuley, was unable to start the game because of injury.

St Pauls is a small but closely-knit club with three sets of brothers - the McStravicks, Finnegans and Donnellys. They can sit back and reflect not only on a first title but an impressive scoring record of 5-40 in their four games. Defensively, St Pauls were no slouches either, conceding only 2-14 and holding the 1992 champions Lamh Dhearg to two points in the semi-finals. The losers did not help their case by having three players sent off; John McManus scored two classy goals for the winners.

Summary: Lamh Dhearg had earlier beaten St Endas in a bizarre First Round game which remained scoreless for the first nineteen minutes. Mickey Boyle eventually totalled 1-3 for the winners, while St Galls' Billy Drake scored 1-9 (all from placed-balls) for his team in the defeat of Rasharkin. Cargin's Eddie Quinn scored their only and decisive goal as they beat St Johns and a late Colm Higgins goal helped Glenravel overcome McDermotts.

The top quarter-final clash was Lamh Dhearg against St Galls. The latter had two players carried off as they fought back from a six-point deficit to lead by 1-8 to 1-7, Joe Donaghy with their goal. But with Billy Drake also injured, St Galls relinquished their title in the final quarter when Frankie Wilson saw Lamh Dhearg home by 0-15 to 1-10.

ST PAULS: Sean McGreevey, Paul McStravick, Greg Finnegan, Charlie Hemsworth, Ryan O'Neill, Charlie McStravick, Aidan Donnelly, Paul McErlean 0-2, Chris Murphy, John McManus 0-4, Donagh Finnegan (c) 0-2, Michael Stevenson, Peter McStravick, Barry O'Neill 0-2, Joe Kennedy 0-3.
Sub: Fergus Donnelly 0-1 for Stevenson (half-time).
CARGIN: Fergal Kelly, Martin Logan, Michael Johnston, Eamonn McCann, Niall Lynn 0-1, Dessie McGuckin, Matthew Gribbin, Raymond McGuckin 0-1, Eddie Quinn 0-1, Stephen Lynn 0-1, Paddy Graffin, Dermot McPeake 0-1, Declan Gallagher, JC Devlin 0-2, Adrian Craig 1-0. Sub: Martin McAuley (c) for S.Lynn.
Referee: Billy Reid (McDermotts).

Above: St Pauls captain Donagh Finnegan receives the McNamee Cup from Antrim Chairman Oliver Kelly (far right). *From left,* Bass Ireland Field Sales Representative Tony Hawkins, Antrim Secretary Gerry Barry, and John Devlin, Bass Ireland Regional Sales Manager.

Below: Mullabawn, beaten finalists in the Armagh Championship.

ARMAGH

Between 1968 and 1978 Clan na Gael were Armagh champions seven times. They qualified for five Ulster Club Finals and won the provincial title three times in-a-row, from 1972-74. Without doubt this was a golden period, but it also gave future Clan na Gael teams a lot to live up to.

Nearly two decades on, there are signs that the club may have another quality side. Captained by Barry McCabe, and containing the exciting talent of 19-year-old Diarmuid Marsden, they have won back-to-back Armagh titles with relative ease. They beat Maghery in the 1993 final by thirteen points and Mullabawn this year by five points.

In the 1994 First Round, Clan na Gael beat Clann Eireann by a massive 23 points, then St Peters by seven, and St Patricks by nine in the semi-finals, 2-13 to 2-4. Sean Duffy and Des Mackin scored St Patricks' goals in the first half but the Clans still led at the interval by 1-8 to 2-2, and ended the contest with a goal from Man of the Match John Campbell. He was also top-scorer in the final, including an important first half goal when Clan na Gael were 0-3 to 0-1 in arrears. Seven minutes into the second half, another Campbell shot rebounded off the crossbar for Dessie McCann to score the decisive goal.

Apart from Clan na Gael, the other story of the championship was Mullabawn reaching their first final since 1964. They stunned Armagh Harps in the quarter-finals with three brilliant second half goals from the McNulty brothers, Paul, Justin and Enda, yet were caught in injury time by John Toner (4-6 to 0-18). A Neil Smyth penalty and superb defensive work by Peter McCreesh saw Mullabawn home in the replay.

Clan Na Gael, Armagh Champions, 1994.

Smyth and Justin McNulty were always in control of Mullabawn's semi-final defeat of Pearse Ogs. The losers did come back from 7-3 at half-time to within two points, thanks to Ger Houlahan, Fergal Harney and five frees by Gary Harney, but Smyth and Rory McDonnell kept Mullabawn's noses in front. Gary Harney had earlier scored 1-7 for the Ogs in their drawn game with Maghery and another five points in the replay.

St Patricks beat Silverbridge in the best game of the First Round, 3-5 to 2-5. Benny Donnelly and Mark McConville goaled for the winners in the first half, Ollie Reel for the losers. McConville wrapped it up with his second goal five minutes from time.

CLAN NA GAEL: Martin Devlin, Paul McKenna, Niall Morrow, Joe Lavery, Dominic Marsden, Gareth McCaugherty, Paddy Murray, Barry O'Hagan, Barry McCabe (c), Paul O'Hagan 0-1, John Campbell 1-2, Diarmuid Marsden 0-1, Paul Henderson 0-1, Barry McAreavey, Dessie McCann 1-0. Sub: Frankie Conn for Murray.

MULLABAWN: Benny Tierney, Raymond Quinn, Colum Byrne, Gerard Larkin, Colum McParland 0-1, Kieran McGeeney, Sean McDonnell,Justin McNulty, Neil Smyth, Paul McNulty, Rory McDonnell, Paddy McGeeney 0-4, Declan Crawley, Gary McParland, Fergal McDonnell 0-1 (c). Subs: Enda McNulty for G.McParland, Bryan Quinn for Crawley.

Ref: J.McKee (Pearse Og).

CAVAN

Holders - Kingscourt	
Name of Cup - Lakeland Dairies Cup	
Initial stages played in four groups with first two qualifying from each for the quarter-finals.	
Group 1: Ramor United, Mullahoran, Bailieboro, Killenkere.	
Group 2: Ballyhaise, Gowna, Cavan Gaels, Cuchullains.	
Group 3: Denn, Crosserlough, Lavey.	
Group 4: Kingscourt, Ballinagh, Killashandra.	
QUARTER-FINALS	
Kingscourt 3-18	Ballyhaise 1-6
Ramor Utd 2-10	Denn 5-5 (R: 2-7 1-10)
Mullahoran 0-11	Crosserlough 0-10
Gowna 1-19	Ballinagh 0-9
SEMI-FINALS	
Kingscourt 2-4	Gowna 1-11
Mullahoran 0-13	Denn 1-7 (R: 0-12 0-12)
FINAL	
Gowna 1-8	Mullahoran 0-9

Martin McHugh, Mickey Moran and Terry Ferguson all had a part to play in the Cavan Championship this year. The Donegal man trained Mullahoran for the semi-finals until he was named county manager, Moran then took over at Mullahoran, while Ferguson did a remarkable job in taking Denn to the verge of the county final.

In the first game of the league section Denn lost to Crosserlough by ten points. And, when the entire management resigned, the players approached Ferguson, from Kells in County Meath, to take over for the remainder of the championship. Denn went on to reach the semi-finals, after a dramatic quarter-final replay with Ramor United. They rattled home three goals in the last four minutes to win by 5-5 to 2-10.

Still, none of the outside names had a say in the eventual destination of the title. Little Gowna, drawn from eleven townlands, landed only their second Cavan crown amid torrential rain at Hugh O'Reilly Park in Cootehill (only the third time for the final to be played outside Breffni Park). "It was a poor final because of the weather", reflects winning manager John O'Dwyer. "We were much better in the semi-final in beating the champions, Kingscourt. That was exhibition stuff". Gowna came from behind on that day after Tommy McCaul's goals had put Kingscourt ahead by 2-3 to 0-6. Team captain Ciaran Brady scored a goal and a point in the last five minutes.

Gowna's supporters were just as pleased with the victory in the final, especially as it was against near neighbours, Mullahoran. Their team laid the foundations in the

Gowna, Cavan Champions, 1994.

opening twenty minutes, racing into a 1-3 to 0-0 lead; Christy Madden's goal proved decisive. Mullahoran had switched county star Damien O'Reilly from full-forward to centre-half-back at the start of the game, but his bustling style was badly missed in the attack. Also, early free-kicks were squandered and Danny Brady shot against the crossbar when presented with an open goal in the sixth minute.

Brothers Dessie and Ciaran Brady linked well in the Gowna forwards while the McCabe boys, Declan at midfield and Dermot at right-half-forward, made significant contributions. Man of the Match was Gowna captain Ciaran Brady, though his namesake and opposite number Kieran Brady also had a fine game, scoring two points from centre-half-back. Unfortunately the contest had a nasty sting in the tail as Damien O'Reilly suffered an eye, cheek and ear injury which required fourteen stitches.

GOWNA: Declan O'Reilly, Kevin Madden, Joe Brady, Damien Duignan, Bernard Morris, Fergal Hartin, Dermot Madden, Laurence Brady 0-1, Declan McCabe, Dermot McCabe 0-2, Dessie Brady 0-1, Christy Madden 1-0, Terry Hartin, Ciaran Brady 0-2 (c), Sean Pearson 0-2 Sub: Martin McCabe for Declan McCabe.
MULLAHORAN: Paul O'Reilly, Michael G.Brady, Gerry Sheridan, Gerry Brady, Sean Brady, Kieran Brady 0-2, Michael Smith 0-1, Christy Shiels 0-1, Michael Fegan 0-2 (c), Norbert Reilly, Michael Fitzsimons, Seamus Gannon, Danny Brady 0-2, Damien O'Reilly 0-1, Cormac Brennan. Subs: David Fegan for Brennan, Eamonn Brady for Reilly, Dan Mel Reilly for Fitzsimons.
Ref: Packie Smith (Killygarry).

DERRY

A First Round classic between Lavey and Dungiven, a quarter-final exit for Castledawson after six marathon games, top-scoring by county defenders Karl Diamond and Tony Scullion, and surprises galore, including Bellaghy beating Ballinascreen to land their 15th title.... and they say the standard of the championship was lowered by players going to America!

Five thousand saw Dungiven dump old rivals and reigning champions Lavey out of the competition in early June, 0-9 to 0-7. Both sides were reduced to fourteen men after only twelve minutes when Seamus Downey and Damien Heavron were

Bellaghy, Derry Champions,1994

sent off. At half-time it was five points each with Brian McCormick on target three times for Lavey. Geoffrey McGonigle matched that total as Dungiven sneaked into the lead going into the last quarter. Lavey responded with a wonderful Henry Downey point; the Derry captain soloed from one 21-yard line to the other, before fisting over the crossbar. 0-7 to 0-7. Dungiven midfielder Brian Kealy, who totalled four points over the hour, regained the lead, and Eunan O'Kane made it 9-7. In added time Fergal Rafferty's shot might have won the game for Lavey but goalkeeper Tony Tracey made a fine save.

The victors might well have expected to at least reach the final yet they were comprehensively beaten by eight points in their next match. Impressive Ballinderry shocked Dungiven with three marvellous goals from Adrian Conway, Declan Bateson and Raymond Bell, the last killing the contest after Dungiven had cut the gap to five.

Meantime, Castledawson were almost in a championship of their own! They beat Glenullin after three Preliminary Round games, then overcame Magherafelt after one replay, before losing to Newbridge in the quarter-finals. Both draws with Glenullin were achieved by late equalisers, from Stephen McLarnon and then Seamus Shivers. In the third game, a fit-again Dermot Heaney helped Castledawson into a 7-0 lead, and to eventual victory.

MacRory Cup star Michael Gribben became their next saviour with a last-minute free to earn a replay with Magherafelt, for whom Gary Coleman scored three points from full forward.

Holders - Lavey	
Name of Cup -John McLaughlin Cup	
PRELIMINARY ROUND	
Kilrea 0-8	Lavey 5-13
Castledawson 0-10	Glenullin 1-4
(Rs: 2-7 1-10, 1-13 0-16 aet)	
FIRST ROUND	
Dungiven 0-9	Lavey 0-7
Ballymaguigan 0-5	Newbridge 1-12
Ballinderry 3-10	Swatragh 3-9
Ballinascreen 2-18	Ballerin 1-2
Drumsurn 2-11	Craigbane 2-12
Bellaghy 1-14	Claudy 0-7
Glen 1-6	Slaughtneil 0-5
Castledawson 2-10	Magherafelt 1-9 aet
(R: 1-9 0-12)	
QUARTER-FINALS	
Ballinderry 3-14	Dungiven 0-15
Glen 1-11	Ballinascreen 1-13
(R: 1-9 1-9)	
Bellaghy 1-11	Craigbane 1-4
Newbridge 0-11	Castledawson 1-6
SEMI-FINALS	
Ballinascreen 0-18	Ballinderry 0-9
Bellaghy 1-13	Newbridge 1-5
FINAL	
Bellaghy 2-10	Ballinascreen 0-8

Above: All Star defender Tony Scullion playing in the forwards for Ballinascreen.

Below: Ballinascreen, beaten finalists in Derry.

The dimissal of Magherafelt's Seamus Quinn helped Castledawson back into the game. The marathon men won the replay by four points, and looked good in the quarter-finals when leading a fourteen-man Newbridge by 1-5 to 0-2 after eighteen minutes. But, they would score just once more as Damien Barton (his brother Paddy had been sent off) and midfielder Paul Gribben inspired Newbridge to a memorable comeback. They finally caught up with Castledawson near the end of a tense second half when Damien McErlean pointed a free. Paul Gribben made the game safe for Newbridge.

Bellaghy had strolled through to the semi-finals, where they had another comfortable victory over Newbridge, 1-13 to 1-5. Karl Diamond punished the losers by converting nine free-kicks (he scored ten points in all). Eunan Cassidy (Bellaghy) and Paddy Barton (Newbridge) scored the goals in the first half.

Tony Scullion rivalled Diamond for the Top Scorer Award with fourteen points in Ballinascreen's run to the final. Revelling in a new full-forward role, the All Star defender's scoring feats included a total of 2-5 in a league game. In the championship semi-final with Ballinderry, Scullion landed three points as Ballinascreen upset the pre-match favourites, 0-18 to 0-9. Eamonn Burns scored ten times (nine frees), though the real source of the 'Screen's success was the dominance of midfielders Hugh Francis Murray and Paul Hickson.

Based on that semi-final performance, Ballinascreen were installed as new favourites, even though the club hadn't won the county title since 1973, and despite the fact that Bellaghy had appeared in 21 finals since 1956 and had won fourteen of their last seventeen. The club with the better tradition won again after a stunning second half display.

With Damien Cassidy in Man of the Match form and John Mulholland pumping long passes from midfield, the Bellaghy forward unit out-scored Ballinascreen by 1-7 to 0-2 in the second period, the losers' second score not arriving until deep into added time. 'Screen had led 4-1 early in the match and were level at 0-6 to 1-3 at the break, but couldn't reproduce their best form. Bellaghy's goals came from a brilliantly-fisted effort by Lewis McPeake after a pass from Damien Cassidy, and from Eunan Cassidy in the second half.

BELLAGHY: Kevin O'Neill, Cathal Diamond, Seamus Birt, Peter Diamond, Damien Brown, Paddy Downey, Gerry McPeake, Danny Quinn (c), John Mulholland, Karl Diamond 0-4, Benny Lee, Louis McPeake 1-0, Jude Donnelly, Damien Cassidy 0-3, Eunan Cassidy 1-3.

BALLINASCREEN: Don Kelly, John McIvor, Michael Murray, Conor Murray 0-1, Ciaran McKenna, Dermot O'Neill, Michael Kelly, Hugh Francis Murray, Paul Hickson, Eugene Murray, Brendan McPeake (c), Sean D.O'Neill, Paddy McEldowney, Tony Scullion 0-1, Eamonn Burns 0-6.

Ref: Phonsey Guyler (Magilligan).

TOP SCORERS:

Karl Diamond (Bellaghy) 0-24; Eamonn Burns (B'screen) 0-22; Eamonn Devlin (C'dawson) 1-15; Enda Gormley (Glen) 1-14; Tony Scullion (B'screen) 0-16

DONEGAL

Holders - Kilcar
Name of Cup- Dr Maguire Cup.

FIRST ROUND (played over two legs, home and away).
Ardara bt Cloughaneely 1-9 0-8 & 0-13 0-8
Downings bt Gweedore 2-5 0-9 (& 1-10 1-10)
Naomh Columba bt Naomh Conaill 1-10 0-8 & 0-11 0-9
Killybegs bt Termon 1-15 0-11 & 0-11 0-7
Aodh Ruadh bt Dungloe 2-13 0-11 & 0-12 0-6.
Ties - St Eunans/Red Hughs and MacCumhaills/Glenfin

PLAY-OFFS

Red Hughs 1-12	St Eunans 0-11
Glenfin 0-13	MacCumhaills 2-13

QUARTER-FINALS

Red Hughs 0-8	Aodh Ruadh 0-11
Naomh Columba 3-11	Kilcar 0-11
Killybegs 0-19	MacCumhaills 2-10
Ardara 4-15	Downings 0-4

SEMI-FINALS

Aodh Ruadh 2-17	Killybegs 2-5
Naomh Columba 3-9	Ardara 1-12

FINAL

Aodh Ruadh 2-10	Naomh Columba 1-10

"There is a great underage structure in our club. We actually use three fields every evening with youngsters playing both hurling and football. The facilities are among the best in the country". Aodh Ruadh midfielder Charles O'Donnell talks proudly of the youth development policy that is beginning to stand to his Ballyshannon club at Senior level.

Since 1987 Aodh Ruadh have won three county Under-21 titles, three Minor titles, one Ulster Minor Club Championship and many other competitions in lower age-groups. This year, the average age of the team that captured the Donegal Senior Championship, for the first time in seven years, was just 22.

"We then went on to dethrone Ulster Club Champions Errigal, Ciaran, and all sixteen men who played that day had represented Donegal at some level or other, so you can see there is plenty of talent in the club", adds O'Donnell.

The boys from Ballyshannon came of age in the Donegal semi-finals with a twelve-point demolition of Killybegs, who were supposedly on their way to a fifth successive final. Inspired by Sylvester Maguire, Val Murray (brother of county midfielder Brian) and John Duffy, Aodh Ruadh, simply overwhelmed their opponents. Brian Roper and Damien Conlon got the goals.

Ballyshannon picked up where they left off in the final and raced into a half-time lead of 1-7 to 0-2. Perhaps a lengthy interval of more than twenty minutes, to introduce past champions to the crowd, distracted Aodh Ruadh for they were then held scoreless for 23 minutes. Naomh Columba, another young and spirited team, were driven on by Noel Hegarty who had returned from the United States to play in the final. Substitute Paul O'Donnell also played a major part, creating a goal for Eugene Doherty and then levelling the scores after Aodh Ruadh's Val Murray had pointed from a 45.

With four minutes remaining and four thousand supporters on their feet, Aodh Ruadh showed enough character to lift their game and win a penalty. Val Murray decided the issue with his second successful spot-kick of the final.

Summary: Elsewhere in the championship new Cavan manager Martin McHugh lined out for Kilcar in their surprising quarter-final defeat by parish rivals Naomh Columba. McHugh was handicapped by a heavily strapped knee while his brother

Above: Errigal Ciaran's Eamonn McCaffrey protects the ball as John Duffy (Aodh Ruadh, 14) prepares to challenge.

Below: Action from Bellaghy against Aodh Ruadh in the Ulster Club Championship.

James retired two minutes before half time. Seamus Carr, Martin Gillespie (penalty) and star of the show Paddy Hegarty scored the winners' goals. Damien Diver was Ardara's star against Downings with two goals in their quarter-final.

AODH RUADH: Paul Kane, Donagh Keon, Eamonn O'Donnell, Diarmuid Keon, Martin McGlynn 0-1, Gavin Burke, Ciaran Keon 0-1, Donal Buggy, Charles O'Donnell 0-1, Brian Roper, Sylvester Maguire (c), Malachy Cullen, Damien Conlon 0-2, John Duffy 0-1, Val Murray 2-2. Subs: Barry Ward 0-2 for Cullen, Shane McGee for Buggy, Paul O'Loughlin for E.O'Donnell.

NAOMH COLUMBA: Kevin Doherty, Pauric Gillespie 0-6, JJ Doherty (c), Patrick Cunningham, Noel McGinley, Dessie Cunningham, Conal Cunningham, Conal Gavigan, Damien Gillespie, Eugene Doherty 1-1, Martin Gillespie, Eunan McIntyre, Noel Hegarty, Paddy Hegarty 0-1, Seamus Carr 0-1. Sub: Paul O'Donnell 0-1 for M.Gillespie. Ref: Liam Brown.

DOWN

Winning an All Ireland Senior title usually means a quiet and frustrating Summer for club players (apart from tournament games). That was largely the case in Down, where the gap between the First Round and the quarter-finals of the county championship was five months (April to September).

Many of the same club players were in Croke Park in September. A typical example is Maurice O'Neill from Castlewellan who "got soaked in the Canal End", but looked forward to marking his hero Mickey Linden in the club semi-finals just three weeks later. "It was an honour for me to play against someone like Mickey because in my book he's the best forward in Ireland".

O'Neill took his chance well, following the Mayobridge dangerman wherever he went and keeping him to one point in each half. "The way I looked at it I had nothing to lose. If Mickey scored five goals, nobody would have said anything about me because the best men couldn't hold him. I just tried to stay close, though credit must go to our players upfield who hassled and harried and made sure the ball coming in to Mickey wasn't the best".

In Linden's defence, he had been struggling with a hamstring injury and would take a break from the county scene. Another of Down's All Ireland heroes, who did not need a rest, was Ciaran McCabe, best remembered for his "Goal of the Championship" in Celtic Park. After just three minutes against Mayobridge, the Castlewellan forward found the net in similar fashion. Brian Dougherty, top scorer in the Ulster Minor Championship, supplied a brilliant pass and McCabe shot to the corner of the net.

By the tenth minute, Castlewellan were seven points ahead; at half-time it was 1-9 to 0-4. Mayobridge were unable to make their second half wind advantage count, while Conor O'Neill scored one of three Castlewellan points for a 1-12 to 0-9 victory. O'Neill, a former county minor

Holders - Downpatrick	
Name of Cup - Frank O'Hare Challenge Cup	
FIRST ROUND	
Downpatrick 2-9	Loughinisland 1-7
Castlewellan 2-15	Ballymartin 1-14
Longstone 1-14	Drumaness 1-6
Burren 3-15	Carryduff 1-5
Bryansford 3-12	An Riocht 0-6
Mayobridge 3-20	Tullylish 0-11
Newry Shamrocks 3-7	Clonduff 3-10
Rostrevor	Leitrim
QUARTER-FINALS	
Castlewellan 2-6	Bryansford 1-6
Mayobridge 3-16	Longstone 2-5
Downpatrick 1-8	Clonduff 0-7
Burren 4-11	Rostrevor 1-10
SEMI-FINALS	
Downpatrick 1-9	Burren 0-10
Castlewellan 1-12	Mayobridge 0-9
FINAL	
Castlewellan 1-9	Downpatrick 0-8

CARRICKDALE
• HOTEL •

**Sponsors of Club Championships in Down and the
All County League in Armagh.**

John McParland of the Carrickdale Hotel oversees the presentation
of the Frank O'Neill Challenge Cup by County Chairman
Jimmy Cousins to Audie McVeigh, captain of Castlewellan,
winners of the Carrickdale Hotel SFC.

**Carrickcarnon, Ravensdale, Dundalk, Co. Louth
Telephone: 042 - 71397/71212/71208 - Fax: 042 - 71740**

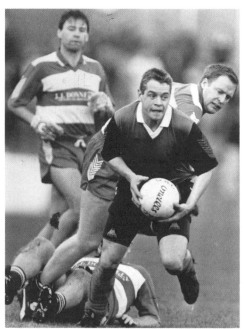

Catlewellan charge... Audie McVeigh leaves three Downpatrick players in his wake in the Down final.

goalkeeper, also scored 2-2 in the quarter-finals against Bryansford.

The quarter-finals saw rare goals from a current county player and a former one, Brian Burns for Bryansford (after switching from full-back to full-forward), and Liam Austin for Rostrevor, who were soundly beaten by Burren. Clonduff came close to toppling the champions Downpatrick, with Ross Carr striking a monster sixty-metre free-kick in the rain at Castlewellan, until a hopeful ball shot off the surface past a stranded Clonduff goalkeeper.

A crowd of five thousand turned up at Newcastle to see Downpatrick survive a semi-final with a Paddy O'Rourke and John "Shorty" Treanor-inspired Burren. Barry Breen eventually won the game for the holders in the last quarter, after Burren had drawn level. The only goal came in the first half when Geoffrey Breen's half-hit shot deceived Donegal goalkeeper Gary Walsh.

The final was played before six thousand at Newcastle, on October 23. It was Downpatrick's fourth final in five years, yet Castlewellan's hunger proved decisive as they landed the title for the first time since 1982. Their defence was outstanding, keeping Downpatrick scoreless for the opening eighteen minutes and restricting them to two scores from play over the hour. Wing-half-forwards Paddy Hardy (Man of the Match) and Conor O'Neill foraged into their own half and still found time to add three points. A wind-assisted Castlewellan led by 0-7 to 0-2 at half-time.

The decisive goal came nine minutes later, when Marty McKibben floated a high ball into the danger zone for his midfield partner Dermot Hawkins to leap highest and flick to the net. Downpatrick came with a late surge, but with Conor Deegan badly handicapped by his All Ireland final injury, Gerard Deegan ruled out and Gregory Deegan a late cry-off, they made little impression on the scoreboard. Kyran Smyth and Barry Breen were Downpatrick's only scorers.

CASTLEWELLAN: Mickey McVeigh, Ruairi O'Neill, Frankie Toner, Maurice O'Neill, Donal Ward 0-1, Martin Laverty, John O'Neill, Martin McKibben 0-3, Dermot Hawkins 1-0, Conor O'Neill 0-2, Kevin Owens, Paddy Hardy 0-1, Brian Dougherty 0-1, Audie McVeigh 0-1 (c), Ciaran McCabe 0-1. Subs: Cormac McCabe for Laverty, John Burns for C.O'Neill.

DOWNPATRICK: TP Louden, Harry Rice, Paul Moore, Mark Trainor, Kevin Donnelly, Paul Evans, Richard Starkey, Conor Deegan, Barry Breen 0-4, Geoffrey Breen, Paul Close, Mark Bohill, Ciaran Prenter, Kyran Smyth 0-4 (c), Ruairi Scullion

Subs: Gregory Deegan for Donnelly, Ian Hynds for C.Deegan.

Ref: Michael Cranny (Warrenpoint).

Summary: Barry Breen was Downpatrick's best player in the championship. He made a comeback from injury in the First Round at the end of April, when he scored two points against Loughinisland, but ended up back in hospital with a nasty shoulder injury which restricted his training with Down. Goals from Gerard Deegan and Ciaran Prenter won the tie for the champions.

Carryduff were missing Greg Blaney for their game with Burren, and when Kevin Blaney was ordered to an early bath (along with Garnet McFerran), the Belfast side crumbled. Burren accumulated 3-9 in the second half, with goals from Shorty Traenor and Jimmy McAlinden. Seamus Savage scored a late goal for the losers. Also in the First Round, Bryansford beat An Riocht with two goals from Paddy Rooney, another from Declan Murray and a fine defensive performance by Gene Morgan.

FERMANAGH

It's unusual for Division Three teams to reach the semi-finals of their Senior Championship, but that's exactly what Aughadrumsee achieved in Fermanagh this year. Joining forces with Tempo from Division Two, they made the last four.

In 1961, Aughadrumsee were Fermanagh champions for the only time, while Tempo won three titles in the early seventies. Neither had reached a final since 1973, but hopes were raised by their impressive joint performances in the early rounds this year.

Four goals by Tommy Mohan sent Irvinestown packing on a 5-11 to 2-6 scoreline, and in the quarter-finals James Carey scored the winning point a minute from time against Hugo Clerkin's Newtownbutler. Seamus Breen got the goal in a 1-7 to 0-9 victory. Enniskillen ruined the fairytale story with an emphatic semi-final win; James Carey put a penalty over the crossbar before Michael McGourty scored the winners' second goal.

Teemore have won the Fermanagh championship twenty times, but only once since 1975. This year they went out in the First Round to St. Patricks after Gerry Quinlan and Declan McGrath had put Teemore ahead in the second half by 2-4 to 1-6. Four successive points and a late goal from Michael Cadden saw St Patricks through. Also in the First Round, Raymond Gallagher scored a hat-trick of goals for Erne Gaels against Brookboro while the holders, Devenish, required a replay to beat Roslea.

The two winners met in the quarter-finals with Devenish squeezing through by a couple of points. However, without the USA-based Mark Gallagher, Ciaran Gallagher and Brian Carty, Devenish lost their title in a poor semi-final to Lisnaskea. 0-3 each at half time, 'Skea pulled away late in the game with two Collie Curran points (one from a penalty).

In the final, only two Lisnaskea players

Holders - Devenish	
Name of Cup - New York Gold Cup	
FIRST ROUND	
Ederney 0-7	Newtownbutler 1-5
Devenish 2-9	Roslea 0-7 (R)
Tempo/Aughadrumsee 5-11	Irvinestown 2-6
Erne Gaels 6-14	Brookeboro 0-6
Derrylin 3-11	Maguiresbridge/Coa 1-1
St Patricks 2-10	Teemore 2-5
Kinawley 0-8	Lisnaskea 0-10
Enniskillen 2-11	Derrygonnelly 0-5
QUARTER-FINALS	
Devenish 0-11	Erne Gaels 1-6
Tempo/Aughadrumsee 1-7	Newtownbutler 0-9
Lisnaskea 1-16	St Patricks 1-8
Enniskillen 2-12	Derrylin 0-6
SEMI-FINALS	
Lisnaskea 0-9	Devenish 0-6
Enniskillen 2-14	Tempo/Aughadrumse 0-4
FINAL	
Lisnaskea 1-9	Enniskillen 1-8

Lisnaskea captain Collie Curran with his family and the New York Gold Cup. *From left,* Conor, Anne Marie, Kevin, Paul and Rebecca.

scored, yet their contributions were enough to beat Enniskillen. Under-21 star Shane King showed excellent free-taking qualities in a personal tally of seven points, while Colm McCreesh's fisted goal nine minutes from time turned the game for Lisnaskea. Simon Bradley had just put Enniskillen in front for the first time at 1-7 to 0-8, after good work by Barry King and Ciaran Woods.

Lisnaskea followed the goal with two points to lead by 1-9 to 0-8 in added time, when Enniskillen were awarded a disputed penalty. John Reihill's long ball came off the crossbar to substitute Michael McGourty who was judged to be fouled in the square. Warren Dixon's successful kick did not affect the outcome; Enniskillen were left to rue eight second half wides while Lisnaskea can point to a brilliant save by Enniskillen keeper Brendan Dooris from Brian McCreesh midway through the half. Keith Swift had an excellent game for the new champions.

LISNASKEA: Cormac McAdam, Martin Woods, Pearse Collins, Damien Teague, Brian O'Donnell, Tony Collins, Keith Swift, Collie Curran (c), Brian McCreesh, Ollie Woods, Shane King 0-7, Eamonn Shannon, Ciaran Woods, Colm McCreesh 1-2, Brendan McCreesh. Sub: Barry King for Shannon.

ENNISKILLEN: Brendan Dooris, Conor McEnhill, Ciaran Lynam, Michael Lilly, Eamonn Beresford, Michael Sheridan, Raymond Curran, John Reihill 0-1, Garvan Gallagher, Gerry Love, Paul Brewster 0-1, Maurice Rooney, Tom Brewster 0-2, Simon Bradley 0-4, Warren Dixon 1-0. Subs: Ollie McShea for Beresford, Michael McGourty for Love.

Ref: Eamonn McPartland (Belcoo).

MONAGHAN

17-year-old Rory Mone will remember Clontibret's championship triumph for the rest of his life. In the semi-finals, he came on as a substitute to score five brilliant points against Castleblayney; in the final, the supersub netted within 35 seconds of being on the field and finished with a tally of 2-1.

Put in the context of his club's first championship win in 26 years, Mone's entrance was quite sensational. He wasn't born until nine years after the 1968 win, but he knew Clontibret had suffered many times at the hands of Castleblayney, including three finals, in that lean period. That's why his club's supporters particularly enjoyed the semi-final, when Clontibret's power and poise reduced the great Nudie Hughes and Blayney to the role of spectators in a nine-point win.

Elsewhere, four Aughnamullan goals saved them in a great game with Drumhowan in the first round, but they eventually fell to Donaghmoyne in the semi-finals. Donaghmoyne were on the way to a first final in 36 years; they had earlier beaten the holders, Scotstown, in the quarter-finals. Eamonn Burns scored the winning point against Scotstown and the same player got the only goal against Aughnamullan.

The 1994 Monaghan final was the first to be played at Clones, and the first all-seater final, as only the Gerry Arthurs and Pat McGrane Stands were opened for the four thousand onlookers. They saw a one-sided show as Clontibret led by six points at the break, and won by five.

At one stage in the first half, the gap was nine points, after goals from Kieran Lavelle and Mick O'Dowd. County player Noel Marron

Holders - Scotstown	
Name of Cup - Mick Duffy Cup	
FIRST ROUND	
Clontibret 3-11	Carrickmacross 0-12
Aughamullen 4-7	Drumhowan 0-12
QUARTER-FINALS	
Augnamullan 1-16	Latton 0-6
Castleblayney 2-13	Magheracloone 1-9
Clontibret 1-6	Emyvale 0-7
Donaghmoyne 0-12	Scotstown 0-11
SEMI-FINALS	
Clontibret 1-15	Castleblayney 0-9
Donaghmoyne 1-6	Aughnamullen 0-7
FINAL	
Clontibret 4-7	Donaghmoyne 1-11

set up Stanley Wilson for a Donaghmoyne goal to make it 2-5 to 1-2 at the break. That's when Rory Mone was told to get ready.

His first goal put more daylight between the sides, though Donaghmoyne scored four points in succession after an injury to Mick O'Dowd, before Rory Mone slammed his second to the roof of the net to finally kill off the challenge. The loser's only consolation was the Man of the Match award, won by Noel Marron.

CLONTIBRET: Michael Thompson, Des Brennan, Barry McShane (c), Brian Morgan, Sean McSkeane, Conor Mone, Declan Mone, Kevin Carragher, Cathal Carragher 0-1, Niall Magennis 0-2, Kieran Lavelle 1-0, Mick O'Dowd 1-1, Mickey Hughes, Pauric McShane 0-1, Kieran Brennan 0-1. Subs: Rory Mone 2-1 for Hughes, Steven McKenna for McSkeane, Shane Magennis for O'Dowd.

DONAGHMOYNE: Patrick Caulfield, Michael Burns, Hugh McGroder, Vincent McConnell, Paul Meegan, Liam Finnegan (c), Tommy Marron, Raymond Marron 0-1, Peter McLoughlin, Adrian McCrossan 0-1, Joe Duffy 0-5, Noel Marron 0-3, Eamonn Burns, Sean McLoughlin 0-1, Michael Deery. Subs: Stanley Wilson 1-0 for Deery, Michael Cumiskey for T.Marron, Eugene Murtagh for Meegan.

Ref: John Mullen (Scotstown).

TOP SCORERS:

Gabriel Bannigan (Aughnamullan) 1-16; Mick O'Dowd (Clontibret) 3-9; Rory Mone (Clontibret) 2-6; Joe Duffy (Donaghmoyne) 0-12; Kieran Lavelle (Clontibret) 2-2

Clontibret, Monaghan Champions, 1994.

TYRONE

The Errigal Ciaran success story began in 1993 when Danny Ball shook a Tyrone jersey in front of his players and appealed to their "pride in Tyrone football". Every player knew what he meant, 'they had all been affected by the gloom that had spread over the county.

Four successive Ulster Championship losses, cruel defeat in the 1992 National League Final, the failure of back-to-back All Ireland Under-21 successes to translate themselves into Senior glory, and poor results in Division Three after the appointment of the "dream team" of Art McCrory and Eugene McKenna.

By this stage, some may well have begun to accept the situation, but not Errigal Ciaran. They saw a winner in Danny Ball, and responded by landing the Tyrone title and the Ulster Club Championship, the first ever to come to the county. Along the way, Errigal defeated champions from Derry, Donegal and Down, counties which had left Tyrone behind in Ulster's dramatic football resurgence.

People began to take notice of Errigal Ciaran when they eliminated Lavey before five thousand at Omagh, late in 1993. It was noticeable that opponents were finding their style of play difficult to handle. Errigal would pull thirteen men into defence and then sweep forward in numbers, playing off their outstanding captain, Peter Canavan.

Holders - Errigal Ciaran	
Name of Cup -O'Neill Cup	
FIRST ROUND	
Errigal Ciaran 3-1	Beragh 1-2
(R: 1-9 2-6)	
Dromore 0-10	Galbally 2-10
Donaghmore 0-9	Dungannon 2-6
Moortown 1-10	Moy 0-9
(R: 0-9 1-6)	
Pomeroy 0-7	Trillick 2-12
Ardboe 1-10	Cookstown 1-14
Carrickmore 2-14	Coalisland 0-7
(R: 1-10 2-7)	
Clonoe 1-4	Omagh 0-9
QUARTER-FINALS	
Dungannon 0-13	Trillick 1-7
Errigal Ciaran 1-13	Galbally 0-5
Carrickmore 2-13	Omagh 1-5
Moortown 1-12	Cookstown 1-9
SEMI-FINALS	
Errigal Ciaran 1-11	Moortown 1-7
Carrickmore 1-8	Dungannon 0-8
FINAL	
Errigal Ciaran 3-5	Carrickmore 1-8

Two dramatic and tempestuous matches followed with Kilcar at Irvinestown, before Downpatrick were beaten in the Ulster Final by 3-7 to 1-8 at Armagh. Peter and Stephen Canavan goaled within minutes of one another in the second half to seal the outcome. In February, Errigal failed in their bid to reach the All Ireland final, losing to Nemo Rangers in Newbridge, 1-13 to 0-11 after extra time.

The rest of Tyrone were proud of their efforts, but every club in the draw for the 1994 Championship also wanted to "have a crack" at the Ulster Champions. The privilege went to Beragh on their return to the Senior Championship after 21 years. It seemed an easy draw, but Errigal needed a Martin McCaffrey point with the very last kick of the game to prevent a First Round sensation. In the replay, Eoin Gormley scored 2-4 as Errigal won by twenty points.

1993 finalists Moortown also came from behind to overcome Moy in a second game, while Ciaran Corr's last-minute point earned Coalisland a replay against Carrickmore. Two Brian Gormley goals decided the issue the next day for Carrickmore.

In the quarter-finals, Peter Canavan missed a penalty but still scored eight points to account for Galbally. Gerard Cavlan scored eight more for Dungannon against

Errigal Ciaran parade before the Tyrone final.

Trillick, Moortown had three points to spare over Cookstown and Carrickmore beat Omagh with some ease. Terence McWilliams was in charge of Omagh after Mickey Moran's seven-year reign, and two more Derrymen were involved in a head-to-head in the semi-finals, Peter Doherty with Carrickmore and Adrian McGuckin with Dungannon.

The teams were level six times in the first game, though Dungannon got off to a great start with an Adrian Kilpatrick goal. Gerard Cavlan later added a penalty, but Brian Gormley replied with 1-4 and Peter Loughran kept his nerve for two pressure free-kicks to level things out. In the replay, Loughran struck with an early goal and added four points to end Dungannon's dreams of a first title in 38 years.

Errigal Ciaran were in a spot of bother in the other semi-final when Finbar Conway struck a first-minute goal for Moortown and Eamonn McCaffrey was sent off. But, that was before a quite superb individual display by Peter Canavan. The captain tormented Chris Lawn on his way to matching Moortown's total of 1-7 with his own, and sending his team through.

Eoin Gormley was the star of the final with a marvellous goal in each half for Errigal Ciaran, the second putting his team four points ahead in the last quarter. Carrickmore's number was called a few minutes later when Canavan's through ball was blasted to the net by Damien Mallon. Raymond Munroe scored a late consolation goal.

Peter Canavan lifted the O'Neill Cup for the second time, and also set a new scoring record for the Tyrone Championship. His final tally of 3-27 bettered the previous record of 2-26, held by Tommy Fiddis, and was twelve points clear of Gerard Cavlan and Brian Gormley in this year's competition.

Tyrone also claim the best-attended club championship in Ulster, with an estimated twenty thousand people watching fourteen First and Second Round games. 4,000 then saw the first semi-final between Carrickmore and Dungannon, while 8,000 were present at the final.

ERRIGAL CIARAN: Cathal McAnenly, Seamus Mallon, Mickey McGirr, Colm McCann, Eamonn Kavanagh, Ciaran McCrory, Christopher Quinn, Pascal Canavan, Hugh Quinn, Stephen Canavan, Damien Mallon 1-1, Brian Neill 0-1, Leo Quinn, Peter Canavan 0-3 (c), Eoin Gormley 2-0. Subs: Martin McCaffrey for Kavanagh, Paudge Quinn for L.Quinn.

CARRICKMORE: Plunkett McCallan, Aidan Loughran (c), Damien Loughran, Gavin McElroy, Eamonn Martin, Conor McElduff, Conor Daly, Raymond Munroe 1-0, Seamus McCallan, Ciaran Loughran 0-1, Peter Kerr 0-1, Brian Gormley 0-1, Pat Tanney 0-2, Fergal Gormley, Peter Loughran 0-3. Subs: Ronan McGarrity for Daly, Conor McAleer for Kerr, Davog McElroy for P.Loughran.

Ref: Barney Taggart (Clonoe).

Champions again! Errigal Ciaran captain Peter Canavan with the O'Neill Cup.

1994 MINOR FINALS

Antrim:	Rasharkin 2-10	Lamh Dhearg 0-6
Armagh:	Silverbridge 0-10	Crossmaglen 1-6
Cavan:	St Finbarrs 1-10	St Killians 0-11
Derry:	Bellaghy 1-10	Ballinderry 0-8(R)
Donegal:	St Eunans 2-18	Ardara 4-7
Down:	Clonduff 3-6	Mayobridge 1-5
Fermanagh:	Roslea 1-5	Enniskillen 0-5
Monaghan:	Castleblayney 4-15	Scotstown 0-2
Tyrone:	Dungannon 1-14	Strabane 1-7

UNDER-21 FINALS

Antrim:	St Pauls 2-4	Rossa 1-6
Armagh:	Crossmaglen 4-11	Killeavey 0-5
Donegal:	Ardara 1-12	Aodh Ruadh 1-10
Tyrone:	Cookstown 1-11	Ardboe 0-5

1994 ULSTER CLUB CHAMPIONSHIP

(for the Seamus McFerran Cup)

Aodh Ruadh 0-15	Errigal Ciaran 1-10
St Pauls 1-9	Clan na Gael 2-9
Castlewellan 2-10	Clontibret 3-9
Gowna 0-11	Lisnaskea 1-7
Bellaghy 0-13	Aodh Ruadh 1-8
Clan na Gael 1-10	Clontibret 2-10
Gowna 1-7	Bellaghy 0-11
Final December 11	
Bellaghy	Clontibret

Silverbridge, Armagh Minor Champions, 1994

Gerard Cavlan celebrates Dungannon's Minor triumph in Tyrone.

SENIOR COUNTY FINAL WINNERS RESULTS

ANTRIM

1902 - Tir na nOg
1903 - Seagan an Diomais
1904 - Ollamh Fodhla
1905 - O'Neill Crowleys
1906 - Seagan an Diomais
1907 - Ollamh Fodhla
1908 - Seagan an Diomais
1909 - Seagan an Diomais
1910 - Seagan an Diomais
1911 - Mitchells
1912 - Mitchells
1913 - Sarsfields
1914 - James Stephens
1915 - James Stephens
1916 - James Stephens
1917 - James Stephens
1918 - James Stephens
1919 - James Stephens
1920 - Rossa
1921 - Rossa
1922 - James Stephens
1923 - Davitts
1924 - Cuchullains
1925 - Cuchullains
1926 - Cuchullains
1927 - Rossa
1928 - O'Connells
1929 - Lamh Dhearg, Toome
1930 - Rossa
1931 - Cuchullains
1932 - Ardoyne
1933 - St Galls
1934 - O'Connells
1935 - Cuchullains
1936 - Cuchullains
1937 - Ardoyne
1938 - Gaedhil Uladh
1939 - Gaedhil Uladh
1940 - O'Donnells
1941 - Sarsfields
1942 - Gaedhil Uladh
1943 - Kickhams, R'town
1944 - Rossa
1945 - St Johns
1946 - Rossa
1947 - O'Connell
1948 - Eire Og
1949 - St Johns
1950 - Rossa
1951 - St Johns
1952 - Rossa
1953 - Rossa
1954 - Kickhams, R'town
1955 - Rossa

1956 - Rossa		
1957 - St Johns		
1958 - Rossa		
1959 - St Johns 2-7	Rasharkin 0-5
1960 - St Johns 4-4	Rasharkin 2-1
1961 - St Johns 0-8	Rasharkin 0-2
1962 - St Johns 1-10	Pearses, Belfast 0-6
1963 - St Johns 1-6	Rasharkin 1-2
1964 -St Johns 1-10	Pearses 2-4 (R)
1965 - St Johns 0-11	Sarsfields 1-3
1966 - Glenravel 1-5	Sarsfields 0-6
1967 - Sarsfields 1-5	Pearses 0-5
1968- Pearses 1-6	St Johns 0-4
1969 - St Johns 2-3	Pearses 0-8
1970 - St Johns 1-9	Sarsfields 0-6
1971 - Lamh Dhearg 1-13	St Johns 1-12
1972 - St Johns 3-11	Lamh Dhearg 0-7
1973 - Rossa 1-7	St Johns 1-4
1974 - Cargin 1-6	Sarsfields 1-3
1975 - St Johns 2-10	Rossa 2-7
1976 - St Johns 2-11	St Teresas 3-5 (R)
1977 - St Johns 3-8	Creggan 1-9
1978 - St Johns 1-15	St Galls 1-7
1979 - St Teresas 2-10	St Johns 2-4
1980 - St Johns 1-7	St Teresas 1-6
1981 - St Johns 2-9	St Teresas 1-5
1982 - St Galls 0-11	St Teresas 2-3
1983 - St Galls 1-7	Lamh Dhearg 0-9
1984 - St Johns 1-8	St Galls 1-6
1985 - Sarsfields 2-8	St Pauls 2-7
1986 - St Johns 0-8	St Pauls 0-6
1987 - St Galls 0-10	Cargin 1-5
1988 - St Johns 2-6	St Galls 0-8
1989 - Rossa 1-10	Cargin 0-5
1990 - St Galls 0-5	Cargin 0-4
1991 - Rossa 1-8	St Pauls 0-7
1992 - Lamh Dhearg*	
1993 - St Galls 0-13	Cargin 0-2
1994 - St Pauls 0-14	Cargin 1-7

* St Johns and Cargin disqualified after their semi-final.

ARMAGH

1889 - Armagh Harps 4-14	Blackwatertown 0-3
1890 - Harps	
1891 - Harps	
1901 - Harps	
1902 - Harps	
1903 - Harps	
1904 - Armagh Tir na nOg w/o	
1905 - Whitecross 2-4	Harps 1-4
1906 - C'glen Red Hands 1-7	Camlough 0-4 (R)
1907 - Camlough 2-1	Bessbrook 1-3

1908 - Creggan Rvrs 1-3	Harps 1-2	1975 - Crossmaglen 0-9	Harps 0-4 (R)
1909 - Bessbrook bt	Harps	1976 - Clan na Gael 1-8	Maghery 0-7
1910 - Camlough 2-1	C'glen Rangers 1-3	1977 - Crossmaglen 1-7	Clan na Gael 0-5 (R)
1911 - C'glen Rangers bt	Camlough	1978 - Carrickcruppen 0-11	Clan na Gael 1-7
1912 - C'glen Rangers bt	Harps	1979 - Carrickcruppen 2-13	Crossmaglen 1-8
1913 - C'glen Rangers 2-2	Culloville 0-1	1980 - Clan na Gael 3-7	Carrickcruppen 1-8
1914 - Killeavy 3-2	Crossmaglen Rgrs 1-1	1981 - Clan na Gael 0-10	Carrickcruppen 0-7
1915 - Killeavy 0-4	Bessbrook 0-2	1982 - Carrickcruppen 0-6	Crossmaglen 0-4
1916 - Bessbrook/Culloville		1983 - Crossmaglen 2-9	Maghery 1-6
1917 - Armagh Yg. Irelands 0-12	C'glen Plunketts 0-5	1984 - Keady 0-7	Harps 0-2
1923 - C'glen Rgrs 0-9	C'glen Geraldines 0-2	1985 - Pearse Og 0-7	Harps 0-3
1924 - C'glen Rgrs 1-1	Killeavy 0-3	1986 - Crossmaglen 3-8	Pearse Og 0-11
1925 - C'glen 1-4	Young Irelands 0-4	1987 - Clann na Gael 3-6	Harps 0-6
1926 - C'glen bt	Young Irelands	1988 - Pearse Og 1-10	Killeavey 0-5
1927 - C'glen 1-8	Young Irelands 1-3	1989 - Harps 3-9	St Pauls 2-8
1928 - Young Irelands 2-4	Forkhill 0-8 (R)	1990 - Sarsfields 0-9	Harps 0-6
1930 - Young Irelands bt	Crossmaglen	1991 - Harps 0-11	Maghery 1-7
1931 - Young Irelands 3-6	Culloville 0-3	1992 - Pearse Og 0-13	Sarsfields 0-3
1932 - Young Irelands 3-2	Crossmaglen 0-5 (R)	1993 - Clan na Gael 2-15	Maghery 1-6
1933 - Crossmaglen 1-1	Young Irelands 0-2	1994 - Clan na Gael 2-5	Mullabawn 0-6
1934 - Young Irelands 2-5	Keady 0-4		
1935 - Tir na nOg 0-4	C'glen 1-2 (Obj)		

CAVAN

1936 - Crossmaglen 1-8	Young Irelands 1-2	1888 - Maghera McFinns 1-4	B'connell First Ulsters 0-1
1937 - Crossmaglen 0-8	Keady 1-0	1890 - Cavan Slashers	
1938 - Keady w/o		1903 - Drumlane Sons of O'Connell	
1939 - Bessbrook 2-5	Young Irelands 1-4	1904 - Drumlane 1-3	Virginia 0-2
1940 - N'hamilton 1-6	Crossmaglen 0-3	1905 - Drumlane	
1941 - N'hamilton bt	Crossmaglen	1907 - Drumlane bt	Crosserlough
1942 - Armagh St Malachys bt	Mullabawn	1909 - Cornafean 1-7	Crosserlough 0-1
1943 - Derrymacash bt	Crossmaglen	1910 - Cornafean 2-1	Denn 0-2
1944 - St Peters 2-8	Crossmaglen 1-3	1911 - Bailieboro bt	Cornafean
1945 - St Malachys 0-7	Silverbridge 0-5	1912 - Cornafean bt	Cross
1946 - Harps 0-7	Crossmaglen 0-2	1913 - Cornafean bt	Bailieboro
1947 - Crossmaglen 3-6	Harps 4-2	1914 - Cornafean bt	Virginia
1948 - Killeavy 2-4	St Peters 0-3	1915 - Cornafean bt	Virginia
1949 - Clan na Gael 0-6	Crossmaglen 0-2	1916 - Virginia 1-2	Belturbet 0-0
1950 - Clan na Gael 1-3	St Peters 0-3	1917 - Cavan Slashers1-4	Crosserlough 0-0 (R)
1951 - St Peters 2-7	Killeavy 1-9	1918 - Cornafean 2-4	Crosserloug 1-1
1952 - Harps bt	Clan na Gael	1919 - Virginia	
1953 - Keady 0-10	Harps 2-3	1920 - Cornafean	
1954 - Clann Eireann 2-4	Clan na Gael 0-1	1921 - Kingscourt Stars	
1955 - Harps 3-9	Killeavy 1-2	1922 - Cavan Slashers 2-3	Virginia 2-4 (Protest)
1956 - Keady 2-7	Harps 0-11	1923 - Templeport	
1957 - Harps 2-2	Keady 0-5	1924 - Cavan Slashers 2-1	Bailieboro 0-5
1958 - Harps 1-2	Keady 0-4	1925 - Cavan Slashers 1-3	Cornafean 0-4
1959 - Carrickcruppen 2-7	Clann Eireann 0-5	1926 - Maghera	
1960 - Crossmaglen 4-8	Clann Eireann 3-3 (R)	1927 - Cavan Slashers 1-5	Virginia 0-4
1961 - Collegeland 4-11	Clann Eireann 4-7	1928 - Cavan Slashers 1-3	Maghera 0-3
1962 - Crossmaglen 2-3	Clann Eireann 0-4	1929 - Cornafean 2-5	Cavan Slashers 2-2
1963 - Clann Eireann 3-6	Crossmaglen 1-4	1930 - Cavan Slashers 1-4	Cornafean 0-4
1964 - Mullabawn 0-10	Derrymacash 1-4	1931 - Cavan Slashers 3-4	Cornafean 0-8
1965 - Crossmaglen 2-5	Clann Eireann 1-3	1932 - Cornafean 5-5	Bailieboro 0-5
1966 - Crossmaglen 4-11	Carrickcruppen 0-5	1933 - Cornafean 4-1	Cavan Slashers 0-3
1967 - Crossmaglen 0-12	Wolfe Tones 0-3	1934 - Cornafean 3-5	Bailieboro 1-2
1968 - Clan na Gael 2-6	Clann Eireann 0-4	1935 - Mullahoran 2-5	Cornafean 1-3
1969 - Clan na Gael 2-6	Crossmaglen 0-4	1936 - Cornafean 3-6	Cavan Slashers 0-5
1970 - Crossmaglen 1-6	Clan na Gael 0-6	1937 - Cornafean	
1971 - Clan na Gael w/o	Carrickcruppen	1938 - Cornafean 2-6	Gowna 0-5
1972 - Clan na Gael 0-8	Crossmaglen 0-7	1939 - Cornafean 1-6	Killinkere 1-5
1973 - Clan na Gael 3-14	Wolfe Tones 0-8	1940 - Cornafean 1-4	Killinkere 0-3
1974 - Clan na Gael 3-13	Carrickcruppen 0-7		

1941 - Cavan Slashers 1-4   Cornafean 1-2
1942 - Mullahoran 1-8   Cornafean 0-10
1943 - Cornafean 3-7   Mullahoran 2-4
1944 - Mullahoran 1-6   Mountnugent 1-4
1945 - Mullahoran 3-8   Bailieboro 1-4
1946 - Mountnugent
1947 - Mullahoran 1-6   Cross 1-4
1948 - Mullahoran 3-5   Cornafean 2-5
1949 - Mullahoran 3-11   Cornafean 0-2
1950 - Mullahoran 2-5   Cornafean 0-6
1951 - Lavey
1952 - Bailieboro
1953 - Cootehill
1954 - Cootehill
1955 - Cootehill
1956 - Cornafean 4-3   Bailieboro 1-7
1957 - Bailieboro
1958 - Crosserlough 3-7   Cavan Gaels 3-4
1959 - Virginia
1960 - Not Finished
1961 - Crosserlough 2-8   Ballinagh 2-3
1962 - Virginia
1963 - Mullahoran 1-10   Bailieboro 0-3 (R)
1964 - Bailieboro
1965 - Cavan Gaels 3-5   Bailieboro 1-10
1966 - Crosserlough 3-13   Ballyconnell 0-0
1967 - Crosserlough 0-18   Cavan Gaels 3-5
1968 - Crosserlough 2-6   Castlerahan 0-8
1969 - Crosserlough 1-9   St Josephs 0-4
1970 - Crosserlough 1-12   Cavan Gaels 0-5
1971 - Crosserlough 1-12   Killygarry 1-4
1972 - Crosserlough 3-8   Laragh 2-6
1973 - Annagh (Redhills/Belturbet)
1974 - Ramor United
1975 - Cavan Gaels 1-11   Crosserlough 0-8 (R)
1976 - St Marys (Castlerahan/Munterconnacht)
1977 - Cavan Gaels 3-12   St Marys 1-6
1978 - Cavan Gaels 1-10   Ballyhaise 0-6
1979 - Laragh United 3-14   Crosserlough 1-7
1980 - Kingscourt 0-10   Crosserlough 0-9
1981 - Kingscourt 1-10   Drumalee 0-4 (R)
1982 - Laragh United 1-10   Bailieboro 1-3
1983 - Laragh United 1-15   Cavan Gaels 2-6
1984 - Laragh United 0-16   Drumalee 2-7
1985 - Ramor United 3-10   Kingscourt 0-7
1986 - Kingscourt 2-14   Ballinagh 0-4
1987 - Kingscourt 1-8   Ramor United 0-6
1988 - Gowna 1-6   Laragh United 0-3
1989 - Kingscourt 1-11   Ramor United 0-8
1990 - Kingscourt 1-12   Mullahoran 0-9
1991 - Kingscourt 3-11   Crosserlough 0-10
1992 - Ramor United 1-9   Bailieboro 0-11
1993 - Kingscourt 2-8   Gowna 0-8
1994 - Gowna 1-8   Mullahoran 0-9

DERRY

1907 - Eire Og
1914 - Clan Chonail 1-4   Emmetts 1-2
1916 - Sarsfields
1917 - St Patricks bt   Glenkeen
1918 - Emmetts

1921 - Derry Guilds bt   St Patricks
1927 - Ballinderry bt   Drumsurn
1928 - Glenullin
1930 - Buncrana bt   St Patricks
1931 - Burt bt   Wolfe Tones
1934 - Ballinascreen
1935 - Ballinascreen
1936 - Loup bt   Park
1937 - Newbridge bt   Limavady
1938 - Lavey bt   Pearses
1939 - Magherafelt 5-7   Dungiven 1-2
1940 - Newbridge bt   Glenullin
1941 - Ballinascreen 2-5   Limavady 1-1
1942 - Magherafelt w/o   Glenullin (R)
1943 - Lavey bt   Faughanvale
1944 - Lavey bt   Derry Mitchells
1945 - Newbridge 3-6   Dungiven 0-3
1946 - Magherafelt 7-8   Sean Dolans 2-6
1947 - Dungiven 2-8   Lavey 2-3
1948 - Newbridge 1-6   Dungiven 0-7
1949 - Magherafelt 2-8   Eoghan Ruadhs 0-7
1950 - Newbridge 3-6   Dungiven 0-6
1951 - Dungiven 4-3   Bellaghy 1-9
1952 - Eire Og 1-2   Desertmartin 1-0
1953 - Desertmartin 4-9   Ballerin 0-2
1954 - Lavey bt   Banagher
1955 - Newbridge bt   Sean Dolans
1956 - Bellaghy 2-9   Drum 1-1
1957 - Ballerin 3-8   Ballymaguigan 2-6
1958 - Bellaghy 3-6   Ballmaguigan 0-7
1959 - Bellaghy 3-4   Desertmartin 1-3
1960 - Bellaghy 1-5   Dungiven 2-1
1961 - Bellaghy w/o   Ballymaguigan
1962 - Ballymaguigan 2-10   Castledawson 1-5 (R)
1963 - Bellaghy 2-12   Newbridge 2-8
1964 - Bellaghy 2-9   Ballerin 1-7
1965 - Bellaghy 3-11   Ballerin 0-10
1966 - Newbridge 2-10   Dungiven 0-3
1967 - Newbridge 0-11   Magherafelt 1-7
1968 - Bellaghy 2-3   Newbridge 0-7
1969 - Bellaghy 1-9   Slaughtneil 0-8
1970 - Newbridge 3-8   Bellaghy 0-13
1971 - Bellaghy 2-12   Lavey 0-5
1972 - Bellaghy 0-14   Ballerin 1-8
1973 - Ballinascreen 2-14   Bellaghy 1-10
1974 - Ballinderry 1-4   Banagher 1-2
1975 - Bellaghy 1-9   Magherafelt 0-3 (R)
1976 - Ballerin 0-9   ungiven 0-3
1977 - Lavey 1-8   Ballinderry 0-7
1978 - Magherafelt 1-4   Banagher 1-3
1979 - Bellaghy 0-14   Magherafelt 0-5 (R)
1980 - Ballinderry 0-7   Lavey 0-4
1981 - Ballinderry 0-7   Banagher 0-5
1982 - Ballinderry 0-7   Dungiven 0-5 aet (R) *
1983 - Dungiven 1-4   Magherafelt 1-3
1984 - Dungiven 0-9   Castledawson 0-8
1985 - Glenullin 1-9   Ballinderry 1-5
1986 - Bellaghy 3-5   Ballinderry 1-6
1987 - Dungiven **

1988 - Lavey 0-11   Newbridge 0-6
1989 - Newbridge 3-4   Castledawson 0-9
1990 - Lavey 3-14   Ballinascreen 1-7
1991 - Dungiven 3-5   Newbridge 0-4
1992 - Lavey 2-6   Ballinascreen 0-9
1993 - Lavey 3-5   Swatragh 0-8
1994 - Bellaghy 2-10   Ballinascreen 0-8
* Declared Void
** Ballinderry and Newbridge disqualified after
semi-final.

DONEGAL

1920 - Bundoran 2-4   Killygordon 1-2
1921 - Killygordon bt   Donegal
1922 - Castlefin
1923 - Ardara 0-3   Ballybofey 0-1
1924 - Donegal 3-2   Dungloe 1-4
1925 - Kilcar
1926 - Ardara 0-5   Letterkenny 0-2
1927 - Letterkenny
1928 - Ardara 1-4   Killygordon 0-3
1929 - Ballyshannon 0-7   Killygordon 0-5
1930 - Dungloe 3-2   Letterkenny 2-3
1931 - Dungloe 2-4   Ballybofey 2-2
1932 - Ballyshannon 1-7   Dungloe 0-1
1933 - Dungloe 3-2   Bundoran 1-3
1934 - Bundoran 1-5   Dungloe 0-4
1935 - Gweedore 2-8   Bundoran 0-3
1936 - Dungloe 2-8   Ardara 2-2
1937 - Ballyshannon 3-8   Gweedore 4-2
1938 - Gweedore 1-7   Ardara 0-5
1939 - Ballyshannon 0-6   Gweedore 0-4
1940 - Dungloe 3-8   Ballyshannon 1-3
1941 - Gweedore 0-10   Glenties 2-3
1942 - Ballyshannon 2-8   Glenties 1-4
1943 - Ballyshannon 1-9   Convoy 2-1
1944 - Gweedore 4-10   St Eunans 3-4
1945 - Gweedore 4 - 5   Ballyshannon 1-6
1946 - Gweedore 0-7   St Eunans 0-6
1947 - Gweedore 1-9   St Eunans 0-3
1948 - St Eunans 1-7   Gweedore 2-1
1949 - Gweedore 2-12   St Eunans 3-4
1950 - St Eunans \ Donegal
1951 - Ballyshannon 1-6   St Eunans 1-5
1952 - Killybegs 0-9   St Eunans 1-5
1953 - Gweedore 1-5   Carndonagh 1-4
1954 - Gweedore 3-6   Donegal 0-5
1955 - Gweedore 1-7   St Eunans 1-4
1956 - St Eunans 0-8   Ballyshannon 1-2
1957 - Dungloe 0-12   Ballyshannon 1-4
1958 - Dungloe 2-6   St Eunans 2-5
1959 - MacCumhaills 2-7   Kilcar 1-6
1960 - St Eunans O -1 1   Gweedore O-3
1961 - Gweedore 2-5   Dungloe 0-6
1962 - MacCumhaills 1-9   Gweedore 1-7
1963 - MacCumhaills 1-6   Kilcar 0-4
1964 - MacCumhaills 1-11   Dungloe 1-3

1965 - St Josephs 1-11   Glenties 0-10
1966 - St Josephs\McCumhaills
1967 - St Eunans 1-13   St Josephs 1-9
1968 - St Josephs 1-10   MacCumhaills 0-5
1969 - St Eunans 0-10   St Josephs 1-4
1970 - St Josephs 1-16   Rosses Rovers 0-4
1971 - MacCumhaills 2-10   Clann na Gael 0-11
1972 - St Eunans 2-12   Clann na Gael 1-8
1973 - St Josephs 1-8   MacCumhaills 1-6
1974 - St Josephs 1-8   St Eunans 1-3
1975 - St Josephs 1-11   MacCumhaills 1-5
1976 - St Josephs 1-13   Four Masters 0-5
1977 - MacCumhaills 0-8   Gweedore 0-5
1978 - Glencolmcille 1-12   Gweedore 0-10
1979 - Bundoran 0-9   MacCumhaills 1-5
1980 - Kilcar 1-13   Ardara 0-8
1981 - Ardara 1-7   Four Masters 0-6
1982 - Four Masters 1-4   Kilcar 0-6
1983 - St Eunans 0-8   Ardara 0-8
1984 - Four Masters 0-9   Ardara 1-2
1985 - Kilcar 0-9   Four Masters 0-7
1986 - Ballyshannon 1-8   Killygordon O-5
1987 - Ballyshannon 2-10   Kilcar 1-7
1988 - Killybegs 2-10   Kilcar 2-8
1989 - Kilcar 1-9   Ballyshannon 0-9
1990 - Naomh Columba 0-10   Killybegs 0-9
1991 - Killybegs 2-7   Red Hughs 0-11
1992 - Killybegs 0-12   Naomh Columba 0-9
1993 - Kilcar 0-12   Killybegs 0-10
1994 - Ballyshannon 2-10   Naomh Columba 1-10

DOWN

1903 - Faugh-a-Ballagh, Newry
1904 - Clann na Banna 1-2   Faugh-a-Ballagh 0-4
1905 - Leitrim
1906 - Faugh-a-Ballagh 0-7   Leitrim 0-4
1907 - Faugh-a-Ballagh bt   Leitrim
1908 - Annsboro 0-11   Faugh-a-Ballagh 0-1
1909 - Faugh-a-Ballagh 2-0   Ballyvarley 1-0
1910 - Clann Uladh, N'ry 2-1   Ballyvarley 1-1
1916 - Mayobridge bt   Downpatrick
1917 - Kilcoo bt   Killyleagh
1919 - Mayobridge 1-2   Leitrim 1-1
1920 - Leitrim 0-2   Rossglass 0-1
1921 - Kilcoo bt   Rossglass
1922 - Rossglass 0-3   Kilcoo 0-1
1924 - Castlewellan 1-2   Mayobridge 0-2
1925 - Kilcoo 2-3   Rathfriland 0-1
1926 - Kilcoo 0-3   Clonduff 0-2
1927 - Kilcoo 0-11   Mayobridge 0-0
1928 - Kilcoo 1-6   Clonduff 1-4
1929 - D'naquoile 2-2   Mayobridge 1-1
1930 - Clonduff 1-3   Mayobridge 1-1
1931 - Rathfriland bt   Rossglass
1932 - Kilcoo 2-6   Rossglass 0-3
1933 - Kilcoo

1934 - Castlewellan 2-5   Ballymartin 0-1 (R)
1935 - Downpatrick 3-1   Kilcoo 0-8
1936 - Castlewellan 1-4   Mayobridge 0-3 (R)
1937 - Kilcoo bt   Mayobridge
1938 - Ballymartin 2-1   Saul 1-1
1939 - Bryansford 1-5   Saul 1-1
1940 - Bryansford 3-4   Kilcoo 2-2
1941 - Bryansford 0-12   Warrenpoint 0-10
1942 - Bryansford 1-9   Newry 2-4
1943 - Warrenpoint 3-3   Bryansford 1-3 (R)
1944 - Clonduff 1-10   Warrenpoint 1-6
1945 - Clonduff 1-7   Castlewellan 0-0
1946 - Newry bt -   Castlewellan
1947 - Clonduff 3-7   Newry 0-5
1948 - Warrenpoint 4-1   Kilcoo 1-5
1949 - Clonduff 1-8   Saul 2-2
1950 - Castlewellan 2-5   Warrenpoint 2-4
1951 - Newry 3-2   Kilkeel 1-6
1952 - Clonduff 2-9   Castlewellan 1-9
1953 - Warrenpoint 1-0   Burren 0-1
1954 - Lisnacree 2-4   Annaclone 0-4
1955 - Ballymartin 4-8   Longstone 0-5
1956 - Newry S.rocks 2-6   Kilwartin 0-5 (R)
1957 - Clonduff 3-4   Cabra 1-3
1958 - Castlewellan 0-8   Clonduff 0-4
1959 - Glenn 3-4   Rostrevor 0-5
1960 - Newry Mitchels 2-10   Ballykinlar 1-4
1961 - Newry S.rocks 1-11   Newry Mitchels 2-6
1962 - Glenn 1-12   Castlewellan 0-4
1963 - Glenn 0-7   Downpatrick 0-5 (R)
1964 - Newry Mitchels 4-2   Ballykinlar 1-10
1965 - Castlewellan 3-10   Clonduff 1-9
1966 - Burren bt   Kilwarlin (R)
1967 - Newry Mitchels 1-9   Downpatrick 1-6
1968 - Newry Mitchels 3-7   Bryansford 2-3
1969 - Bryansford 1-11   Burren 1-6
1970 - Bryansford 3-11   Burren 0-4
1971 - Bryansford 2-12   Tullylish 1-7
1972 - Downpatrick 2-5   Loughinisland 0-8
1973 - Bryansford 0-16   Loughinisland 1-7
1974 - Bryansford 3-5   Loughinisland 0-8
1975 - Loughinisland 1-7   Rostrevor 0-9
1976 - Rostrevor 1-9   Warrenpoint 1-5
1977 - Bryansford 3-9   Burren 2-5
1978 - Downpatrick 0-11   Warrenpoint 1-6
1979 - Castlewellan 2-10   Rostrevor 1-4
1980 - Clonduff 0-7   Glenn 1-3
1981 - Burren 1-10   Saval 2-6 (R & AET)
1982 - Castlewellan 2-5   Clonduff 1-5 (R)
1983 - Burren 0-9   Clonduff 0-4
1984 - Burren 3-14   An Riocht 0-5
1985 - Burren 0-10   Loughinisland 0-5
1986 - Burren 0-13   Longstone 0-7
1987 - Burren 0-12   Bryansford 1-6
1988 - Burren 1-10   Loughinisland 0-7
1989 - Loughinisland 1-12   Bryansford 0-7

1990 - Downpatrick 0-12   Burren 1-5
1991 - Downpatrick 1-7   Castlewellan 1-5
1992 - Burren 4-7   Rostrevor 1-6
1993 - Downpatrick 3-6   Bryansford 0-8
1994 - Castlewellan 1-9   Downpatrick 0-8

FERMANAGH

1904 - Teemore
1905 - Teemore
1906 - Teemore
1907 - Enniskillen
1908 - Enniskillen
1909 - Enniskillen
1910 - Teemore
1911 - Teemore
1912 - Teemore
1913 - Teemore
1914 - Teemore
1915 - Teemore
1916 - Teemore
1917 - Teemore
1918 - Irvinestown
1919 - Wattlebridge
1920 - Wattlebridge
1924 - Teemore
1925 - Killyrover
1926 - Teemore
1927 - Knockninny Harps
1928 - Lisnaskea
1929 - Teemore
1930 - Enniskillen Gaels
1931 - Lisnaskea
1932 - Knockninny
1933 - Belnaleck
1934 - Newtownbutler
1935 - Teemore
1936 - Lisnaskea
1937 - Lisnaskea
1938 - Lisnaskea
1939 - Lisnaskea
1940 - Newtownbutler
1941 - Lisnaskea
1942 - Lisnaskea
1943 - Lisnaskea
1944 - Newtownbutler
1945 - Lisnaskea
1946 - Lisnaskea 4-4   Irvinestown 0-7
1947 - Lisnaskea 4-9   Teemore 1-6
1948 - Lisnaskea 8-3   Ros lea 2-3
1949 - Belleek 3-8   Lisnaskea 2-5
1950 - Lisnaskea 1-8   Belleek 1-4
1951 - Lisnaskea 1-6   Belleek 1-3
1952 - Irvinestown 2-2   Roslea 1-1
1953 - Newtownbutler 0-6   Irvinestown 0-4
1954 - Lisnaskea 2-10   Belleek 1-8
1955 - Roslea 0-9   Lisnaskea 0-4

1956 - Roslea 0-8	Aughadrumsee 0-2
1957 - Roslea 1-3	Derrygonnelly 0-3
1958 - Roslea 2-5	Tempo 1-2
1959 - Newtownbutler	
1960 - Devenish/Mulleek bt	Newtownbutler
1961 - Aghadrumsee 1-4	Newtownbutler 0-5
1962 - Roslea 2-9	Kinawley 0-9
1963 - Devenish 3-4	Roslea 1-7
1964 - Newtownbutler 1-8	Devenish 2-3
1965 - Devenish 2-5	Tempo 0-5
1966 - Devenish 1-8	Newtownbutler 1-4
1967 - Devenish 3-4	Newtownbutler 0-7
1968 - Ederney 3-7	Newtownbutler 2-6
1969 - Teemore 0-12	Irvinestown 1-8
1970 - Tempo 2-15	Belcoo 0-4
1971 - Teemore 2 -8	Brookeboro O-1 1
1972 - Tempo 1-8	Teemore 1-6
1973 - Tempo 1-12	Roslea 1-5
1974 - Teemore 0-10	Erne Gaels 0-1
1975 - Teemore 1-8	Devenish 2-4
1976 - Enniskillen 1-12	St Patricks 0-4
1977 - Lisnaskea 0-11	Enniskillen 0-7
1978 - Enniskillen 2-4	St Patricks 1-4
1979 - Belleek Erne Gaels 2-10	Teemore 1-10
1980 - Lisnaskea 0-10	Enniskillen 0-6
1981 - Belleek 3-8	Belcoo 1-4
1982 - Roslea 3-10	St Patricks 1-6
1983 - Teemore 2-5	Lisnaskea 0-7
1984 - Roslea 0-7	St Patricks 0-2
1985 - Devenish 1-10	Belcoo 0-6
1986 - Roslea 0-9	Devenish 0-5
1987 - Enniskillen 0-7	Roslea 0-5
1988 - Newtownbutler 1-10	Belcoo 0-8
1989 - Devenish 0-9	Roslea 0-8
1990 - Devenish 2-7	Lisnaskea 0-8
1991 - Lisnaskea 1-13	Newtownbutler 1-9
1992 - Enniskillen 1-11	Lisnaskea 2-6(R)
1993 - Devenish 1-15	Kinawley 2-5
1994 - Lisnaskea 1-9	Enniskillen 1-8

MONAGHAN

1888 - Iniskeen 0-7	Carrickmacross 0-0
1904 - Donaghmoyne 0-5	Inniskeen 0-2
1905 - Inniskeen 2-4	Donaghmoyne 0-9
1906 - Donaghmoyne 1-5	Carrickmacross 0-3
1907 - Castleblayney 0-9	Monaghan Harps 0-4
1908 - Carrickmacross 1-3	Inniskeen 0-1
1909 - Carrickmacross 2-12	Currin 1-1
1910 - Carrickmacross 0-2	Monaghan 0-0
1911 - Monaghan 3-1	Greenan's Cross 2-1
1913 - Carrickmacross w/o	Ture
1914 - Carrickmacross 2-0	Magherarney 1-1
1915 - Magherarney bt	Castleblayney
1916 - Castleblayney bt	Clones
1917 - Castleblayney bt	Clontibret
1918 - Carrickmacross bt	Clontibret
1919 - Carrickmacross 1-15	Clontibret 0-0

1922 - Monaghan 2-4	Ballybay 0-3
1923 - Monaghan bt	Castleblayney
1924 - Castleblayney bt	Clones
1925 - North Sel. bt	South Sel.
1926 - Castleblayney bt	Clones
1927 - Killeevan 1-8	Castleblayney 0-7
1928 - Corcaghan 1-3	Carrickmacross 0-3
1929 - Killeevan 1-4	Killanny 1-1
1930 - Latton 2-1	Inniskeen 0-4
1931 - Castleblayney 3-5	Killeevan 0-2
1932 - Castleblayney 2-2	Killeevan 0-1
1933 - Castleblayney 3-6	Inniskeen 3-2
1934 - Donaghmoyne 2-3	Carrickmacross 0-0
1935 - Donaghmoyne 3-2	Castleblayney 0-8
1936 - Castleblayney	
1937 - Castleblayney 1-6	Donaghmoyne 1-4
1938 - Inniskeen 0-6	Killeevan 1-2
1939 - Castleblayney 2-9	Donaghmoyne 2-4
1940 - Castleblayney 2-2	Inniskeen 1-3
1941 - Castleblayney 2-5	Donaghmoyne 2-4
1942 - Donaghmoyne 2-6	Clones 0-6
1943 - Clones 1-6	Inniskeen 0-7
1944 - Killeevan 1-6	Castleblayney 2-2
1945 - Donaghmoyne 1-6	Clones 2-2
1946 - Castleblayney 4-3	Killanny.1-4
1947 - Inniskeen 3-6	Castleblayney 1-8
1948 - Inniskeen 3-4	Castleblayney 1-3
1949 - Clontibret 0-11	Carrickmacross 2-3
1950 - Clontibret 2-11	Killanny 1-2
1951 - Clontibret 5-7	Castleblayney 0-3
1952 - Clontibret 1-6	Inniskeen 1-3
1953 - Ballybay 2-8	Donaghmoyne 0-6
1954 - Ballybay 2-9	Clontibret 0-5
1955 - Clontibret 1-6	Ballybay 0-6
1956 - Clontibret 3-8	Ballybay 3-6
1957 - Ballybay 1-8	Clontibret 0-4 (R)
1958 - Clontibret 0-7	Donaghmoyne 0-4
1959 - Ballybay 3-7	Clontibret 0-5 (R)
1960 - Scotstown 1-5	Castleblayney 1-4
1961 - Scotstown 1-10	Castleblayney 2-0
1962 - Ballybay 1-10	Castleblayney 1-7
1963 - Castleblayney 0-5	Ballybay 0-3 (R)
1964 - Castleblayney 1-9	Scotstown 1-4
1965 - Castleblayney 1-5	Clontibret 0-3
1966 - Castleblayney 0-6	Scotstown 0-3
1967 - Castleblayney 2-9	Clontibret 1-10
1968 - Clontibret 1-6	Scotstown 0-8
1969 - Ballybay 3-5	Castleblayney 0-5
1970 - Castleblayney 1-10	Clontibret 0-9
1971 - Castleblayney 1-10	Clontibret 2-4
1972 - Castleblayney 2-14	Ballybay 2-8
1973 - Castleblayney 3-8	Ballybay 3-5
1974 - Scotstown 1-10	Castleblayney 0-8
1975 - Castleblayney 2-10	Scotstown 2-5
1976 - Castleblayney 0-9	Ballybay 0-5 (R)
1977 - Scotstown 2-7	Ballybay 1-4 (R)
1978 - Scotstown 1-8	Castleblayney 1-3

1979 - Scotstown 2-4	Castleblayney 1-4	1957 - Omagh 1-7	Derrylaughan 0-3
1980 - Scotstown 0-10	Monaghan 1-5 (R)	1958 - Clonoe 1-5	Carrickmore 1-3
1981 - Scotstown 1-14	Castleblayney 1-8 (R)	1959 - Clonoe w/o	Omagh
1982 - Castleblayney 0-10	Ballybay 0-7	1960 - Clonoe 2-7	Donaghmore 2-0
1983 - Scotstown 3-4	Ballybay 0-10	1961 - Carrickmore 2-5	Moy 0-5
1984 - Scotstown 0-11	Inniskeen 0-4	1962 - Stewartstown 3-3	Derrylaughan 0-3
1985 - Scotstown 2-6	Castleblayney 0-11	1963 - Omagh 2-10	Galbally 0-5
1986 - Castleblayney 2-11	Emyvale 0-5	1964 - Clonoe 2-5	Derrylaughan 0-4
1987 - Ballybay 0-9	Monaghan 0-4 (R)	1965 - Clonoe 0-10	Derrylaughan 0-3 (R)
1988 - Castleblayney 3-10	Clontibret 0-7	1966 - Carrickmore 0-10	Derrylaughan 0-4
1989 - Scotstown 1-8	Castleblayney 0-7	1967 - Derrylaughan 0-9	Carrickmore 0-6
1990 - Castleblayney 2-13	Inniskeen 3-9	1968 - Ardboe 1-8	Coalisland 0-7
1991 - Castleblayney 3-12	Monaghan 0-8	1969 - Carrickmore 1-10	Coalisland 1-9
1992 - Scotstown 0-9	Castleblayney 0-7 (R)	1970 - Eglish 2-7	Augher 1-8
1993 - Scotstown 0-9	Clontibret 1-5	1971 - Ardboe 2-9	Carrickmore 1-9
1994 - Clontibret 4-7	Donaghmoyne 1-11	1972 - Ardboe 1-9	Stewartstown 1-4

TYRONE

1904 - Coalisland 3-7	Strabane 0-1	1973 - Ardboe 2-6	Augher 1-4
1905 - Strabane 1-4	Donaghmore 0-4	1974 - Trillick 1-9	Carrickmore 1-3
1907 - Coalisland 0-8	Fintona 0-2 (R)	1975 - Trillick 1-11	Owen Roes 2-3
1908 - Dungannon 2-9	Fintona 0-5	1976 - Augher 3-4	Ardboe 1-7
1913 - Fintona 2-1	Coalisland 0-1	1977 - Carrickmore 0-11	Dromore 1-7
1916 - Cookstown 3-1	Kilskeery 2-1	1978 - Carrickmore 1-6	Dromore 0-4
1917 - Cookstown 1-2	Omagh 1-1 (R)	1979 - Carrickmore 0-8	Fintona 1-4
1919 - Moy 2-2	Omagh 1-1	1980 - Trillick 1-6	Omagh 0-6 (R)
1924 - Stewartstown 0-18	Omagh 0-4	1981 - Derrylaughan 2-3	Carrickmore 1-5
1925 - Dungannon 4-4	Ballygawley 1-1	1982 - Augher 2-6	Dromore 1-5
1926 - Ballygawley 2-2	Ardboe 0-3	1983 - Trillick 1-9	Ardboe 0-8
1927 - Donaghmore 1-7	Ardboe 0-9	1984 - Ardboe 0-8	Omagh 0-7
1928 - Coalisland 2-4	Donaghmore 1-3	1985 - Augher 0-8	Gortin 0-3
1929 - Dungannon 4-3	Coalisland 1-6	1986 - Trillick 1-10	Dungannon 2-5 (R)
1930 - Coalisland 1-2	Dungannon 0-2	1987 - Ardboe 1-6	Trillick 0-5 (R)
1931 - Ballygawley 2-1	Washingbay 1-3	1988 - Omagh 2-6	Clonoe 2-4
1933 - Dungannon 2-2	Omagh 2-1	1989 - Coalisland 1-11	Ballygawley 0-6
1934 - Washingbay 3-1	Omagh 1-4	1990 - Coalisland 4-6	Omagh 2-7
1935 - Dungannon 2-5	Omagh 2-1	1991 - Clonoe 1-13	Coalisland 1-6
1936 - Dungannon 1-4	Carrickmore 0-4	1992 - Moortown 2-6	Dromore 0-5
1937 - Trillick 2-8	Donaghmore 0-2	1993 - Errigal Ciaran 0-11	Moortown 0-10
1938 - Fintona 0-3	Cookstown 0-0	1994 - Errigal Ciaran 3-5	Carrickmore 1-8
1940 - Carrickmore 1-5	Dungannon 0-5 (R)		
1941 - Moortown 1-5	Clonoe 0-6		
1942 - Moortown 2-5	Omagh 0-1		
1943 - Carrickmore 4-3	Moortown 0-4		
1944 - Dungannon 2-2	Moortown 0-3		
1945 - Strabane 3-11	Dungannon 4-4		
1946 - Coalisland 1-6	Dromore 0-3		
1947 - Dungannon 2-6	Moortown 1-2		
1948 - Omagh 1-3	Clogher 0-2		
1949 - Carrickmore 4-1	Derrytresk 0-6		
1950 - Moortown 1-6	Dungannon 2-1		
1951 - Dungannon 3-9	Moortown 0-1		
1952 - Omagh 2-4	Clonoe 1-1		
1953 - Omagh 3-6	Clonoe 2-3		
1954 - Omagh 1-8	Dungannon 0-5		
1955 - Coalisland 2-6	Dungannon 2-4		
1956 - Dungannon 2-6	Clonoe 1-5		

COUNTY TITLES ROLL OF HONOUR

30 - Castleblayney

23 - St Johns, Belfast

22 - Crossmaglen

20 - Lisnaskea, Teemore

15 - Bellaghy, Rossa

14 - Cavan Slashers/Gaels, Clan na Gael, Scotstown

13 - Armagh Harps

12 - Cornafean, Gweedore

10 - Ballyshannon, Bryansford, Dungannon

HURLING CHAMPIONSHIPS

ANTRIM SHC	
Holders - Cushendall	
Name of Cup - Volunteer Cup	
Dunloy 4-19	Gort na Mona 0-3
Loughgiel 1-11	Cushendall 3-14
QUARTER-FINALS	
Dunloy 3-17	Ballycastle 2-8
Rossa 2-14	Cushendall 2-11
St Johns 5-10	St Pauls 0-7
Cushendun 7-11	Sarsfields 0-2
SEMI-FINALS	
St Johns 1-9	Rossa 1-7
Dunloy 3-13	Cushendun 1-7
FINAL	
Dunloy 1-18	St Johns 1-5

In 1990, Dunloy Cuchullains won the Antrim Under-21 title for the seventh year in-a-row. Most of the team also received medals for winning the Senior Championship the same year; Dunloy looked set for a long reign at the top of Antrim hurling.

However, Dunloy's new kids on the block learned a few harsh lessons as Cushendall took the next three Senior Championships. In 1994, they returned wiser and fitter to fulfil their potential and win the title by the proverbial mile. Dunloy scored an impressive eleven goals and 67 points in four games, while none of their opponents got within twelve points.

New manager Phonsie Kerins must take some of the credit, while on the field the McMullan brothers, Seamus and Frankie, the Elliott boys Shane, Nigel and Alastair, and the O'Kanes, Gary and Gregory, pulled together magnificently. Seamus Boyle also stepped into the injured Dominic McMullan's boots at full-back.

In the quarter-final, Eamonn McKee set Dunloy on course for victory over Ballycastle with a superb goal early in the second half. Colm McGuckian and Jarlath Elliott scored further goals to seal the issue. Ballycastle's goal-scorers were Martin McElroy and Brian Donnelly.

The turning point in the semi-final with Cushendun came after seventeen minutes; Jarlath Elliott was carried off injured and Cushendun's Conor McNeill was sent off. Dunloy trailed at that point by 1-3 to 0-5 (goal by Paul Graham), but substitute Jarlath Cunning came on to score a goal in each half for a 3-11 to 1-7 final scoreline. Alistair Elliott grabbed Dunloy's second goal just twenty seconds into a second half in which Cushendun failed to score.

City club St Johns were underdogs in the final but acquitted themselves well in the first half. Packie Nolan's early goal (from goalkeeper Paddy Nugent's long puck-out) merely served to bring out the best in Dunloy, as Eamonn McKee goaled on six minutes and Frankie McMullan revelled in his new forward role.

Paul Montgomery put a 23rd minute St Johns penalty over the bar as Dunloy took a half-time lead of 1-5 to 1-3. In the second half Seamus

Dunloy's Gary O'Kane holds aloft
the Antrim SHC trophy

McMullan and Fergal Collins were sent to the line but Dunloy captain Gary O'Kane, full-forward Gregory O'Kane (0-6) and Alistair Elliott (0-5) steered their team to the title.

Back at the start of the year Cushendall had pretentions of winning the title, and so becoming only the second club to land a four in-a-row, but they surprisingly fell to the very club they were trying to emulate, O'Donovan Rossa.

In a quite sensational contest at Casement Park, Cushendall led 7-1 after a first quarter in which Rossa's Collie Murphy missed a penalty. Still, the Belfast men closed to 0-8 to 1-4 by half time, and with superb work at midfield by Jim Close and Jim Connolly (they scored nine of Rossa's total), they were in front going into the last ten minutes by 1-11 to 0-10. Cushendall struck back with a point from James McNaughton and a goal from Mark McCambridge to level the tie.

Noel Murray then swung the pendulum back towards Rossa with a point, only for the exceptional Danny McNaughton to raise the roof with a goal for Cushendall. Trailing by 2-11 to 1-12, Rossa responded yet again with a Noel Murray goal and points from Collie Murphy and Joe McCaffrey, to win a rousing contest, 2-14 to 2-11.

But, after all their efforts, Rossa went out in the semi-finals to St Johns, 1-9 to 1-7. Despite being without team captain Shane Caldwell, the men from Corrigan Park had a first title in 21 years in their sights as they hustled and outplayed the favourites. The accuracy of Paul Montgomery (final tally of 0-7) saw the Johnnies ahead at half time 7-5, and although Collie Murphy goaled from Ger Rogan's through ball, Antrim football captain Locky McCurdy replied with a decisive goal ten minutes from time for St Johns, following a 65 from John Cousins.

Summary: In the Preliminary Round of the championship, Jackie Carson and Alastair McGuile scored the important goals as Cushendall beat Loughgiel, while in the First Round Rory McQuillan grabbed a hat-trick and Gary McNeill two more, as Cushendun defeated Sarsfields by a massive thirty points.

DUNLOY: Shane Elliott, Brian Og Cunning, Seamus Boyle, Sean McIlhatton, Seamus McMullan, Gary O'Kane (c), Seamus Mullan, Tony McGrath 0-2, Colm McGuckian 0-1, Nigel Elliott 0-1, Michael Maguire, Frankie McMullan 0-3; Eamonn McKee 1-0, Gregory O'Kane 0-6, Alastair Elliott 0-5.
Subs: Paul Molloy for Maguire, Jarlath Cunning for McKee.
ST JOHNS: Paddy Nugent, Aidan Darragh, Mickey Carlin, Mickey O'Neill, John Cousins, Liam Donnelly, Paul Morgan 0-1, Ronan Heenan 0-1, Fergal Collins (c), Paul Montgomery 0-3, Packie Nolan 1-0, Locky McCurdy, Conor McCaffrey, Donal Kennedy, Brendan McGibbon. Subs: Donal Gallagher for McGibbon, Collie Donnelly for Nolan, Brian McFall for Heenan.
Ref: John McCartan (St Pauls)

ANTRIM WINNERS/RESULTS

1901 - Brian Oge	1911 - Sean Mitchells	1921 - Rossa	1931 - Cushendun Emmetts
1902 - Lamh Dhearg	1912 - Sean Mitchells	1922 - Tir na Og	1932 - O'Connells
1903 - O'Neill Crowleys	1913 - McQuillans, Ballycastle	1923 - Carey	1933 - Ballycastle
1904 - Tir na Og	1914 - Ballycastle	1924 - Loughgiel	1934 - St Johns
1905 - Tir na Og	1915 - Seagan An Diomis	1925 - Loughgiel	1935 - Glenariffe
1906 - Carey Faughs	1916 - Carey	1926 - Tir na Og	1936 - O'Connells
1907 - O'Neill Crowleys	1917 - James Stephens	1927 - O'Connells	1937 - Glenariffe
1908 - Seagan An Diomis	1918 - O'Donovan Rossa	1928 - O'Connells	1938 - Loughgiel
1909 - Brian Ogs	1919 - Rossa	1929 - Loughgiel	1939 - Tir na Og
1910 - Seagan An Diomis	1920 - Loughgiel Shamrocks	1930 - O'Connells	1940 - O'Connells

1941 - O' Connells		1969 - St Johns 3-8	Ballycastle 0-4
1942 - O'Connells		1970 - Loughgiel 8-9	Ballycastle 4-8
1943 - Loughgiel		1971 - Loughgiel 4-11	Glenariff 1-5
1944 - Ballycastle		1972 - Rossa 2-15	St Johns 3-11
1945 - O'Connells		1973 - St Johns 4-10	Ballycastle 3-12
1946 - Rossa		1974 - Sarsfields 3-12	Loughgiel 3-7
1947 - Sean Mitchels		1975 - Ballycastle 3-14	Sarsfields 2-10
1948 - Ballycastle		1976 - Rossa 3-17	Dunloy 0-12
1949 - Rossa		1977 - Rossa 2-10	Ballycastle 1-7
1950 - Ballycastle		1978 - Ballycastle 2-11	St Johns 1-6
1951 - St Johns		1979 - Ballycastle 3-15	Cushendall 0-11
1952 - Ballycastle		1980 - Ballycastle 4-11	Cushendall 2-8
1953 - Ballycastle 3-2	Rossa 2-4 (R)	1981 - Cushendall 3-8	Ballycastle 0-16 (R)
1954 - Ballycastle 4-5	Loughgiel 3-2	1982 - Loughgiel 5-9	Ballycastle 3-8
1955 - Rossa 4-7	Ballycastle 3-1	1983 - Ballycastle 1-14	Loughgiel 2-10
1956 - Loughgiel 0-11	Rossa 2-2	1984 - Ballycastle 1-18	Cushendall 2-6
1957 - Rossa bt	Ballycastle	1985 - Cushendall 4-13	Loughgiel 1-12
1958 - Rossa 7-1	Loughgiel 4-2	1986 - Ballycastle 1-20	St Johns 0-7
1959 - Rossa 4-3	Carey 2-5	1987 - Cushendall 4-12	Rossa 1-11
1960 - Rossa 2-11	Loughgiel 3-3	1988 - Rossa 2-10	Cushendall 1-10 (R)
1961 - St Johns 5-7	Carey 1-7	1989 - Loughgiel 2-14	St Johns 1-6
1962 - St Johns 5-7	Loughgiel 3-8	1990 - Dunloy 2-10	Rossa 1-10 (R)
1963 - Loughgiel 3-6	Dunloy 3-2	1991 - Cushendall 1-5	St Johns 0-7
1964 - Ballycastle 2-3	Loughgiel 0-3	1992 - Cushendall 2-8	Ballycastle 0-9
1965 - St Johns 3-5	Loughgiel 2-6	1993 - Cushendall 1-18	Ballycastle 1-7
1966 - Loughgiel 5-5	Glenravel 2-9 (R)	1994 - Dunloy 1-18	St Johns 1-5
1967 - Loughgiel 4-14	Mitchels 0-0	**ROLL OF HONOUR**	
1968 - Loughgiel 3-13	Rossa 4-7	Ballycastle 16, Loughgiel 15, Rossa 14.	

ARMAGH

Holders - Keady
Name of Cup - Cardinal MacRory Cup
FIRST ROUND

Cuchullains 3-11	Killeavey 2-4
Derrynoose 1-10	Lurgan 2-5

SEMI-FINALS

Keady 0-11	Cuchullains 1-6
Middletown 4-12	Derrynoose 1-4

FINAL

Keady bt	Middletown

CAVAN

Mullahoran are the current champions. The four other hurling clubs in the county are Bailieboro Shamrocks, Woodford Gaels (Kildallon, Ballyconnell and Killashandra), Cavan Gaels and Cavan College of Further Education.

DONEGAL

Holders - Burt
FINAL - Burt 4-7   Naomh Mura (Inch) 1-4

DERRY

Holders - Slaughtneil
Name of Cup - Fr.Michael Collins Cup
SEMI-FINAL
Slaughtneil 6-11   Ballinascreen 2-9
FINAL
Lavey 3-21   Slaughtneil 4-8

Slaughtneil caused a bit of panic in Lavey's defence by scoring four goals in the last ten minutes of the final, but with fourteen points from Oliver Collins already in the bag, Lavey were not going to be caught. This was Lavey's seventh title in ten years and they now trail Dungiven on the County titles Roll of Honour by one, 13-12. Dungiven's haul includes a record six in-a-row from 1972-77, while Lavey captured four titles in the 1940s. Slaughtneil were champions four times in the late sixties, while St Finbarrs, Loup, Banagher, Ballinascreen and Mitchels, Coleraine, all have two titles each. In the early part of the century, the crown rested in Derry City six times and twice in Donegal (with Burt and Aileach).

LAST TEN DERRY FINALS		
1984 - Derry 1-12	Ballinascreen 1-5	
1985 - Lavey bt	Dungiven	
1986 - Lavey 5-9	Ballinascreen 0-6	
1987 - Dungiven 2-9	Lavey 3-5	
1988 - Lavey bt	Ballinascreen	
1989 - Dungiven 2-4	Ballinascreen 1-6	
1990 - Lavey 5-18	Drum 2-6	
1991 - Lavey 3-12	Dungiven 0-8	
1992 - Lavey bt	Slaughtneil	
1993 - Slaughtneil bt	Lavey	
1994 - Lavey 3-21	Slaughtneil 4-8	

DOWN

There can't be many clubs in Ulster that have played in 23 of their last 25 Senior County Finals, but Ballycran from the Ards Peninsula can boast of such a record. Since 1970, they have won twelve and lost eleven Down Championship Finals.

Four of those defeats came in consecutive years from 1988-91, while 1992 was one of

DOWN
Holders - Ballycran
Name of Cup - Jeremiah McVeigh Cup
SEMI-FINALS
Ballygalget 3-18 Leitrim 0-7
Ballycran 2-9   Portaferry 0-13
FINAL
Ballycran 1-10   Ballygalget 0-12

those rare times when Ballycran did not get past the semi-finals. But, with five disappointments behind them, Ballycran lifted themselves onto a higher plain by regaining the Down title in 1993 and adding the Ulster Club Championship for the first time since 1976.

The new era began for Ballycran after they survived three incredible games with Ballygalget to decide the 1993 Down Championship. Trailing by five points in the third game, Kevin Blaney came to the rescue with two goals for a memorable 2-17 to 2-15 triumph, after extra time.

Next, Antrim's eighteen-year stranglehold on the Ulster Club Championship ended with Ballycran's surprisingly comfortable defeat of the then champions, Cushendall, by 2-10 to 0-12. In the All Ireland semi-finals in February, the Down men lost to Toomevara from Tipperary by 1-13 to 1-5 in Croke Park.

With their appetite whetted, Ballycran set about retaining the Down title, but such is the closeness of the Ards clubs that the champions required another double-goal rescue act by Kevin Blaney to overcome Portaferry in the semi-finals, 2-9 to 0-13.

In the final with Ballygalget, at St Patricks Park in Portaferry, Hugh Gilmore scored the game's only goal after twelve minutes when he doubled on a sideline cut from Man of the Match John McCarthy. Backed up by Danny Hughes and a strong half-back line, Ballycran added points from Conor Arthurs and Kevin Blaney to lead at the break, 1-6 to 0-3.

Ballygalget's Kevin Coulter blasted a penalty over the crossbar, but the anticipated comeback began to materialise when Martin Coulter and Brendan Gallagher reduced the gap to three. Entering the last ten minutes the tension mounted when Tom Coulter and then Gallagher left the minimum between them.

With John McCarthy helping out, Ballycran defended desperately and were relieved to see Martin Coulter's effort fall inches wide. Two long-distance frees from Tom Coulter also missed the target as Ballycran held out for a 1-10 to 0-12 victory.

BALLYCRAN: Noel Keith, Bill Hughes, Paddy Dorrian (c), Hugh Torney, Michael Braniff, Dermot Woods, Stephen McAree, John McCarthy 0-1, Danny Hughes 0-1, Conor Arthurs 0-2, Dermot O'Prey 0-4, Sean Masterson 0-1, Seamus Mallon, Hugh Gilmore 1-0, Kevin Blaney 0-1. Subs: Conor Mallon for Torney, Michael Blaney for S.Mallon.

BALLYGALGET: Graham Clarke, Gerard Monan, Paddy Braniff (c), Paddy Monan, Tom Coulter 0-2, Gerard Coulter, Kevin Coulter 0-1, Paddy Savage, Barry Coulter, Brendan Gallagher 0-4, Martin Bailie 0-1, Barry Smyth, Martin Coulter 0-2, Paul Coulter, Philbin Savage 0-1. Sub: Colin Smyth for P.Coulter.

Ref: H.P.McCusker (Ballela).

DOWN WINNERS/RESULTS

1903 - Faugh-a-Ballagh (Newry)		
1904 - Faugh-a-Ballagh		
1905 - Clann na Boirce (Newcastle)		
1906 - Clann na Boirce		
1907 - Faugh-a-Ballagh		
1908 - Faugh-a-Ballagh		
1909 - Faugh-a-Ballagh		
1910 - Ballyvarley		
1912-20 - Kilclief		
1925 - Kilclief		
1926 - Portaferry		
1927 - Leitrim		
1928 - Leitrim		
1929 - Portaferry		
1930 - Faugh-a-Ballagh		
1931 - Kilclief		
1932 - Kilclief		
1933 - Kilclief		
1934 - Clann Ulagh (Newry)		
1935 - Kilclief		
1936 - Ballela		
1937 - Ballela		
1938 - Portaferry		
1939 - Kilclief		
1940 - Ballela		
1941 - Ballela		
1942 - Kilclief		
1943 - Kilclief		
1944 - Kilclief		
1945 - Kilclief		
1946 - Clann Ulagh		
1947 - Kilclief		
1948 - Ballela		
1949 - Ballycran		
1951 - Ballela 2-3	Ballycran 1-3	
1952 - Ballela bt	Kilclief	
1953 - Ballycran 8-10	Leitrim 2-3	
1954 - Kilclief 5-7	Ballycran 4-6	
1955 - Kilclief 4-6	Ballygalget 3-4	
1956 - Kilclief bt	Ballygalget	
1957 - Ballycran bt	Portaferry	
1958 - Ballycran bt	Ballygalget	

1959 - Ballygalget 1-10	Portaferry 0-4	
1960 - Ballycran 2-10	Portaferry 0-6	
1961 - Ballycran 6-10	Portaferry 0-2	
1962 - Void		
1963 - Portaferry 4-2	Ballygalget 4-1	
1964 - Ballygalget 2-8	Ballycran 4-0	
1965 - Portaferry 2-13	Ballygalget 3-3	
1966 - Ballygalget 1-13	Ballycran 1-11	
1967 - Ballycran 7-6	Portaferry 2-11	
1968 - Portaferry 1-17	Ballycran 3-6	
1969 - Portaferry 2-8	Ballygalget 1-8	
1970 - Ballygalget 3-12	Ballycran 1-7	
1971 - Portaferry 4-5	Ballycran 2-8	
1972 - Ballycran bt	Portaferry	
1973 - Ballygalget bt	Portaferry	
1974 - Ballycran 3-5-	Portaferry 0-13	
1975 - Ballygalget 1-10	Ballycran 0-12	
1976 - Ballycran 5-9	Portaferry 1-5 (R)	
1977 - Ballycran 1-13	Ballygalget 0-2	
1978 - Portaferry 1-13	Ballycran 1-7	
1979 - Ballycran 1-6	Ballygalget 0-4	
1980 - Ballycran 3-6	Ballygalget 2-7 (R)	
1981 - Portaferry 2-12	Ballycran 1-11	
1982 - Ballygalget 1-9	Ballycran 0-11	
1983 - Ballygalget 4-8	Ballycran 2-8	
1984 - Ballycran 2-10	Ballygalget 1-ll	
1985 - Ballycran 2-14	Portaferry 2-12	
1986 - Ballycran 3-6	Portaferry 1-11	
1987 - Ballycran 0-17	Ballygalget 1-8	
1988 - Portaferry 2-15	Ballycran 3-5 (R)	
1989 - Portaferry 0-14	Ballycran 1-8	
1990 - Ballygalget 3-13	Ballycran 2-12	
1991 - Portaferry 0-10	Ballycran 1-5	
1992 - Ballygalget 0-11	Portaferry 0-10	
1993 - Ballycran 2-17	Ballygalget 2-15	
AET (R)		
1994 - Ballycran 1-10	Ballygalget 0-12	

ROLL OF HONOUR

Kilclief 23, Ballycran 19, Portaferry 13, Ballygalget 10.

FERMANAGH FINALS	
1988 - Lisbellaw 4-3	Lisnaskea 0-7
1989 - Lisbellaw 0-12	Lisnaskea 0-7
1990 - Enniskillen 4-4	Lisbellaw 2-9 (R)
1991 - Lisbellaw 1-16	Enniskillen 0-10
1992 - Lisbellaw 3-8	Donagh 1-8
1993 - Lisbellaw 6-13	Donagh 1-4
1994 - Lisbellaw 1-15	Enniskillen 2-2

MONAGHAN

Clontibret are the current champions. The other three clubs are Monaghan Harps (1993 winners), Castleblayney and Carrickmacross.

TYRONE	
Holders - Dungannon	
Name of Cup - Benburb Cup	
QUARTER-FINALS	
N.Colmcille 0-6	Omagh 3-9
Killyclogher 2-9	Shamrocks 1-4
Clan na Gael 0-1	Dungannon 8-18
SEMI-FINALS	
Killyclogher 4-8	Carrickmore 2-5
Dungannnon 5-15	Omagh 0-3
FINAL	
Killyclogher 4-5	Dungannon 0-10

LAST TEN TYRONE FINALS	
1985 - Carrickmore 4-12	Killyclogher 2-3
1986 - Carrickmore 0-10	Dungannon 0-4 (R: 2-3 0-9)
1987 - Carrickmore 5-6	Killyclogher 1-8
1988 - Carrickmore 2-8	Omagh 1-6
1989 - Carrickmore 3-8	Dungannon 2-6
1990 - Carrickmore 3-9	Dungannon 2-5
1991 - Killyclogher 1-9	Dungannon 1-6 (R: 2-7 2-7)
1992 - Dungannon 0-11	Killyclogher 1-5
1993 - Dungannon 1-15	Carrickmore 4-1
1994 - Killyclogher 4-5	Dungannon 0-10
ROLL OF HONOUR	
Dungannon 14, Carrickmore 12, Killyclogher 6, Omagh 3.	

1994 ULSTER CLUB CHAMPIONSHIP

RESULTS	
Killyclogher 2-10	Castleblaney 1-11
Keady 5-16	Burt 3-6
Keady w/o	Mullahoran
Killyclogher 1-9	Lisbellaw 0-8
SHIELD FINAL	
Keady 4-12	Killyclogher 5-3
SEMI-FINALS	
Dunloy 2-13	Ballycran 1-9
Lavey 2-18	Keady 1-2
FINAL	
Dunloy 3-9	Lavey 1-12

Henry Downey, the man who lifted the Sam Maguire as Derry football captain in 1993, set the pattern for the 1994 Ulster Club Hurling Final at Casement Park with a scrambled goal in the first minute for the underdogs from Lavey. The South Derry boys proceeded to take the game to the Antrim champions and threatened a major upset when they led by six points in the second half.

Oliver Collins had scored five points in the first half for Lavey, several of them from long-distance frees, and he proved a handful for Gary O'Kane. But, as the game progressed a pre-match injury took it's toll on Collins and he was moved to full-forward.

Lavey's half-time lead of 1-7 to 1-3 was extended by two Henry Downey frees, before Dunloy finally halted Lavey's brave challenge with two splendid goals and three points, in a devastating eight-minute spell. Gregory O'Kane smashed the first goal to the Lavey net with a great shot from 20 yards, and the second came when Seamus McMullan's long ball was batted overhead by Nigel Elliott, past a startled Shane Coyle.

Dunloy's fitness and superior finishing had eventually told, the same qualities that had counted in the semi-final defeat of Ballycran at Armagh. Gregory O'Kane pointed eight times in that 2-13 to 1-9 victory, the goals from Alastair Elliott and Eamonn McKee.

DUNLOY: S.Elliott, B.Cunning, S.Boyle, S.McElhatton, S.McMullan 0-1, Gary O'Kane (c), S.Mullan, T.McGrath, C.McGuckian 0-2, N.Elliott 1-0, M.Maguire, F.McMullan, A.Elliott 1-1, Gregory O'Kane 1-4, E.McKee 0-1.
LAVEY: S.Coyle, Ciaran McGurk, C.McGurk, J.Young, E.Downey, P.McCloy, B.Ward, J.McGurk, A.McCrystal 0-1, S.Downey, O.Collins 0-6, H.Downey 1-3, F.McNally, Michael Collins 0-2, Martin Collins. Sub: B.Regan for McCrystal (59 mins).
Ref: A.Sweeney (Dublin).

Dunloy, Antrim and Ulster Champions, 1994

ULSTER FINALS

1971 - Loughgiel 6-14	Ballygalget 2-5	1983 - Ballycastle 4-11	Ballygalget 2-3
1972 - Loughgiel 3-8	Portaferry 1-12	1984 - Ballycastle 1-14	Ballycran 1-3
1973 - Rossa 2-9	Ballycran 3-2	1985 - Cushendall 0-19	Ballycran 0-10
1974 - Ballycran 3-5	Sarsfields 3-2	1986 - Ballycastle 1-14	Lavey 1-8
1975 - Ballygalget 4-6	Ballycastle 1-9	1987 - Cushendall 3-10	Ballycran 1-6
1976 - Ballycran 0-8	Rossa 0-7	1988 - Rossa 0-13	Lavey 0-11
1977 - Rossa 1-13	Ballycran 2-6	1989 - Loughgiel 1-14	Portaferry 2-9
1978 - Ballycastle 2-14	Portaferry 2-7	1990 - Dunloy 0-17	Ballygalget 2-4
1979 - Ballycastle 0-11	Ballycran 0-8	1991 - Cushendall 1-16	Portaferry 2-4
1980 - Ballycastle 1-20	Ballycran 0-13	1992 - Cushendall 2-12	Ballygalget 1-10
1981 - Cushendall 7-19	Portaferry 3-5	1993 - Ballycran 2-10	Cushendall 0-12
1982 - Loughgiel 1-9	Ballygalget 0-9	1994 - Dunloy 3-9	Lavey 1-12

1994 UNDER-21 FINALS

Antrim -	Loughgiel 4-7	Rossa 1-6
Tyrone -	Dungannon 1-5	Carrickmore 0-4

MINOR FINALS

Antrim -	Loughgiel 2-13	St Pauls 2-7
Down -	Ballygalget 3-10	Ballycran 2-9
Derry -	Banagher 4-7	Drum 0-6

17

THE EAMONN COLEMAN SAGA

The most sensational story in Ulster in 1994 was the sacking/non-reappointment of Eamonn Coleman as manager of Derry, while his team was still technically All Ireland Champions. County Chairman Harry Chivers broke the news to Coleman in early September by telephone to Chicago, from where the former hero returned five days later to find that Mickey Moran was the new manager.

What followed has been one of the most controversial passages in the history of Derry football. Senior players refused to play for the county in protest at Coleman's dismissal; they became engaged in a series of meetings and counter-meetings over a two-month period with the new management, the old management, and the County Board.

Outside Derry, GAA folk ask "What's going on up there?" with a certain bewilderment at how a county can fall so quickly from it's greatest moment. I have

compiled a diary of the relevant events, from conversations and from newspaper accounts of meetings, which I understand to have been accurate.

In early 1991, Eamonn Coleman returned from exile in London as the "the player's choice" to manage Derry. He would win 40 of 47 matches, including the 1992 National League Final and the 1993 All Ireland Final. However, there were problems behind the scenes.

In August 1993, a few weeks before the All Ireland semi-final with Dublin, Gardai are called to a hotel where the Derry team had gone after a challenge game with Meath in Navan. It was alleged that a County Board Official had struck team captain Henry Downey during a row over sponsorship of playing gear, though the Gardai left without taking further action. Angry players were told the County Board would deal with the individual concerned after the All Ireland. In the meantime he was not allowed on the team coach or in the dressing-room.

The way we were. Eamonn Coleman, Mickey Moran and the Sam Maguire Cup.

Eamonn Coleman talks in Bundoran.

September 20th - On the last leg of the journey back to Derry with the Sam Maguire, the "banned" County Official, a long-serving member, was allowed onto the celebration bus from the border to Maghera.

September 26th - "Cash or I Quit" screams a Sunday Press front page headline, relating to an Eamonn Coleman interview with Liam Hayes. He was reported to have threatened to leave for London unless he received "adequate compensation for the work and travelling I am putting in". Coleman claimed he could earn 400 pounds a week in London.

October - At a number of Awards functions Coleman made a point of paying tribute to the rest of his management team, Mickey Moran, Denis McKeever and Harry Gribben.

October 10, Castlebar - Players stop changing when the "banned" County Board official enters the dressing-room before a league game with Mayo. Coleman asks the official, the Senior representative of the Board on the trip, to leave. Other County Board members are upset to hear of the incident.

December - Coleman reveals at a book function in Bundoran that he received fifty pounds a week in expenses from the Derry County Board, and that his request for one hundred pounds a week had been rejected. "I don't think it is an unreasonable figure when you consider the time and effort put into the job, and I am not in it for the money. In the two weeks before the All Ireland final I didn't work at all, but got no compensation from the Board. I am not talking about professionalism, all I want is compensation for what I lost, and there is a distinction". Coleman also claimed that he knew of three club managers in Derry who were getting more, and that he had been offered the same but "I am going to stay with the boys".

1994 - Coleman coaches Tyrone Junior side Kildress. He had previously been refused permission to coach Dungiven (early 1993) and was told after the All Ireland final that he could not manage a club side in Derry while he was county manager.

May 29th, 1994 - Derry lose to Down in the First Round of the Ulster SFC. Coleman was criticised for leaving his son too long on Mickey Linden and, to a lesser extent, for not playing Johnny McGurk, Damien Barton and Seamus Downey. The manager said he intended to carry on and bring a very good Derry side back next year. The contracts for the management team would come up for renewal in September.

Mid-June - Coleman, Moran, McKeever and Gribben met and agreed to stay on as the management team. Coleman would spend the summer managing the St Brendans club in Chicago, the others would watch the Derry Championship while he was away.

June/July - A number of Derry players leave to play in America after the elimination of top sides, Lavey, Dungiven and Swatragh, from the Derry Championship. Five of the team that started in Celtic Park had no involvement beyond the First Round of the competition and six more were free after the quarter-finals. At one stage it was reported that seventeen of the county panel were Stateside, some in Chicago and some, like Henry Downey, in Philadelphia.

August - Nominations for county manager. Some clubs didn't nominate, others presumed there would be no contest and others may not have wanted Coleman.

Late August in Chicago - Anthony Tohill tells Coleman of rumours back home that he might not be re-appointed. On phoning Harry Gribben, Coleman is told the County Board want to contact him. A few days later County Chairman Harry Chivers phoned Coleman to ask if he wanted his name to go forward for the coming year. When Coleman answered "yes", he says he was asked several questions, including what he would do about the resignation of Mickey Moran as coach/selector "if he was re-appointed", and about Derry's loss to Down.

September 4th - A week after their last conversation, Chivers phoned Coleman to say "You are not being re-appointed", adding that he could not give reasons why. No announcement is made to the public.

Thursday, September 8th - Moran lets his name go forward after hearing that interviews for the vacant manager's post were to be held. (It was also suggested that the post had been offered to former manager Frank Kearney). "I was put under considerable pressure to go forward as Eamonn wasn't going to be re-appointed by the Board. It was essential to keep the present squad together after four years of hard work, and this could only be done by letting my name go forward".

Friday 9th - Moran is interviewed for the Derry job.

Saturday 10th - Coleman flies into Dublin to hear that Moran had been appointed Derry manager (along with McKeever and Gribben).

Sunday 11th - Coleman and Moran are interviewed on RTE Radio. Coleman says he feels "stabbed in the back" by the new management team, Moran said he would resign if he did not have the support of the players.

Monday 12th - Coleman meets Denis McKeever but has no contact with Gribben or Moran.

Tuesday 13th - Moran meets a group of senior players in Toomebridge. Enda Gormley voices his support for Coleman and asks for the previous management team to be reinstated. His view is endorsed by the rest, who tell Moran that it wasn't necessarily their preference of Coleman over him as much as their anger at the treatment of the old manager. Joe Brolly told Moran he was right to expect loyalty from the players but asked "who has been loyal to Eamonn?". Moran gave the players three options (one of which was to try and get Coleman back) and left before the end of the meeting, with the understanding that he would approach the County Board. However, at the first training night at Greenlough only six players turn up and the others again meet Moran afterwards. When the new manager insists he is staying, the players want a meeting with the County Board.

Early October - Derry beat Tyrone in the O'Fiach Cup at Crossmaglen with only three of their All Ireland winners (Tony Scullion, Dermot Heaney and Eamonn Burns). A County Board official confirms there would be no chance of Coleman being reinstated, and that the new set-up would carry on with replacement players if need be. He also claims that clubs in Derry supported the decision to change the management and that, apart from the players, there was little support for Coleman within the county, "I have not had one angry phone call over the matter".

He added, "Coleman had not in fact been the manager for the past two years. He was only made that by the media, but really he has been part of a team of four. It follows that the manager wasn't sacked, just one of the team who was not re-appointed". The Official's parting comment was "there are things that went on which you will never know about".

October 6th - Tohill, McGilligan, McKeever and Henry Downey meet the County Board in Claudy to ask them to re-consider. After giving their views they are thanked but told that decisions relating to the management of Derry football team were taken by the Board "in the best interests of Derry football". Coleman met the County Board the same evening and was given a number of reasons for his non-reappointment. First, they were unhappy with his "Cash or I Quit" story which they viewed as critical of the Board and as a public

"Play for the Jersey", Tony Scullion.

demand for greater expenses. Second, they did not like the manager admitting at a book function that he was being paid fifty pounds a week in expenses by the Board. Third, they felt his commitment to Kildress undermined his commitment to Derry, and fourth, the Board alleged Coleman encouraged players to play for him in America in the Summer. I understand there were two further reasons, both to do with financial matters. At the end of the meeting, a Board member thanked him for what he had done for Derry football. Coleman told him to save his gratitude, he didn't need it and didn't want it. The Board said they would not be commenting publicly on a private matter which they now considered to be closed.

Sunday, October 9th - The Sunday Independent describes the situation in Derry as an "undignified disaster". The Sunday Press interviews Gary Coleman. "It's all very depressing. There's nothing I want more than to put on that Derry jersey, that means everything in the world to me but the way da has been treated is wrong, it's very wrong".

Monday, 10th - Coleman meets the players in Ballymaguigan. "Thank you for your loyalty but it is too late to save me. Your careers are short as it is, now go back for the sake of Derry football. That's bigger than Mickey, me and the County Board". Afterwards, Coleman added "they are a great bunch of lads, we have had a very special relationship over the last few years and it is a great pity that it is being destroyed. I know them and they want to win another All Ireland, but at the moment they are angry and upset".

Wednesday, 12th - The players meet with Mickey Moran. Henry Downey expresses misgivings but says they are prepared to "get on with it", providing there would be no recriminations. But, just as it looked like a return, a new member of the panel (goalkeeper Johnathan Kelly) asked why he had not received official notice to attend training. He was informed that he was no longer a member of the panel, something which angered senior players present. They felt that Kelly had been victimised for supporting Coleman. Moran was asked why he wasn't prepared to step down for the good of Derry football. He refused to answer "such a question" and the meeting broke up after fifteen minutes. At training, 24 players turned up, but the squad had been enlarged to about 45.

Friday, 14th - Brian McGilligan publicly backs Moran. "Mickey has been appointed by the Board and as far as I am concerned we now have to accept their decision. The players have made their point, cleared the air and there's little more that can be done". However, the team to play Laois is not picked until Friday evening and includes only two recognised names, Tony Scullion and Eamonn Burns. Some regulars were suspended, others were to play for Lavey in the Ulster Club Hurling Final and others were still involved in the Ulster Club Football Championship. Others were plainly boycotting the county set-up, like Anthony Tohill who would play for soccer's Intermediate League side Park on the Saturday, but then feel the wrath of Derry supporters when attending the game with Laois the following day.

Sunday, 16th - Derry lose to Laois at Celtic Park by 1-17 0-8, their heaviest defeat in years. In a television interview, Moran issues an ultimatum to the stayaway players to return to training by Wednesday.

Tuesday, 18th - Moran's ultimatum did not have the desired effect. One senior player said "Mickey did a lot of damage when he blamed everything on the players", though others, like Joe Brolly, were ready to go back and indicated as much to Moran. The manager in turn withdrew the ultimatum and restored Johnathan Kelly to the panel. Some of the players looked set to return the following week.

Sunday, 23rd - "Coleman: A player's man nailed by the Board", is the heading as Eamonn Coleman talks to David Walsh of the Independent. "I want to clear my name" said Coleman, "The County Board left things in such a way that it looked like they had something on me. The truth is that they did not have one reason to dismiss me like they did. I did nothing wrong! The reasons they give are silly, incidental things which the Board just wanted to throw at me". Coleman said his work with Kildress never interfered with his job with Derry, "it was on a different night, and anyway Mickey Moran trained Omagh for years when he was with Derry. I had to bring in Eugene Young on Friday evenings for Moran. The Board does not appear to have any problems with that". Coleman described the Board's comments about encouraging players to go to America as "damaging, malicious and without foundation. Derry players have been going over there for years, clubs were queueing up for Tohill and the others, they were going

one way or another. I didn't even speak to my own son about going out". A spokesman for St Brendan's said Coleman "never asked us for any money and he never asked us to get him any players. We had Tohill, Burns, and McKeever before we contacted Eamonn. We had a good relationship with the clubs and sent Eamonn Burns home to play in the semi-finals". Coleman said he had left the meeting with the County Board convinced he had not been told the true reason for his sacking. "I honestly feel I was sacked because I put the team before the Board". He referred to the incident in Mayo with the "banned" County Official, as the "beginning of the end, the start of differences with the Board. My loyalty was to the players first and the Board second, I was the one identified with the players". Harry Chivers refused to answer questions from the same reporter, "the Derry Board is only answerable to clubs in Derry".

Wednesday, 26th - Brolly, McNicholl, McKeever and Tohill rejoin and train with the squad. Others were reported to be annoyed that Brolly had offered Moran an escape from his ultimatum, and were determined not to return. They wanted either an entirely new management team or the return of Coleman.

Joe Brolly.

Sunday, 30th - Defeat by Donegal at Ballybofey but an improved performance. Joe Brolly spoke after the game about why he and others had stayed away. "We stayed out for very genuine reasons. We felt there was a clear perception that the Board behaved possibly dishonestly in relation to Eamonn Coleman. We were in a very, very difficult position and ultimately we realised that Derry football is bigger than the 25 men who won All Ireland medals. The Board has been there for 25 years and will be there for another ten. Team management and politics, that's their affair. All the players can do is play football or not. We took it as far as we could, there was no alternative but to come back".

Thursday, November 3rd - Henry Downey plays for Derry under lights at Burren against Antrim. The bulk of the other "stayaway" players also return or indicate they will play when fit, or free from other commitments.

Notes: The Derry County Convention is set for December 19th. Mickey Moran is the Derry delegate to Central Council.

MANAGERS

Cavan, Donegal and Fermanagh also changed managers this year. Martin McHugh accepted an approach from Cavan (which had been made before he and Donal Reid lost out to PJ McGowan for the Donegal job). McHugh's selectors are Donal Donohoe from Laragh, Paddy McNamee from Munterconnacht and Mickey Reilly from Redhills. Former Railway Cup star Jim McDonnell is an adviser.

PJ McGowan's backroom team includes Seamus Gallagher from Kilcar, Dublin-based Sean Ferriter, Tom Comack from Dungloe, Michael Lafferty and trainer Patsy McGonagle. The new boss has a wealth of coaching and managerial experience, including a spell with Fermanagh and two All Ireland Under-21 titles with Donegal. Incidentally, he played against Peter McGrath in the 1974 Ulster Final.

Terry Ferguson arrived in style for his first match in charge of Fermanagh. Minutes after playing for Kells in Meath, he travelled by helicopter to arrive in Lisnaskea just before Fermanagh played in the B Championship! Ferguson, whose father is from Down, was approached after Brian McEniff and Danny Ball had turned down the job, and after Hugh McCabe had not been re-appointed. McCabe had refused to attend an interview to put his plans to a five-man committee, "it didn't make sense to go for an interview for a job I already had. I had had the job for two and a half years and took it on when no-one else would have it". McCabe, who described the affair as "rather shoddy", effectively ruled himself out of the running.

FOOTBALL MANAGERS

	SENIOR	UNDER-21	MINOR
Antrim	PJ O'Hare	Same	Tommy Hall*
Armagh	Jim McCorry	Same	Bro.Ennis**
Cavan	Martin McHugh	Same	Ray Cullivan
Derry	Mickey Moran	J.J.Kearney	John McGoldrick**
Donegal	PJ McGowan	Donal Reid	Anthony Molloy
Down	Peter McGrath	Donal Bell	PJ McGee**
Fermanagh	Terry Ferguson	Same	Ciaran Carey
Monaghan	Michael McCormick	Same	Kevin Treanor
Tyrone	Art McCrory\	Frank Martin*	Mickey Harte\
	E.McKenna		Fr.Gerard McAleer

* Resigned ** 1995 Manager still to be appointed.

Note: Peter McGrath is by far the longest-serving senior manager, having taken over from Jackie McManus in the Autumn of 1989. Jim McCorry has been Armagh boss since late 1991 (when he replaced Paddy Moriarty) while the Antrim and Tyrone management teams came into their positions in 1992 (succeeding Hugh Murphy and John Donnelly respectively). Michael McCormick has been with Monaghan for two seasons.

Donegal man in Cavan, Martin McHugh

New Donegal boss, PJ McGowan

Still in charge, Peter McGrath

HURLING MANAGERS

Antrim:	Dominic McKinley	**UNDER-21s**	
Armagh:	Paddy Connolly	Antrim:	Jim McLean
Cavan:	Sean Farrell	Down:	Cathal McGrattan
Derry:	Joe McGurk	Tyrone:	Ciaran McHugh
Donegal:	John O'Brien	**MINORS**	
Down:	Sean McGuinness	Antrim:	Olcan McFetridge/Mickey McCallin
Fermanagh:	Seamus Doonigan	Down:	Seamus Fay
Monaghan:	Dave Ryan	Derry:	Mark Cassidy
Tyrone:	Brendan Harkin	Tyrone:	Gerard O'Connor/Terry McGowan

18

SPONSORS

When Derry and Tyrone met in the Ulster Senior Football Championship three years ago, neither side carried a sponsor's logo on it's jerseys. This year, all but one senior football team in the province had the name of a sponsor on it's shirts. Progress indeed, yet the single most significant development this year was the first ever sponsorship of the All Ireland Senior Football Championship.

According to GAA President Jack Boothman, the Bank of Ireland paid "a very large figure, substantial in fact" to become official sponsors of the Provincial and All Ireland competitions. The deal was announced in May and will run for five years, but it does not include hurling or any other level of football. It also prevents the Bank of Ireland's competitors from having their name on jerseys in the Senior Championship. This explains why Down Minors had the "Ulster Bank" logo on their shirts at Celtic Park, only to be followed by the Down Seniors with blank jerseys.

All Ireland Champions Down, sponsored by the Ulster Bank.

	FOOTBALL	HURLING
Antrim	—	Mackies
Armagh	Newry Building Supplies	Same
Cavan	Cavan Co-op Mart	—
Derry	Sperrin Metals	—
Donegal	Donegal Parian China	—
Down	Ulster Bank	Same
Fermanagh	Tracey Concrete	Fort Lodge Hotel
Monaghan	Westenra Hotel	—
Tyrone	WJ Dolan	—

Burren captain Malachy Murdock shakes hands with Kyan Smyth of Downpatrick before their semi-final

Devoted Burren men Malachy and Ciaran Murdock were the last people expected to join forces with Armagh, but that's exactly what the men behind Newry Building Supplies did in September this year! Easily the most intriguing new sponsorship deal of 1994, Malachy, current club captain at the famous Burren club, and his brother Ciaran, Managing Director of the company, reacted favourably to an approach by Armagh County Chairman Gene Duffy, even though their headquarters is only a few hundred yards away from the Marshes.

"We're an expanding and ambitious company", explained Company Director Malachy, "we are making a name for ourselves outside Down and this deal is a good way of carrying that on. Mind you, as a Down man I will certainly be supporting my home county come Ulster Championship time, unless they go out. Then I'll support Armagh!" The Armagh package covers county teams at Senior, Under-21 and Minor level, in football and

New Tyrone sponsor W. J. Dolan (right) shares a joke with Declan O'Neill, County Chairman, Eugene McKenna and Ciaran Corr.

hurling for three years. Down's package with the Ulster Bank is similar while Monaghan's deal includes their Under-21 and Minor football teams.

Aghyaran building and civil engineering contractor Willie John Dolan is the only one-man sponsor of a senior county team in Ireland. As well as backing Tyrone, he is also behind the Border Rally Championship which involves six events along the border. In 1993, he won the Irish Tarmac National Championship (Group N).

SENIOR CHAMPIONSHIP SPONSORS		
	FOOTBALL	HURLING
Antrim	Bass Ireland	Same
Armagh	Guinness	Same
Cavan	Meadowview Restaurant	—
Down	Carrickdale Hotel	Same
Monaghan	ACC Bank	—

Notes: Bass Ireland's deal for both Antrim Championships runs for three years. The Carrickdale Hotel also sponsors the Armagh All County Football League and the Minor, Intermediate and Junior Club Championships in Down. The Meadowview Restaurant sponsors Cavan's Junior Football Championship.

Sperrin Metal meets Magee Tailored as Eamonn Coleman shakes hands with Brian McEniff.

19

BASS ULSTER GAA WRITERS AWARDS

The Bass Ulster GAA Writers Association was founded on March 28th, 1988, with Adrian Logan as Chairman, Kevin Hughes Vice-Chairman, Eamonn O'Hara Secretary and Tony McGee Treasurer. With five other gaelic games writers, the group met with Bass Ireland Ulster Brewery Public Relations manager Brian Houston to agree overall sponsorship.

More than 200 hundred people, including Meath's Bernie Flynn with the Sam Maguire and guest speaker Jimmy Magee, attended the first Annual Awards Banquet in Belfast. The Sam Maguire Cup has since become a regular at the top table for an event which now attracts up to 650 guests while the Writers Association has grown in membership. Monthly Award winners receive a sports voucher to the value of £100 and a specially commisioned GAA Vase with the Writers crest, supplied by Belleek Pottery, Ltd.

ANNUAL WINNERS

1988
Personality	- Jim Nelson
Handball	- Una Mulgrew (St Pauls)
Camogie	- Sarah Anne Quinn (Derry)
Club	- Burren

1989
Personality	- Terence McNaughton
Footballer	- Martin McHugh
Hurler	- Olcan McFetridge
Club	- O'Donovan Rossa, Belfast
Communications	- John Graham (M'ghan)

1990
Personality	- Brian McEniff
Footballer	- Martin Shovlin
Hurler	- Ciaran Barr
Club	- Lavey
Handball	- Ciaran Curran
Camogie	- Mary Lundy (Antrim)
Referee	- Damien Campbell (Ferm)
Communications	- Pat Nugent (Armagh)

1991
Personality	- Peter McGrath
Footballer	- Greg Blaney
Hurler	- Terence McNaughton
Club	- St Pauls, Belfast
Handball	- Michael Finnegan (Cavan)
Camogie	- Bernie McNally (Queens)
Referee	- Gerry McClorey (Antrim)
Communications	- Pat Nugent

1992
Personality	- Brian McEniff
Footballer	- Martin McHugh
Hurler	- Noel Keith
Services to GAA	- Brother Ennis
Club	- Lamh Dhearg (Antrim)
Handball	- Michael Finnegan
Camogie	- Ann Higgins
Referee	- Tommy McDermott (Cavan)
Communications	- Bernie Mullan (Derry)

1993
Personality	- Eamonn Coleman
Footballer	- Henry Downey
Hurler	- Paul McKillen
Services to GAA	- Jim McKeever
Club	- Errigal Ciaran
Handball	- Joe Kelly (Armagh)
Camogie	- Ursula McGivern (Armagh)
Referee	- Dessie Slater (Tyrone)
Communications	- Gerry McClorey

1994
Personality	- Peter McGrath
Footballer	- Mickey Linden
Hurler	- Dominic McKinley
Services to GAA	- Brian McEniff
Club	- Dunloy
Handball	- St Pauls, Belfast
Camogie	- Mary Black
Referee	- Catherine McAllister (Camogie)
Communications	- Seamus McAleenan (Camogie)

1988

Familiar faces among the 1988 Monthly and Annual Award winners. *Back, left to right;* Sean Donegan, Terence McNaughton, Kevin McCabe, Seamus Horisk of Bass Ireland, Joey Cunnningham and Nudie Hughes. *Front;* John Kelly, (former) Sales, Belleek Pottery Ltd., Una Mulgrew, Sarah Anne Quinn, Gloria Murdock (Burren Secretary) and Jim Nelson.

1994

Winner takes all! Annual Award Winners from 1994. *Back, left to right;* Michael Murray (St. Pauls), Mary Black, Seamus McAleenan, Catherine McAllister, Martin Cochrane (Dunloy), Brian McEniff. *Front;* Liam Meaney, Managing Director Tennents Ireland, Adrian Logan, Chairman UGAAWA, Peter McGrath, Bob Magee, Managing Director Bass Ireland, Mickey Linden, Dominic McKinley.

MONTHLY WINNERS

1988
May - Joey Cunningham (Armagh)
June - Kevin McCabe (Clonoe)
July - Nudie Hughes (Monaghan)
Aug - Terence McNaughton (Antrim)
Sept - Sean Donegan (Newtownbutler Mgr)
Oct - Danny McNaughton (Antrim)
Nov - Donegal SF team
Dec - St Pauls GAC, Belfast

1989
Feb - Ciaran Barr (Antrim)
Special Award - Kevin Armstrong (Rossa)
Mar - St Marys TC, GFC (Belfast)
Aprl - Mickey Linden (Down)
May - Adrian McGuckin (St Pats, Maghera)
June - Harry McClure (Tyrone)
July - John McGoldrick (Tyrone)
Aug - Dessie Donnelly (Antrim)
Sept - Derry MF team
Oct - Jim McConville (Ulster)
Nov - Fergus Caulfield (Monaghan)

1990
Jan - Ciaran Curran (Loughmacrory)
Feb - Dessie Ryan (Queens GFC)
Mar - Gerry McClorey (Antrim)
Aprl - Peter Quinn (GAA President)
May - Celtic Park Development Committee
June - Ciaran McGurk (Armagh)
July - Martin Gavigan (Donegal)
Aug - Niall Patterson (Antrim)
Sept - Brian McAlinden (Sarsfields, Armagh)
Oct - Seamus McMullan (Antrim)
Nov - PJ Carroll (Leitrim Manager)

1991
Jan - Mattie McGleenan (Tir Connail Gaels)
Feb - Bernie McNally (Queens)
Mar - Anthony McGurk (Lavey)
Aprl - Peter Canavan (Tyrone)
May - PJ McGowan (Fermanagh Manager)
June - Henry Downey (Derry)
July - Peter McGrath (Down)

Aug - Peter Withnell (Down)
Sept - Paddy O'Rourke (Down)
Oct - Chris Mageean (Down)
Nov - Adrian Cush (Tyrone)
Dec - Nudie Hughes (Castleblayney)

1992
Jan - Ciaran Curran (Loughmacrory)
Feb - Grace McMullan (UUJ)
Mar - Peter McGinnity (St Michaels Coach)
Aprl - Dermot Heaney (Derry)/Adrian Cush (Tyrone)
May - Henry Downey (Derry)
June - Enda Gormley (Derry)
July - Sean McGuinness (Down Manager)
Aug - Matt Gallagher (Donegal)/
       Danny Ball (Tyrone U-21 Manager)
Sept - Anthony Molloy (Donegal)
Oct - Paddy Walsh (Antrim)
Nov - Hugh McCabe (Fermanagh Manager)

1993
Feb - Tony Boyle (Donegal)
Mar - Danny Hughes (Down)
Aprl - Ray Morgan (St Colmans Coach)
May - Ray McCarron (Monaghan)
       /Anthony Tohill (Derry)
June - Ger Houlahan (Armagh)
July - Anthony Tohill (Derry)
Aug - Henry Downey (Derry)
Sept - Eamonn Coleman (Derry)
Oct - Noel Keith (Down)
Nov - Conor Deegan (Downpatrick)
Dec - Danny Ball (Errigal Ciaran Manager)

1994
Feb - Jim Nelson (Antrim Manager)
Mar - Peter Canavan (Tyrone)
Aprl - Ger Houlahan (Armagh)
May - Jim Carty (Fermanagh U-21 Manager)
June - Fay Devlin (Tyrone)
July - Joe McGoldrick (Fermanagh Hurling)
Aug - Conor Deegan (Down)
Sept - Mickey Linden (Down)
Oct - Noel Sands (Down)

ULSTER GAA WRITERS ASSOCIATION:

Chairman - Adrian Logan (UTV) (Outgoing)

Vice-Chairman - John McAviney (Freelance Photographer, Monaghan)

Secretary - Michael Breslin (Fermanagh Herald) Treasurer - Tony McGee (Irish News)

Members - John Campbell (Belfast Telegraph), Peter Campbell, Michael Daly (Donegal Democrat), Des Fahy (Irish Times), Eamonn Gaffney (Anglo-Celt, Cavan), John P.Graham (Freelance, Monaghan), John Haughey, Eamonn O'Hara (Irish News), Kevin Hughes (Sunday World, Tyrone Times), Owen McCann (Editor, Gaelsport), Dominic McClements (Tyrone Times), Liam McDowell (Freelance, Belfast), Michael McGeary (Sunday Life), Seamus McKinney (Derry People & Donegal News), Oliver McVeigh (Photographer, Tyrone Times), Jerome Quinn (BBC).

N.B. John McAviney is to replace Adrian Logan as Chairman.

Eamonn Coleman receives the September 1993 Monthly Award from Regional Sales Manager, Seamus Horisk. Anthony Tohill looks on.

Tyrone's Fay Devlin with his cheque and Belleek Vase for winning the June Award in 1994. Paul Gormley, Regional Distribution Manager, made the presentation. Looking on are, *from left:* Fergal Logan, Danny Barr, Eamonn McCaffrey and Paul Doris.

1993 Hurler of the Year Paul McKillen

St.Colmans Manager Ray Morgan accepts the April 1993 Award from PR Manager Brian
Houston. They are joined by Peter McGrath and three of the Hogan Cup winners.

20

NATIONAL FOOTBALL LEAGUE
1993-94

"We're hearing that Westmeath have beaten Derry at Enniskillen, we hope to go there in a minute to confirm it". Des Cahill couldn't believe his ears, and neither could the rest of us listening to Sunday Sport on RTE Radio on April 4.

The last we knew, Derry were leading at half-time, by 0-8 to 1-2, now we were supposed to believe the Division Four side had dumped the All Ireland champions out of the league on a scoreline of 3-6 to 0-11! Derryman Seamus Mullan came on air a few minutes later to assure us it was true. The details were thus - in the first half Anthony Tohill hit the post with a penalty and Larry Giles scored Westmeath's goal. John Fleming got another in the second half, but Derry still led by 0-10 to 2-3 with fifteen minutes to go. Then, a slip by Johnny McGurk let Ger Heavin set up Giles for his second goal and give Westmeath the lead. At the end, wild scenes greeted the county's first qualification for a national senior semi-final.

While Westmeath celebrated, the rest of us tried to make sense of the result. We knew Derry were without Damien McCusker, Gary Coleman (his calf muscle injury required three levels of stitching and almost fifty stitches in total), Tony Scullion and Kieran McKeever (sent off against Kildare) but surely they had enough defensive cover in the squad to cope with the Division Four side? Eamonn Coleman helped us out, "the best team won", he explained.

Derry were in good company as Down, Donegal and Dublin were all eliminated on that crazy afternoon. Four Division One favourites fell to teams from lower divisions.

QUARTER-FINALS	
Armagh 2-13	Dublin 1-9
Derry 0-11	Westmeath 3-6
Donegal 0-7	Laois 0-8
Down 1-9	Meath 0-13
SEMI-FINALS	
Meath 0-15	Westmeath 0-11
Armagh 3-11	Laois 1-9
FINAL	
Meath 2-11	Armagh 0-8

Ger Houlahan was Armagh's hero at Breffni Park, with 2-6 against League Champions, Dublin. His first goal, in the eighteenth minute, gave Armagh a nine-point lead; only superb goalkeeping by John O'Leary kept the score down in the early exchanges as the Dubs reeled under an Armagh onslaught. Houlahan's second goal killed off Dublin thirteen minutes into the second half and only for a last-minute penalty Armagh's winning margin would have been ten points.

At Croke Park, Donegal failed to score from play for 55 minutes against Laois, until Marty Carlin brought them level at seven points each. However, the same player then missed a free (Declan Bonnar had been replaced) and Laois went straight upfield to win the match with a Delaney free-kick. John Cunningham had earlier been sent off.

The second game at headquarters also had an exciting finish, with Trevor Giles kicking the Meath winner from a free, just after Down had levelled. A cheeky goal from James McCartan and a point from Conor Deegan had wiped out Meath's four-point lead, bu then Bernie Flynn was fouled by Starkey. Down manager Peter

Armagh's Ger Houlahan salutes his second goal against Dublin in Breffni Park

McGrath wasn't pleased, "We gave away far too many free-kicks in scoreable positions. Eight points from frees (seven to Giles) is just terrible". However, McGrath did take something out of the experience. "I watched the Meath game on video and noticed that the play became far too punctuated, with us taking a lot of time over frees and other deadball situations. We knew therefore that we had to try and speed up the game against Derry in the Championship, even though it would take up a lot of energy".

Armagh arrived for their semi-final with Laois in a fleet of taxis, ordered in a panic when the team coach failed to arrive at their hotel. Not surprisingly, Laois started better, 4-1 up after thirteen minutes, but when Armagh settled into their stride there was going to be only one winner. Houlahan judged a high, bouncing ball in the Spring sunshine to perfection, and stabbed it past the Laois goalkeeper for a goal, and a half-time lead of 1-6 to 0-5. Jim McConville scored an opportunist goal three minutes after the break and Diarmuid Marsden gloriously wrapped things up late on when he ran on to a long punt from John Grimley. Armagh supporters were ecstatic; their team had dispatched Dublin and now Laois with scintillating forward play to reach the final of the National League. They were to be the next Ulster success story.

On the morning of the final the Sunday Press agreed. "Armagh to shade it", they predicted, though still warning that Meath had won nine

NATIONAL LEAGUE FINAL		
	Armagh	Meath
1 min Cm O'Rourke		0-1
6 mins Devine		0-2
8 mins Dowd		0-3
10 mins Cl O'Rourke	0-1	
11 mins Giles (F)		0-4
22 mins Giles (F)		0-5
24 mins Giles (F)		0-6
27 mins O'Hagan (F)	0-2	
28 mins Houlahan	0-3	
29 mins Smyth	0-4	
Half-Time 30:00		
31 mins Flynn		1-6
35 mins Cl O'Rourke	0-5	
36 mins Giles (F)		1-7
39 mins McGurk	0-6	
39 mins Smyth	0-7	
45 mins Giles (F)		1-8
47 mins Giles (F)		1-9
51 mins Flynn		2-9
56 mins Gillic		2-10
58 mins Giles		2-11
59 mins McQuillan	0-8	
Full-Time 61:00		

of thirteen finals they had played at Croke Park since 1986. Armagh's last league final was in 1985.

Sean Boylan had plans for Armagh dangermen Ger Houlahan and Diarmuid Marsden. Martin O'Connell was supposed to be an emergency full-back, yet he caught an early ball cleanly above Houlahan's head, to set the pattern for their one-to-one confrontation. Other Meath defenders seemed to know when the Armagh forwards were

going to make a move before they knew themselves! Neil Smyth and Jarlath Burns won the midfield battle, but because of close-marking the passes didn't get through. Smyth was left to carry the ball forward himself, with some success (he scored two points).

36-year-old Colm O'Rourke had given Meath a first minute lead with a high kick that appeared to go over a post. Cavan whistler Tommy McDermott over-ruled his umpires and gave the point. Benny Tierney did well to stop O'Rourke from adding a goal soon after, but the reliable Trevor Giles and the elusive Tommy Dowd had Meath 6-1 in front after 26 minutes. Armagh's only score had come from Cathal O'Rourke, yet they had chances. Houlahan's drive thundered off the black spot while O'Hagan and O'Rourke both shot wide.

Just before before the break, Armagh came to life with three quick points, but Meath responded decisively at the start of the second half. Dowd and O'Rourke combined to set up Flynn for a classic goal, and a five-point lead. Armagh clawed their way back with a superb point from McGurk but costly frees (for jersey-holding) and a missed goal effort by Smyth, highlighted the gap in experience and standard of finishing. In the last quarter, Brian Stafford set up Flynn for his second goal while McGurk's last-minute penalty was easily saved.

Armagh's supporters were hugely disappointed. After all the hype, their team had flattered to deceive. Perhaps they should have listened to the honesty of Diarmuid Marsden, when he observed before the final. "We were pretty ordinary in Division Three, our scoring rate wasn't that good and we had some very close calls. We lost to Cavan and drew with Tyrone, and only for full points before Christmas we wouldn't have made it to the play-offs".

1993-94 RESULTS

October 10, 1993
DIVISION ONE
Clare 0-6 — Dublin 0-8
Donegal 1-15 — Down 0-9
Kerry 2-11 — Kildare 0-10
Mayo 1-9 — Derry 2-14
DIVISION TWO
Fermanagh 0-7 — Leitrim 2-11
Galway 0-9 — Louth 1-9
Laois 0-14 — Roscommon 0-12
Meath 1-12 — Cork 0-6
DIVISION THREE
Antrim 0-11 — Cavan 0-8
Offaly 3-8 — Tyrone 1-14
Tipperary 1-5 — Armagh 1-14
Wexford 2-10 — Monaghan 0-9

October 24
DIVISION ONE
Derry 3-16 — Donegal 0-7
Down 0-10 — Mayo 0-9
Dublin 2-12 — Kerry 0-13
Kildare 0-14 — Clare 1-7
DIVISION TWO
Cork 2-12 — Fermanagh 1-8
Leitrim 0-8 — Meath 1-10
Louth 1-8 — Laois 0-11
Roscommon 0-9 — Galway 0-12
DIVISION THREE
Armagh 2-7 — Offaly 0-5
Cavan 1-15 — Wexford 1-14
Monaghan 0-14 — Antrim 0-14
Tyrone 1-12 — Tipperary 0-7

November 6
DIVISION ONE
Clare 0-8 — Down 1-5
Donegal 0-11 — Dublin 0-7
Kerry 0-13 — Derry 1-12
Mayo 1-10 — Kildare 1-9
DIVISION TWO
Fermanagh 0-11 — Louth 1-13
Galway 2-11 — Leitrim 0-11
Laois 1-9 — Cork 1-8
Meath 1-9 — Roscommon 2-7
DIVISION THREE
Antrim 3-2 — Armagh 1-10
Offaly 1-8 — Monaghan 2-5
Tipperary 1-10 — Cavan 0-7
Wexford 1-7 — Tyrone 2-9

November 21
DIVISION ONE
Derry 3-12 — Clare 1-5
Down 1-12 — Kerry 0-10
Dublin 1-19 — Mayo 0-8
Kildare 1-10 — Donegal 0-7
DIVISION TWO
Cork 2-14 — Galway 1-6

Leitrim 1-7 — Laois 1-6
Louth 0-9 — Meath 0-14
Roscommon 0-12 — Fermanagh 0-10
DIVISION THREE
Armagh 0-9 — Wexford 0-7
Cavan 2-7 — Offaly 2-5
Monaghan 0-13 — Tipperary 1-13
Tyrone 1-10 — Antrim 2-8

February 6, 1994
DIVISION ONE
Down 0-6 — Derry 0-8
Donegal 3-7 — Mayo 0-12
Kerry 2-8 — Clare 0-3
Kildare 1-4 — Dublin 0-7
DIVISION TWO
Cork 0-6 — Leitrim 0-5
Galway 0-8 — Laois 0-8
Louth 0-12 — Roscommon 0-5
Meath 0-12 — Fermanagh 0-6
DIVISION THREE
Armagh 0-8 — Tyrone 1-5
Cavan 1-10 — Monaghan 1-6
Tipperary 1-7 — Offaly 0-10
Wexford 3-7 — Antrim 1-7

February 20
DIVISION ONE
Derry 0-7 — Kildare 0-5
Donegal 0-10 — Clare 1-5
Dublin 1-7 — Down 1-7
Kerry 1-9 — Mayo 1-5
DIVISION TWO
Fermanagh 0-9 — Galway 1-8
Laois 1-11 — Meath 0-10
Leitrim 0-9 — Louth 0-5
Roscommon 0-6 — Cork 1-12
DIVISION THREE
Antrim 1-9 — Tipperary 1-10
Cavan 0-10 — Armagh 0-9
Monaghan 0-11 — Tyrone 0-8
Offaly 0-9 — Wexford 2-6

March 13
DIVISION ONE
Clare 2-8 — Mayo 0-7
Down 0-11 — Kildare 0-8
Derry 2-6 — Dublin 0-15
Kerry 0-11 — Donegal 0-9
DIVISION TWO
Galway 0-8 — Meath 1-10
Laois 2-11 — Fermanagh 0-4
Leitrim 1-8 — Roscommon 0-6
Louth 1-6 — Cork 0-7
DIVISION THREE
Antrim 1-8 — Offaly 0-2
Armagh 1-6 — Monaghan 0-6
Tipperary 1-8 — Wexford 1-13
Tyrone 2-14 — Cavan 0-6

PLAY-OFFS

DIVISION ONE

| Donegal 1-8 | Down 0-10 |
| Down 2-12 | Kerry 0-11 |

DIVISION THREE

Tyrone 2-10	Cavan 2-6
Tyrone 2-10	Wexford 0-10
(Tyrone promoted)	

DIVISION FOUR

| Longford 2-8 | Westmeath 2-10 |

QUARTER-FINALS

Armagh 2-13	Dublin 1-9
Derry 0-11	Westmeath 3-6
Donegal 0-7	Laois 0-8
Down 1-9	Meath 0-13

SEMI-FINALS

| Meath 0-15 | Westmeath 0-11 |
| Armagh 3-11 | Laois 1-9 |

FINAL

| Meath 2-11 | Armagh 0-8 |

FINAL LEAGUE TABLES AND TOP SCORERS

DIVISION ONE

	Pld	Pts
Derry	7	12
Dublin	7	10
Donegal	7	8
Down	7	8
Kerry	7	8
Kildare	7	5
Clare	7	3
Mayo	7	2

Charlie Redmond (Dublin)	2-25
Niall Buckley (Kildare)	0-29
Aidan O'Keefe (Clare)	1-23
Enda Gormley (Derry)	1-21
Sean McElligott (Kerry)	1-17
Kevin O'Neill (Mayo)	0-19
Manus Boyle (Donegal)	0-18
Ross Carr (Down)	0-14

DIVISION TWO

	Pld	Pts
Meath	7	10
Laois	7	10
Louth	7	9
Cork	8	8
Leitrim	8	8
Galway	7	7
Roscommon	7	4
Fermanagh	7	0

Damien Delaney (Laois)	3-35
Brian Stafford (Meath)	0-31
Stefan White (Louth)	2-21
Aidan Rooney (Leitrim)	0-25
Niall Finnegan (Galway)	0-21
Collie Curran (Fermanagh)	0-20
Colin Corkery (Cork)	1-12

DIVISION THREE

	Pld	Pts
Armagh	7	11
Cavan	7	8
Wexford	7	8
Tyrone	7	8
Antrim	7	7
Tipperary	7	7
Monaghan	7	4
Offaly	7	3

Ronan Carolan (Cavan)	0-36
Adrian Cush (Tyrone)	4-21
Ray McCarron (Monaghan)	2-22
Eamonn McCaffrey (Tyrone)	1-21
John Toner (Armagh)	1-15
Ger Houlahan (Armagh)	1-13
Conal Heatley (Antrim)	2-10

TEAMS:

DERRY v WESTMEATH at Enniskillen:
D.Kelly, J.McGurk, B.McCormick, F.McCusker, K.Diamond, H.Downey, J.McElhennon, B.McGilligan 0-1, A.Tohill, D.McNicholl, D.Heaney, D.Cassidy, J.Brolly 0-5, S.Downey 0-2, E.Gormley 0-3 Subs: E.Burns for Cassidy, R.Ferris for McCormick, O.Collins for McNicholl.
Ref: Sean McHale (Mayo).

DONEGAL v LAOIS at Croke Park:
G.Walsh, JJ Doherty, M.Gallagher, P.Hegarty, D.Reid, J.Cunningham, N.Hegarty, M.McShane, B.Murray, J.McHugh, M.McHugh, J.McMullan, D.Bonnar 0-2, M.Boyle 0-4, J.McGuinness. Subs: A.Molloy for McShane, P.Carr for Bonnar, M.Carlin 0-1 for McGuinness. Ref: Tommy Sugrue (Kerry).

DOWN v MEATH at Croke Park:
N.Collins, C.Murray, M.Magill, R.Starkey, G.McCartan 0-6,C.Deegan 0-1, E.Burns, B.Burns, G.Colgan, Ggy.Deegan, G.Blaney, Grd.Deegan, M.Linden 0-1, C.McCabe 0-1, J.McCartan 1-0. Subs: P.Withnell for Ggy.Deegan, P.Higgins for Murray. Ref: S.O'Keeffe.

ARMAGH v MEATH at Croke Park:
B.Tierney, D.Clarke, G.Reid, J.Rafferty, D.Horisk, K.McGeeney, M.McQuillan 0-1, N.Smyth 0-2, J.Burns, C.O'Rourke 0-2, K.McGurk 0-1, D.Marsden, B.O'Hagan 0-1, G.Houlahan 0-1, J.McConville. Subs: J.Grimley for O'Hagan, D.Mackin for Marsden, J.Toner for O'Rourke. Ref: T.McDermott.

ULSTER'S TOP SCORERS

DERRY (8 games)	
Enda Gormley	1-24
Joe Brolly	2-21
Anthony Tohill	4-11
Damien Cassidy	1-10

DONEGAL (9 games)	
Manus Boyle	1-28
Declan Bonnar	0-14
John Duffy	0-8
Marty Carlin	1-3

DOWN (10 games)	
Gregory McCartan	0-23
Ross Carr	0-15
Mickey Linden	0-13
James McCartan	1-6

ARMAGH (10 games)	
Ger Houlahan	4-23
John Toner	1-15
Diarmuid Marsden	3-14
Barry O'Hagan	0-18

TYRONE (9 games)	
Adrian Cush	5-27
Eammon McCaffrey	2-21
Peter Canavan	2-13
Plunkett Donaghy	2-5

FERMANAGH (7 games)	
Collie Curran	0-20
Paul Brewster	0-10
Mark Gallagher	0-9
Brian Carty	0-5

CAVAN (8 games).	
Ronan Carolan	0-39
Adrian Lambe	2-9
Fintan Cahill	2-3

ANTRIM (7 games)	
Conal Heatley	2-10
Frankie Wilson	0-13
Mickey Boyle	2-7
Paul McErlean	1-3

MONAGHAN (7 games)	
Ray McCarron	2-22
Michael Slowey	0-8

Armagh's Des Mackin in the National League Final.

21

NATIONAL HURLING LEAGUE
1993-94

"We actually believed we could win the league, but in the end, we made an awful mess of it", reflects the then Antrim captain Dominic McKinley, on a disappointing finish to the National League. They lost a quarter-final to Clare by 2-17 to 0-10 at Croke Park.

Anrim's optimism had been well-founded. A five-game unbeaten run, dating back to a draw with Down in mid-November, and including victories over Wexford, Limerick, Waterford and Galway, was mightily impressive and worthy of fourth place in Division One.

The league had started so badly.Tipperary came to Casement Park in October and easily defeated a young and experimental Antrim team by fifteen points. Two weeks later, Antrim lost in Cork but scored three goals, two from Jackie Carson, in a gritty performance.

Against Down, Antrim collected their first point thanks to two goals from Alastair Elliott, one of them late on. Sean McGuinness's team, determined to make up for their 1993 Ulster final drubbing, had raced into a second half lead with points from the accurate Dermot O'Prey (eight in all) and goals from Noel Sands and Michael Blaney.

Antrim's first league win came in February at Wexford, with Sean Paul McKillop scoring all three goals. Home victories over Limerick and Waterford followed swiftly as the Northerners grew in confidence. (Interestingly, thirteen of the Antrim team that beat Limerick by four points in Casement Park in late February also played in the All Ireland semi-final against the same county in August).

Qualification for the quarter-finals was secured in Ballinasloe, where Antrim accounted for Galway. "After that, we had thoughts on meeting Galway again in the semi-finals", recalls McKinley "we had such high expectations but we didn't prepare for the quarter-final with Clare and fell flat on our faces. It was a terrible embarrassment, we had been too confident'.

The second half against Clare was particularly embarrassing as the Munster side steadily pulled away from Antrim to win by thirteen points, helped by a most unfortunate goal when goalkeeper Brendan Prenter lost sight of a high ball in the sun and allowed it to drop into the Antrim net.

Antrim had the consolation of staying in Division One, whlch is more than can be said for Down. Sean McGuinness raged about the relegation system of "three up and three down", pointing out that the odds are stacked heavily against the smaller counties. He had taken Down into the top flight a few year's earlier for the first time.

It had taken an exceptional effort to beat the then All Ireland champions Kilkenny in Nowlan Park to avoid the drop the previous year, but this time there was no escape. Down opened brightly enough with a draw in Waterford, and picked up another point against Antrim before Christmas, but ended the league with only one victory.

RESULTS

October 18, 1993
DIVISION ONE
Antrim 1-12	Tipperary 4-18
Galway 2-14	Wexford 1-10
Limerick 1-13	Cork 0-13
Waterford 0-11	Down 1-8

DIVISION THREE
Carlow 4-18	Mayo 0-2
Monaghan 1-9	Armagh 3-8
Roscommon 1-9	Derry 0-11
Wicklow 1-12	Kildare 2-9

DIVISION FOUR
Leitrim 2-7	Donegal 2-11
Longford 3-12	Sligo 0-6
Louth 1-9	Fermanagh 2-10
Tyrone 4-15	Cavan 1-4

November 1
DIVISION ONE
Cork 2-21	Antrim 3-11
Down 2-9	Galway 2-15
Tipperary 1-17	Limerick 3-8
Wexford 1-13	Waterford 1-12

DIVISION THREE
Armagh 0-9	Roscommon 1-10
Derry 3-14	Monaghan 0-5
Kildare 4-8	Carlow 5-14
Mayo 1-6	Wicklow 2-19

DIVISION FOUR
Cavan 1-8	Leitrim 0-13
Donegal 2-7	Tyrone 2-13
Fermanagh 1-8	Longford 1-8
Sligo 1-3	Louth 5-22

Nov 14
DIVISION ONE
Antrim 2-12	Down 2-12
Galway 0-15	Cork 0-13
Limerick 1-12	Wexford 1-9
Tipperary 0-11	Waterford 0-10

DIVISION THREE
Wicklow 3-14	Derry 2-7
Carlow 3-9	Armagh 1-6
Monaghan 4-10	Mayo 3-9
Roscommon 0-12	Kildare 0-7

DIVISION FOUR
Longford 4-6	Donegal 1-6
Leitrim 1-12	Sligo 1-3
Louth 8-27	Cavan 1-2
Tyrone 2-11	Fermanagh 1-14

February 13, 1994
DIVISION ONE
Cork 1-8	Waterford 0-5
Down 0-9	Limerick 1-13
Tipperary 1-11	Galway 3-12
Wexford 2-7	Antrim 3-7

DIVISION THREE
Armagh 1-9	Wicklow 0-10
Derry 1-10	Carlow 2-12
Kildare 2-10	Monaghan 4-4
Mayo 0-5	Roscommon 2-13

DIVISION FOUR
Cavan 0-4	Longford 3-11
Donegal 1-4	Louth 5-13
Fermanagh 4-8	Leitrim 1-2
Sligo 3-10	Tyrone 1-12

February 27
DIVISION ONE
Antrim 1-11	Limerick 1-7
Down 2-12	Wexford 2-8
Galway 4-10	Waterford 0-9
Tipperary 0-15	Cork 0-17

DIVISION THREE
Armagh 1-8	Derry 3-9
Carlow 3-11	Wicklow 1-9
Mayo 0-5	Kildare 3-10
Roscommon 2-15	Monaghan 1-2

DIVISION FOUR
Donegal 2-6	Cavan 0-6
Fermanagh 1-10	Sligo 0-3
Leitrim 2-7	Tyrone 5-6
Louth 1-12	Longford 3-3

March 6
DIVISION ONE
Antrim 1-11	Waterford 0-11
Cork 2-12	Wexford 2-8
Limerick 1-9	Galway 1-9
Tipperary 3-12	Down 3-2

DIVISION THREE
Kildare 2-10	Derry 2-10
Mayo	Armagh
Monaghan 3-3	Carlow 2-16
Wicklow 2-16	Roscommon 1-8

DIVISION FOUR
Cavan 1-5	Fermanagh 5-11
Longford 1-6	Leitrim 0-7
Sligo 3-10	Donegal 1-11
Tyrone 0-9	Louth 0-10

March 20
DIVISION ONE
Down 0-10	Cork 3-15
Galway 0-8	Antrim 1-9
Tipperary 1-17	Wexford 1-14
Waterford 1-13	Limerick 1-13

DIVISION THREE
Armagh 1-5	Kildare 0-11
Derry 3-14	Mayo 0-7
Monaghan 1-6	Wicklow 0-9
Roscommon 0-8	Carlow 1-10

DIVISION FOUR

Cavan 2-6	Sligo 1-14
Donegal 1-10	Fermanagh 1-12
Leitrim 1-6	Louth 5-6
Longford 1-9	Tyrone 1-15

QUARTER-FINALS

Antrim 0-10	Clare 2-17
Tipperary 2-18	Kilkenny 1-12

SEMI-FINALS

Clare 0-10	Galway 1-13
Tipperary 2-13	Cork 1-13

FINAL

Tipperary 2-14	Galway 0-12

DIVISION ONE

	Plyd	Pts
Galway	7	11
Cork	7	10
Tipperary	7	10
Antrim	7	9
Limerick	7	8
Down	7	4
Waterford	7	2
Wexford	7	2

Top Scorers

Antrim: Sean Paul McKillop 4-9
Gregory O'Kane 0-17, Alistair Elliott 3-8.
Down: Noel Sands 3-6, Chris Mageean 1-13
Dermot O'Prey 0-13

Antrim's Ronan Donnelly chases Andrew Whelan of Clare in their NHL Quarter-final.

22
PICTURE ALBUM

Above: Down's Greg McCartan doesn't look pleased to see Aidan Morris.
Previous page, top, Michael Magill, Barry Breen and Eamonn Burns line up to block
Adrian Kilpatrick's path to goal in the Ulster Final.
Previous page, Below: Goal! Adrian Cush (hidden by Tyrone 9) sends the ball to the Down net.

ULSTER FINALISTS

Above: Down, *back, left to right*, Eamonn Burns, Conor Deegan, Paul Higgins, Barry Breen, Brian Burns, Neil Collins, Greg Blaney, Aidan Farrell, Gary Mason. *Front*, Ross Carr, Michael Magill, Mickey Linden, DJ Kane, Greg McCartan, James McCartan.

Below: Tyrone, *back, left to right*, Paul Devlin, Pascal Canavan, Plunkett Donaghy, Gareth McGirr, Eamonn McCaffrey, Adrian Kilpatrick, Joe Cassidy, Finbar McConnell, Mattie McGleenan. *Middle*, Adrian Cush, Peter Canavan, Stephen Lawn, Chris Lawn, Aidan Morris, Ciaran Corr, Fergal Logan, Fay Devlin, Ciaran Loughran, Brian Gormley, Paul Donnelly. *Front*, Ronan McGarrity, Seamus McCallin, Terence O'Neill, Sean McLaughlin.

Above: The Donegal team beaten by Tyrone at Breffni Park. *Back, left to right*, Matt Gallagher, Mark Crossan, John Joe Doherty, Brian Murray, Gary Walsh, Barry McGowan, Declan Bonnar, Joyce McMullan. *Front*, John Cunningham, Manus Boyle, Martin McHugh, Tony Boyle, Noel Hegarty, Anthony Molloy, James McHugh.

Below: Dungannon, Tyrone Minor Champions, 1994.

Above: Action from the 1994 Ulster Hurling Final.
Below: Fermanagh's Joe McGoldrick wins the Bass GAA Writers Award for July. He is pictured with his wife, Frances, and boys Ciaran and Niall. Also in the group: *front,* Michael McGurn and Seamus Donegan, *back,* Sean Treacy, Chairman Patsy Dolan, John McElroy, Fabian Burns, Fionnuala Donegan and Tony Jackman. John Devlin, Bass Ireland, made the presentation.

NEWRY BUILDING SUPPLIES

OFFICIAL SPONSORS OF ARMAGH SENIOR, UNDER 21 AND MINOR FOOTBALL AND HURLING TEAMS

Managing Director Ciaran Murdock surrounded by Armagh folk!
Seated: Jarlath Burns, *back row*: PRO Pat Nugent.
Centre: Chairman Gene Duffy.
Far right: Manager Jim McCorry.

NEWRY   BUILDING   SUPPLIES   LIMITED
RAMPART RD., GREENBANK IND. EST., NEWRY, CO. DOWN, N.IRELAND BT34 2QU
TEL: (08) 0693 67626   FAX (08) 0693 67666   COMPANY REG. No. N.I. 19569

Member of the
Timber Trade
Federation

23

CHURCH & GENERAL
NATIONAL LEAGUE FIXTURES/RESULTS
1994-95

FOOTBALL

October 16, 1994

DIVISION ONE

Derry 0-8	Laois 1-17
Down 0-7	Donegal 0-8
Dublin 0-7	Meath 1-8
Kerry 2-12	Kildare 0-8

DIVISION TWO

Armagh 2-13	Mayo 1-10
Cork 0-12	Clare 2-7
Leitrim 1-7	Tyrone 0-9
Louth 1-17	Galway 0-15

DIVISION THREE

Cavan 0-11	Antrim 0-10
Fermanagh 1-19	Longford 0-8
Roscommon 0-14	Tipperary 1-10
Westmeath 2-6	Wexford 1-5

DIVISION FOUR

Monaghan 1-18	Kilkenny 0-10
Sligo 2-6	Offaly 0-7
Waterford 1-12	London 2-5
Wicklow 1-15	Carlow 0-8
Limerick (bye)	

October 30

DIVISION ONE

Donegal 0-15	Derry 2-6
Kerry 1-12	Dublin 1-11
Laois 2-14	Down 0-11
Meath 0-12	Kildare 0-7

DIVISION TWO

Clare 1-9	Leitrim 0-4
Galway 0-10	Armagh 0-8
Mayo 1-4	Louth 1-8
Tyrone 1-8	Cork 0-10

DIVISION THREE

Antrim 0-7	Westmeath 2-7
Longford 1-8	Roscommon 1-13
Tipperary 1-6	Fermanagh 2-9
Wexford 1-5	Cavan 1-6

DIVISION FOUR

Carlow 1-7	Monaghan 3-11
Limerick 0-11	Waterford 0-8
London 0-8	Sligo 2-13

Offaly 0-9	Wicklow 0-14
Kilkenny (bye)	

November 13

DIVISION ONE

Derry 1-11	Kerry 2-6
Down 0-8	Meath 0-4
Dublin 1-8	Donegal 0-12
Kildare 2-7	Laois 0-7

DIVISION TWO

Armagh 3-3	Clare 2-6
Cork 1-9	Mayo 0-7
Leitrim 0-9	Galway 0-6
Louth 1-9	Tyrone 1-7

DIVISION THREE

Cavan 1-8	Tipperary 0-6
Fermanagh 1-4	Wexford 1-8
Roscommon 0-10	Antrim 0-8
Westmeath 1-8	Longford 0-11

DIVISION FOUR

Kilkenny 1-8	Sligo 1-10
Monaghan 1-10	Limerick 0-5
Wicklow 1-14	London 0-3
Waterford 2-9	Offaly 2-6
Carlow (bye)	

November 27

DIVISION ONE

Donegal 1-8	Kildare 1-11
Kerry 0-18	Down 1-8
Laois 1-8	Dublin 0-15
Meath 0-8	Derry 0-9

DIVISION TWO

Clare 0-9	Louth 0-4
Galway 0-10	Cork 1-10
Mayo 1-7	Leitrim 0-13
Tyrone 0-8	Armagh 0-7

DIVISION THREE

Antrim 0-12	Fermanagh 0-7
Longford 2-7	Cavan 2-11
Tipperary 1-6	Westmeath 1-9
Wexford 0-9	Roscommon 0-13

DIVISION FOUR

Carlow 1-13	Waterford 1-5
Kilkenny 0-7	Limerick 0-6
London 1-8	Monaghan 2-13
Sligo 1-10	Wicklow 1-7
Offaly (bye)	

December 4

DIVISION FOUR

Kilkenny	Carlow
Limerick	Sligo
Monaghan	Offaly
Waterford	Wicklow
London (bye)	

February 12

DIVISION FOUR

Carlow	Limerick
Offaly	London
Sligo	Waterford
Wicklow	Kilkenny
Monaghan (bye)	

February 19, 1995

DIVISION ONE

Derry	Down
Dublin	Kildare
Laois	Donegal
Meath	Kerry

DIVISION TWO

Armagh	Louth
Leitrim	Cork
Mayo	Galway
Tyrone	Clare

DIVISION THREE

Antrim	Wexford
Cavan	Westmeath
Fermanagh	Roscommon
Longford	Tipperary

DIVISION FOUR

Kilkenny	Waterford
London	Carlow
Monaghan	Sligo
Offaly	Limerick
Wicklow (bye)	

March 5

DIVISION ONE

Down	Dublin
Kerry	Laois
Kildare	Derry
Meath	Donegal

DIVISION TWO

Clare	Mayo
Cork	Armagh
Galway	Tyrone
Louth	Leitrim

DIVISION THREE

Fermanagh	Westmeath
Roscommon	Cavan
Tipperary	Antrim
Wexford	Longford

DIVISION FOUR

Carlow	Offaly
Limerick	Wicklow
London	Kilkenny
Waterford	Monaghan
Sligo (bye)	

March 19

DIVISION ONE

Donegal	Kerry
Dublin	Derry
Kildare	Down
Laois	Meath

DIVISION TWO

Armagh	Leitrim
Clare	Galway
Cork	Louth
Tyrone	Mayo

DIVISION THREE

Cavan	Fermanagh
Longford	Antrim
Westmeath	Roscommon
Wexford	Tipperary

DIVISION FOUR

Limerick	London
Offaly	Kilkenny
Sligo	Carlow
Wicklow	Monaghan
Waterford (bye)	

QUALIFYING TEAMS

Top four from Division One
Top two from Division Two
Top one from Divisions Three/Four

QUARTER-FINALS

Winner Div 1   v   Winner Div 4 (A)
Runner-up Div 1   v   Winner Div 3 (B)
Third Div 1   v   Second Div 2 (C)
Fourth Div 1   v   Winner Div 2 (D)

SEMI-FINALS

A v D
B v C

NB: Two teams are to be relegated and promoted from Divisions One, Two and Three.

HURLING

October 9, 1994
DIVISION ONE

Clare 0-14	Kilkenny 0-9
Cork 0-18	Limerick 1-8
Laois 1-9	Galway 2-17
Tipperary 2-14	Antrim 1-7

DIVISION TWO

Dublin 2-11	Carlow 1-8
Meath 1-7	Down 1-8
Offaly 3-15	Waterford 1-5
Wexford 6-14	Kerry 2-20

DIVISION THREE

Armagh 2-13	Monaghan 0-4
Derry	Roscommon
Kildare 0-12	Wicklow 2-15
Louth 0-6	Westmeath 6-13
London (bye)	

DIVISION FOUR

Donegal 3-10	Leitrim 2-9
Fermanagh 3-11	Mayo 0-10
Sligo 1-5	Longford 2-5
Tyrone w/o Cavan	

October 23
DIVISION ONE

Antrim 3-9	Cork 2-12
Galway 1-10	Clare 3-12
Limerick 2-9	Tipperary 1-15
Kilkenny 1-14	Laois 0-6

DIVISION TWO

Carlow 1-9	Wexford 1-18
Down 3-6	Offaly 2-6
Kerry 1-10	Dublin 1-8
Waterford 0-15	Meath 2-6

DIVISION THREE

London 2-10	Derry 0-6
Monaghan 0-7	Louth 2-11
Roscommon 4-5	Armagh 2-5
Westmeath 1-4	Kildare 1-3
Wicklow (bye)	

DIVISION FOUR

Leitrim w/o	Cavan
Longford 0-6	Fermanagh 2-10
Mayo 1-10	Sligo 1-7
Tyrone 3-10	Donegal 2-6

November 6
DIVISION ONE

Clare 2-8	Antrim 1-6
Galway 0-15	Cork 2-8
Laois 1-6	Limerick 1-6
Tipperary 1-10	Kilkenny 2-12

DIVISION TWO

Dublin 1-9	Waterford 1-14
Meath 0-6	Kerry 2-12
Offaly 2-13	Carlow 1-9
Wexford 3-10	Down 0-12

DIVISION THREE

Derry 6-13	Monaghan 1-5
Kildare 0-6	London 1-9
Louth 3-8	Roscommmon 2-11
Wicklow 1-14	Armagh 1-10
Westmeath (bye)	

DIVISION FOUR

Donegal 0-9	Longford 1-9
Fermanagh 1-13	Tyrone 0-4
Sligo 2-3	Leitrim 2-8
Mayo w/o Cavan	

November 20
DIVISION ONE

Antrim 1-11	Laois 2-11
Galway 1-13	Tipperary 0-11
Kilkenny 2-10	Cork 3-3
Limerick 1-8	Clare 2-8

DIVISION TWO

Carlow	Meath
Down 1-8	Dublin 0-10
Kerry 1-6	Offaly 1-13
Waterford 2-13	Wexford 2-12

DIVISION THREE

Armagh 3-7	Louth 1-12
Roscommon 0-11	Kildare 0-6
Westmeath 2-6	Derry 0-10
Wicklow 1-8	London 2-10
Monaghan (bye)	

DIVISION FOUR

Leitrim 0-2	Fermanagh 5-15
Longford w/o	Cavan
Mayo 2-17	Donegal 1-13
Tyrone 4-7	Sligo 3-10

December 4
DIVISION THREE

Derry	Louth
Kildare	Monaghan
London	Armagh
Wicklow	Westmeath
Roscommon (bye)	

February 12, 1995
DIVISION THREE

Armagh	Derry
Louth	Wicklow
Monaghan	Roscommon
Westmeath	London
Kildare (bye)	

February 26
DIVISION ONE

Cork	Tipperary
Kilkenny	Galway
Laois	Clare
Limerick	Antrim

DIVISION TWO

Carlow	Kerry
Down	Waterford
Dublin	Wexford
Meath	Offaly

DIVISION THREE
Kildare	Armagh
Monaghan	London
Roscommon	Westmeath
Wicklow	Derry
Louth (bye)	

DIVISION FOUR
Cavan	Donegal
Longford	Mayo
Sligo	Fermanagh
Tyrone	Leitrim

March 12
DIVISION ONE
Clare	Tipperary
Galway	Limerick
Kilkenny	Antrim
Laois	Cork

DIVISION TWO
Kerry	Down
Offaly	Dublin
Waterford	Carlow
Wexford	Meath

DIVISION THREE
Derry	Kildare
London	Louth
Roscommon	Wicklow
Westmeath	Monaghan
Armagh (bye)	

DIVISION FOUR
Donegal	Sligo
Fermanagh	Cavan
Leitrim	Longford
Mayo	Tyrone

March 26
DIVISION ONE
Antrim	Galway
Cork	Clare
Limerick	Kilkenny
Tipperary	Laois

DIVISION TWO
Carlow	Down
Meath	Dublin
Waterford	Kerry
Wexford	Offaly

DIVISION THREE
Armagh	Westmeath
London	Roscommon
Louth	Kildare
Monaghan	Wicklow
Derry (bye)	

DIVISION FOUR
Fermanagh	Donegal
Mayo	Leitrim
Sligo	Cavan
Tyrone	Longford

QUALIFYING TEAMS

Top Two from Division One
(straight into Semi-finals)
Third & Fourth from Division One,
Winner and
Runner-up from Division Two

QUARTER-FINALS

Third Div 1   v   Second Div 2 (A)
Fourth Div 1   v   First Div 2 (B)

SEMI-FINALS

Winner Div 1   v   B
Second Div 1   v   A

NB: Three teams are to be relegated from and promoted to Division One; One team is to be relegated from and promoted to Divisions Two and Three.

PLAYING RULES EXPERIMENTS FOR NATIONAL LEAGUES 1994-95

FOOTBALL

1. A player who takes a hand pass from a team mate shall not be permitted to play the ball away with the hand(s).
2. When a team is awarded a free for an aggressive foul any player on that team will be permitted to take the free kick from the hands.
3. All kick-outs shall be taken from the 13 metre line.

HURLING

4. A player shall only take the ball in the hand once before playing it away.
5. A player shall not be permitted to kick the ball from the hand(s).

HURLING AND FOOTBALL

6. That an exclusion zone, with an arc of 10 metres from the centre of the 20 metre line, be established. All players shall be outside the exclusion zone when a penalty kick/puck is being taken.

1995 GAA CALENDAR

(excluding National League dates).

JANUARY
29 - Railway Cup Semi-finals
    (Football and Hurling)

FEBRUARY
4 - MacRory Cup Quarter-finals
5 - Railway Cup Finals
11 - MacRory Cup Quarter-finals
19 - Sigerson Cup Semi-finals,
    All Ireland Club Hurling Semi-finals.
25 - MacRory Cup Semi-finals
26 - Sigerson Cup Final,
    All Ireland Club Football Semi-finals.

MARCH
4 - Fitzgibbon Cup Semi-final.
5 - Fitzgibbon Cup Semi-final.
17 - All Ireland Club Finals,
    MacRory Cup Final.

APRIL
2 - NFL/NHL Play-offs,
    All Ireland Colleges Semi-finals.
9 - NFL/NHL Play-offs/Quarter-finals.
16 - NFL Quarter-finals.
23 - NHL Quarter-finals.
30 - NFL Semi-finals,
    All Ireland Colleges Finals.

MAY
7 - NHL Final.
14 - NFL Final
21 - Ulster SFC - Down v Donegal
28 - Ulster SFC - Armagh v Derry (A)

JUNE
4 - Ulster SFC - Fermanagh v Tyrone (B)
11 - Ulster SFC - Cavan v Antrim (C)
18 - Ulster SFC - Monaghan v Down/Donegal (D)
25 - Ulster SFC - Semi-final (A v B)

JULY
2 - Ulster SFC - Semi-final (C v D)
9 - Ulster SHC - Final
23 - Ulster SFC - Final

AUGUST
6 - All Ireland Hurling Semi-finals
13 - All Ireland Football Semi-final
20 - All Ireland Football Semi-final
27 - All Ireland Under-21 Football Final

SEPTEMBER
3 - All Ireland Hurling Final
10 - All Ireland Under-21 Hurling Final
17 - All Ireland Football Final

OCTOBER
9/23 - NHL
16/30 - NFL

NOVEMBER
6/20 - NHL
13/27 - NFL

DECEMBER
4 - All Ireland Club Hurling Quarter-final,
    Britain v Munster,
    NFL (Division Four only), NHL
    (Division Three only).
11 - All Ireland Club Football Quarter-Final,
    Britain v Munster.